SECURED TRANSACTIONS AND PAYMENT SYSTEMS

Problems and Answers

EDITORIAL ADVISORY BOARD

Little, Brown and Company
Law Book Division

SECURED TRANSACTIONS AND PAYMENT SYSTEMS

Problems and Answers

JOHN F. DOLAN

Professor of Law
Wayne State University

Little, Brown and Company
Boston   New York   Toronto   London

Library of Congress Catalog Card No. 94-79546

ISBN 0-316-18910-3

EB-M

Published simultaneously in Canada
by Little, Brown & Company (Canada) Limited

Printed in the United States of America

For Patrick, Allison, and Shane

Contents

Contents

PART TWO

PAYMENT SYSTEMS   121

Payment Systems: Problems   121

Payment Systems: Answers   **157**

xii   Contents

Preface

The Uniform Commercial Code is the product of more than 200 years of commercial law development in case reports and scholarly commentary. The commercial lawyers and law teachers who drafted the Code were familiar with that history. They were part of the commercial subculture of the law, and they drew their Code not on a fresh tablet but on a tradition of much learning.

As all cultures and subcultures do, commercial law has its own language and its own corporate memory. Being unfamiliar with that language and memory, students may find that they have not come to the course in Secured Transactions or the course in Payments Systems sufficiently acculturated to make sense of the Code.

Using the Book

You can use this book in two ways. Your professor may assign it in the Secured Transactions or Payment Systems course and have your class prepare designated problems for each session. I use the problems in this fashion by lecturing on a subject and the next day going over the problems that generate questions.

You can also use the book as a study tool — to prepare for class and to review for exams. In that case, the book works best as a reference tool to explain specific sections that are problematic. When you use the book in this fashion, it will often be profitable to do a cluster of problems because the problems are arranged not according to the sequence of the Code sections but according to the way the sections interact in a typical commercial transaction. Code rules tend to be part of a complex of rules, and seeing that complex is helpful in understanding the Code. The table of Uniform Commercial Code citations, the index, and the subject headings will help you find the relevant problems.

You might find it worthwhile to read the short introductory comments that precede the problems, though those comments will often repeat textual discussion or class lecture. The introductory comments are not essential. Read them if they help.

Problems and Answers

Generally, the problems begin with simple questions, often that have obvious answers. That method builds gradually on knowledge that is necessary for the more confusing aspects of the provision.*

From time to time as you proceed with the questions, you may want to check your answers against the answers in the book. But remember that the purpose of the problems and the answers is not to test but to explain.

The agencies that sponsor the Code are currently redrafting or have recently redrafted much of it. There will soon be a new article for secured transactions (Article 9). There is already a new article for negotiable instruments (Article 3) and a significantly revised article for bank collections (Article 4). One of the sponsoring agencies is now redrafting the article on letters of credit (Article 5), and the article on investment securities (Article 8) is very close to completion. The problems here usually deal with the official text of the Code; but because many states have not adopted the new Article 3 or the revised Article 4, there are problems in this book for both old and new Article 3 and old and revised Article 4.

The problems do not attempt to make you an expert. They do not go into the complex issues and often do not cover exceptions to the rule of a section. Sometimes the problems do not cover sections that your teacher will want to cover. But these problems cover most of the basics, so that you will be in a position after you do them to deal with the more sophisticated questions. Commercial law study in law school does not make you a complete commercial lawyer. It can make you literate in commercial law, however. These problems and answers are a step toward that end.

A Final Note on the Code

Finally, remember that we have a commercial code to provide convenient access to the rules of commercial law. Lawyers do not try to memorize the rules of the Code. Commercial law study and practice yield a certain measure of working familiarity with those rules, of course; and accomplished Code lawyers can cite chapter and verse as they discuss commercial matters. Most lawyers, however, use the Code as a reference, just as you will use it. Most commercial law teachers do not expect you to memorize Code rules. It is sufficient to know that there is a rule, to know where to find it, and to know how to apply it according to its purpose. When you find the rule, this little book will help you understand it.

---

*Sometimes, the root of trouble with the Code is not an inability to understand Code sections as much as it is a lack of familiarity with the commercial transaction itself that the section governs. If you are unfamiliar with commercial activity, at times it may help to consult a companion to this book that describes the transactions that the rules of commercial law govern, J. Dolan, Uniform Commercial Code: Terms and Transactions in Commercial Law (1991). Familiarity with the commercial transaction itself will make some commercial law provisions clearer.

Acknowledgments

I prepared these problems over a period of ten years teaching commercial law courses at Wayne State University Law School, with visiting stints at the University of Michigan Law School and Hastings College of the Law. Students always have an impact on teaching materials, and here that impact is signal. Foremost thanks, then, go to my students, primarily those at Wayne, whose thoughts and questions largely framed this exercise.

Special thanks are also due three deans who facilitated the effort: John Reed, James Robinson, and, especially, Stephen Calkins. The Richard J. and Elizabeth Schomer Barber Fund and a Gershenson Fellowship provided financial support, for which I am also grateful.

Finally, it is fitting to acknowledge here the hospitality of my colleagues at the Molengraaff Institute at the University of Utrecht where, during a pleasant fall semester in 1993, I completed the manuscript.

John F. Dolan

October 1994

SECURED TRANSACTIONS AND PAYMENT SYSTEMS

Problems and Answers

PART ONE

SECURED TRANSACTIONS

Secured Transactions: Problems

Section 1. Transferring Property Interests: Security of Property, Good-Faith Purchase, and Fraudulent Conveyance

It is helpful to think of a secured transaction as a transfer of a property interest, a transfer of one of those sticks in the bundle of sticks that comprise ownership of an asset, in this case, a personal property asset. A lien, a claim, a special property interest, and a security interest are examples of interests in personal property that may be the subject of a transfer or conveyance. The law of secured transactions is law that governs the transfer of those property interests and the respective rights and liabilities that attend them.

You can facilitate your study of Uniform Commercial Code Article 9 by pausing to consider the transfer categories. Generally, transfers fall into one of three categories, under which the taker receives (1) exactly the same interest as that of the transferor, (2) an interest greater than that of the transferor, or (3) an interest less than that of the transferor.

The second kind of transfer is rather famous in commercial law and has its own name: good-faith purchase. The third is also common. It is the fraudulent conveyance against which commercial law must take precautions and impose penalties. The first kind of conveyance is the most common of all but it has no name, though it lends itself to poetic license or Latin logic. "No stream can rise higher than its source." "*Nemo dat quod non habet.*" The less erudite among us refer to the first rule as the security-of-property or the no-more rule: the taker receives no more rights than its transferor enjoyed. Professor Harris calls the first rule the "*nemo dat*" rule. Professors Jackson and Baird call it the derivation principle. Sometimes the first rule allows a party to come within the "shelter" or under the "umbrella" of its transferor. All these appellations are descriptive.

The following problems illustrate the operation of the three rules and hint at the policies that produced them.

Problems

1. Dealer entered into a contract to sell earth moving equipment to Mine Co. on credit. Mine Co. agreed to pay 10 percent of the total price at the time of delivery and the balance in 120 equal monthly installments. Mine Co. took delivery of the equipment at its mine on May 1. The check it gave Dealer bounced. It is now December 15, and Mine Co. has made none of the monthly payments. Dealer tells you that the equipment is sitting on a parcel of real estate near the mine, and that Dealer could easily take a flatbed truck and remove the equipment. What do you tell Dealer? Does Dealer have any interest in the equipment? Is title to the equipment in Dealer or Mine Co.?

2. §2-401(1)(second sentence). Woolen Co. delivered wool to Distributor Co. under a contract of conditional sale providing that Distributor would pay only for wool it sold to garment companies and that title to the wool would remain in Woolen Co. until such sales occurred. What interest does Woolen Co. have in the wool on Distributor's premises? What interest does it have in wool Distributor sold to a garment manufacturer? Can Distributor's creditors defeat Woolen Co.'s claim to the wool? Would your answers differ if Woolen Co. names Distributor its agent for purposes of soliciting orders from the garment industry?

3. Seller Co., a tool and die business, agreed to sell all of its assets to Buyer Co. with payment of the purchase price to be made over a five-year period. Seller and Buyer also agreed that title to the tools and dies would remain in Seller Co. and that in the event Buyer does not pay all of the purchase price, Seller could repossess the goods. What interest does Seller have in the goods?

4. §2-403(1). In each of the following cases, on May 1 A conveyed all of his rights in a shipment of toluene to B. What does B get:
   a. If A has absolute ownership rights in the cargo?
   b. If, on April 30, A had granted a security interest to C?
   c. If, on May 2, A conveyed his interest in the cargo to C? (Why might the law fashion a different answer to this question if B had left the cargo in A's possession?)
   d. Identify the policies that your answers to each of the foregoing questions serve.

5. §2-403(1). On May 1, Seller granted a security interest in an aircraft to First Bank. On May 2, Seller sold the aircraft to Buyer Co. On May 3, Buyer Co. granted a security interest to Second Bank. Seller Co. and Buyer Co. are now insolvent and have defaulted on their respective obligations to the banks. Both banks claim the equipment. If you assume that both security agreements are fully enforceable, which bank should prevail? Would your answer differ if First Bank's security interest is invalid with respect to Buyer Co.?

6. §2-403(1). On May 1, A lost his gold watch, and B found it. On May 2, B conveyed the watch to C. If A sues C to obtain possession of the watch,

what result? How would you describe C's interest in the watch if A could not find C? (Assume that C is unaware of A's interest in the watch.) Answer the preceding questions assuming that B did not find the watch but stole it. Are there considerations of public policy that dictate one result in the case of loss and another in the case of theft?

7. Owner, who collected portraits, delivered a Whistler to Auctioneer, telling Auctioneer, "Put this up for bids at the auction Saturday but don't sell it. I merely want to know what kind of bids it will generate." Auctioneer duly put the portrait up for bids. Collector bid $500,000 for it. Owner refuses to deliver the painting or to accept Collector's offer of payment. Who owns the painting? Is title in Collector? §2-401(2). Does it matter? §2-401 (preamble). Did Auctioneer have actual authority to sell the painting? Did he have apparent authority? If he had apparent authority, can Collector hold Owner? Should he be able to hold Owner?

8. *§2-403(2), (3).* Smith took his yacht to Dealer, who sold yachts, and asked Dealer to solicit bids. Dealer entered into a sales contract with Jones, who has paid for the yacht and taken delivery. In a dispute between Smith and Jones, who will prevail? Why does the law deprive Smith of his title? Was Smith at fault? Was Jones? Who can more efficiently avoid this loss? Would your answer differ if Smith took the yacht to Dealer solely for purposes of having the yacht stored at Dealer's premises? That Smith delivered the yacht to Dealer with instructions to charter it to vacationers, with Smith receiving 60 percent of the receipts and Dealer receiving the balance? (Bear in mind that neither Smith nor Jones wants a cause of action against Dealer, though the loser in the dispute would surely have such a cause of action. In the real world, dealers that behave this way are usually insolvent when their misconduct comes to light.)

9. *§2-403(1)(b).* Manufacturer sold a carload of greige goods to Middle, who took delivery and paid for the goods with a check that later bounced. Before Manufacturer could do anything about it, however, Middle sold the goods to Dealer. In a dispute between Manufacturer and Dealer, who prevails? Would your answer be different if you knew that Manufacturer had never delivered the goods to Middle? That Dealer had never paid Middle? (See the definition of "value" in §1-201(44).) Why does the statute protect Dealer's expectation interest?

10. *§2-403(1)(a).* Owner shipped 100 cartons of short sleeved women's blouses to Jones, a poor credit risk. Owner, misled by Jones' misstatements, believed that Jones was Reed, a wholesaler of impeccable credit reputation. Jones then sold the blouses to several retailers. In a dispute between Owner and the retailers, who prevails? Did Owner intend that Jones take title to the garments? If Owner had sued Jones before he entered into a contract with the retailers, could Owner have maintained successfully that he had title to the blouses?

11. See *Uniform Fraudulent Transfer Act §4.* Ace Electric Co. owed First Bank $400,000. When Ace defaulted under the terms of the loan agreement and note, the bank sued and obtained a judgment against Ace. During the

course of that lawsuit, Ace, whose sole stockholder is Joe Ace, sold all of its assets (most of them consisting of trucks, tools, and other equipment) to Joe for "one dollar and other good and valuable consideration." First is now seeking to levy against the assets. Will it succeed?

12. *§2-402(2).*   On May 1, Edison Co. purchased a truck from Dealer, paying $20,000, but left the truck on Dealer's lot with plans to pick it up a week later. On May 2, First Bank, a creditor of Dealer, made a claim on the truck. In a dispute between First and Edison, who prevails? Would it matter that Edison had left the truck with Dealer to have it undercoated? Would it matter that Edison had left the truck with Dealer for a month? What result in the foregoing fact settings if the buyer is Dealer's sole shareholder?

Section 2.   Scope

Article 9 of the Uniform Commercial Code is a signal achievement. Its architects — Gilmore, Kripke, and Llewellyn, among others — rationalized a system of law governing personal property security that had up until then defied rationalization in the United States and that still defies it elsewhere. It is a tribute to the Code drafters that Article 9 achieved ubiquitous adoption in the U.S. and ubiquitous regard, though not emulation, abroad. Parties often disguise secured transactions, treating them as sales, consignments, leases, or retention of title arrangements. A remarkable achievement of the Article is its scope provision, which looks through the disguises and lets the realities govern the application of the statute. The scope provision is not without its problems, but by and large it has been an outstanding success.

The following problems illustrate it and the difficulties that attend it. Some problems in this section deal with the transactions that the drafters felt should be excluded from the operation of the Article.

Problems

13. *§9-102(1)(b).*   May, a garment manufacturer, sells all of its accounts receivable ("accounts" in Article 9 parlance) to Finance Co. with the understanding that Finance Co. will collect them and charge May back for any account that is bad. Should Finance Co. comply with Article 9? Would your answer differ if May sold the accounts to the finance company without recourse (with the understanding that the finance company would take the loss on bad accounts)? What is the difference between the sale of accounts and the creation of a security interest in accounts?

14. *§9-102(1)(b) and §9-104(f).*   Dealer sells battery-powered forklift trucks. He has found a new line of customers: independent supermarket operators. The operators need credit, however, and Dealer has agreed to 120-day terms. Dealer insists that the purchasers sign installment sales contracts (which are chattel paper in Article 9 parlance) obligating the purchasers to make monthly payments for the trucks and granting Dealer a security interest in the trucks to secure those payments. Dealer finds that the volume of his paper has risen to the point that he can no longer afford to carry it. Dealer, therefore, approaches Bank and asks Bank to take the paper as collateral for a loan. Must Bank comply with Article 9? Would your answer differ if Dealer sold the paper to Bank? What if Dealer sold its paper to New Dealer along with all of the other assets of Dealer's business?

15. *§9-104(j).*   Mortgage Co. generates second mortgages by lending money to customers of home improvement contractors. The contractors steer the customer to Mortgage Co., which lends the money directly to the customer to pay for the home improvement. Mortgage Co. takes a second mortgage on the customer's home from the customer as security for the note it also takes. It then quickly turns the note and mortgage over to National Bank, which usually pays Mortgage Co. 95 percent of the face amount of the note. Must the bank comply with Article 9? Is the bank's interest in the note a security interest? Is its interest in the mortgage? Does it matter whether Mortgage Co. sells the note and the mortgage to the bank or whether it grants the bank a security interest in the note and the mortgage?

16. *§9-104(a) and comment 1.*   First National Bank loaned $1 million to rock star Andy Swinger for a Lear jet that Swinger is buying. First National took a security agreement under Article 9 that properly creates a security interest in the aircraft. Thus, in Article 9 parlance the security interest "attached." The bank also filed a financing statement in the office designated by Article 9 as the place to file for security interests in Swinger's personal property. Is it accurate to say that having complied with Article 9, the bank can now safely conclude that it is adequately protected? Would the answer be any different if the collateral were a yacht registered under the Federal Ship Mortgage Act? A patent?

17. When Swinger went to the bank to borrow for the aircraft, he also wanted to borrow additional sums for an investment he planned to make in a Las Vegas casino. In which of the following assets might he grant the bank a security interest under Article 9?
    a. Sums due from a recording company under a recording contract. §9-106.
    b. A claim against Andy Zinger for pirating Swinger's songs. §9-104(k).
    c. Sums due from American Casualty Co. for losses Swinger sustained when thieves stole his Grammy. §9-104(g).
    d. One Thousand pounds Swinger has on deposit with the O'Connell Street Branch of the Bank of Ireland. §9-104(*l*).

Section 3.   *The Concept of Security*

If a security interest is a property interest, as most agree it is, there must be rules for its creation. The Code rule is that it is created by the voluntary act or sufferance of the debtor, the party that is conveying the security interest to the secured party or is allowing the secured party to retain a security interest. A security interest arises when the debtor grants it to the secured party or when a seller of goods retains a security interest in them with the buyer's acquiescence.

Problems

18. Seller entered into a contract to sell a drill press on credit to Buyer. More than ten days after delivery, Buyer had not paid. What might Seller do to obtain payment from Buyer? May Seller sneak into Buyer's premises and retrieve the press?

19. *Bankruptcy Code §362.*   Assume the same facts as in the preceding problem with the additional fact that Seller retained a perfected security interest in the press. How would this additional fact alter your answers to the preceding question? Would Buyer's bankruptcy have any effect on Seller's actions? What effect would Buyer's bankruptcy have on Seller's position in Problem 18?

20. *§9-307(1).*   In the preceding problem assume Buyer sold the press to Sub-Buyer. Can Seller recover the press from Sub-Buyer? Would it matter whether Sub-Buyer is a buyer in ordinary course, that is, a buyer without knowledge of Seller's claim who buys in the ordinary course of business from a merchant who sells goods of the kind? Should the law prefer ordinary course Sub-Buyer to Seller?

Section 4.   *Creating the Security Interest: The Security Agreement*

A security interest is not a lien or claim that arises by operation of law. It arises by virtue of a voluntary transfer. The Code forges this feature of the security interest through the concept of "attachment." Attachment occurs only when the parties satisfy certain Code requirements that protect the debtor by insisting that the transaction reveal that the debtor created the security interest voluntarily. Those requirements also relate to the scope of the interest transferred.

Problems

21. *§9-201.*   On May 1, Debtor granted Secured Party a perfected security interest in Debtor's plastic molding machine. Which of the following parties are bound by the conveyance?
  a. Debtor.
  b. Secured Party.
  c. Debtor's unsecured creditors.
  d. *X*, to whom Debtor sells the machine on May 2.

e. *Y*, to whom Debtor grants a security interest in the machine on May 2.

f. *Z*, who causes the sheriff to levy on the machine on May 3.

g. Debtor's trustee in bankruptcy when Debtor files a petition in bankruptcy on May 4.

22. Would any of your answers to the foregoing question differ if

   a. Debtor retained possession of the machine and granted the security interest to Secured Party orally? §9-203.

   b. Secured Party failed to perfect its security interest? §9-301.

   c. Debtor holds title to the machine? §9-202.

   d. Secured Party holds title to the machine? §9-202.

23. *§9-203(1)(a), (c).* On May 1, Debtor Co., a hardware wholesaler that purchases from manufacturers and sells to hardware retailers, entered into a security agreement granting First Bank a security interest in all of Debtor's "inventory, equipment, and accounts, now owned or hereafter acquired or arising." The secured party, First Bank, made a loan to Debtor of $100,000. In which of the following items of property does Bank have a security interest on May 1? On August 1?

   a. A truckload of snow shovels Debtor acquired on May 10.

   b. Sums due from retailers for sales Debtor made to the retailers during June.

   c. Two electrically operated forklift trucks Debtor purchased on May 30 for use in its warehouse.

   d. Sums due Debtor under a software copyright license it entered into with a national chain of food wholesalers, the software being something Debtor developed to keep track of inventory.

   e. Thirteen checks Debtor received from retailers as proceeds from June sales of hinges, door knobs, kickplates, and other brass items.

24. Assume in the foregoing problem that Debtor's president, Joe, went to the bank to borrow the funds he needed as working capital. While he was at the bank, the loan officer asked him to sign a number of documents, including a loan agreement, a promissory note, a financing statement, and the security agreement. Joe went about signing the documents but inadvertently failed to sign the security agreement, a fact that did not become evident until six months later when Debtor Co. filed a petition in bankruptcy. Do these altered facts change any of your answers to the preceding question? Would it matter that the bank discovered the missing signature on August 1 and required Joe to execute the security agreement at that time?

25. *§1-201(37).* At the time of Debtor Co.'s default, it maintained 15 work stations located throughout the warehouse where warehouse employees fed data into a central processing unit that kept track of the inventory. The computer hardware that comprised this inventory control system and that consisted of 15 terminals, a central processing unit, printers, and various peripherals was leased to Debtor by Computer Leasing Co. Under the terms of the lease, which ran for 2 years and had 18 months to run, Debtor paid rent monthly and had the right to terminate the lease at any time. What right, if any, does First Bank have in the computer hardware?

26. On May 1, three farm producers delivered cattle to the slaughterhouse of Samuels & Co. under a contract of sale. Samuels could not pay the producers immediately because the purchase price depended on the weight of the slaughtered animals and the grade that government inspectors gave them. Traditionally, it took a day for the cattle to be slaughtered, dressed, weighed, and graded; shortly thereafter, Samuels would write a check to the producers. On May 2, before Samuels could write the checks to the three farmers, its creditors forced Samuels into bankruptcy. One of the creditors, Commercial Finance, Ltd., had taken a properly signed security agreement from Samuels on April 10, some three weeks before the producers delivered the cattle in question. The security agreement described Commercial's collateral as "all inventory of cattle, now owned or hereafter acquired." The farmers can show that on May 1, Samuels' liabilities greatly exceeded its assets, that is, on May 1, Samuels was insolvent. Under the common law, then, Samuels is guilty of fraud at law, taking delivery of goods on credit while insolvent. Under both the common law and §2-702(2) of the Code, the farm producers have the right to reclaim the cattle they delivered on May 1. Samuels' interest in the cattle on that date was title voidable by the producers. Assume that there is no state or federal statute that preempts application of the Code to this problem.

    a. Is Commercial a purchaser? §1-201(32), (33).
    b. Has it given value? §1-201(44)(b).
    c. Has it acted in good faith? Even if it knew that Samuels had inventory for which Samuels had not paid? §1-201(19).
    d. If the farm producers retained title to the cattle, how does the Code characterize their interest? §2-401(1)(second sentence).
    e. If your or the law's answers to questions a through c are in the affirmative, does Commercial defeat the producers? §2-403(1).
    f. Does the fact that under §9-312(3) the producers had a method to defeat Samuels support the Article 2 analysis implicit in the answers to the above questions?

27. *§9-204(3).* On May 1, CNC, Ltd. sold two pieces of robotic equipment to ABC Manufacturing Co. To pay for the equipment, ABC borrowed most of the purchase price from First Bank and granted First Bank a security interest in the two pieces of equipment to secure the loan. On December 1, First Bank extended credit to ABC to cover ABC's payroll. ABC is now in default on both loans. First Bank has sold the equipment for $2 million. The balance on the first loan is $1.75 million. May First Bank use the $250,000 excess to satisfy the December advance? Would your answer differ if the security agreement recited that the security interest secured

    a. all debts due from ABC to First Bank for equipment?
    b. all debts of any kind whatsoever?

28. *§2-401(1).* Assume in the foregoing question that ABC did not seek a loan from First Bank but purchased the machines for 10 percent down with the balance payable in monthly installments over a period of 60 months. Assume that in the written sales contract, the parties agreed that title to the equipment would remain in CNC until all of the payments were made. If ABC defaults in its installment obligation, may CNC repossess the machines?

29. On May 1, Beer Distributors, Inc. entered into a working capital loan agreement with First Bank. Under the terms of the agreement, First Bank extended a $1 million line of credit in Beer's favor. The agreement required Beer to grant the bank a security interest in all of its inventory, then owned or thereafter acquired. Beer turns its inventory over once every 45 days. Under the terms of the security agreement, First Bank allowed Beer to sell its inventory in the ordinary course of its business, so that by the middle of June, Beer held none of the inventory that it held on May 1. Every week, however, Beer received shipments of beer from its brewery suppliers. Beer defaulted on its bank loan on September 1.
    a. Does First Bank have any interest in the after-acquired inventory? §9-204(1).
    b. Does it matter that First Bank left the inventory in the possession of Beer with power to sell it? §9-205.

30. On May 1, XYZ Manufacturing granted First Bank a security interest in all of its equipment. On May 5, XYZ obtained a metal stamping machine. On May 10, XYZ defaulted on its loan to the bank. Does First Bank have the right to repossess the stamping machine?

31. *§9-203(1).* In each of the following illustrations, indicate the date on which the security interest of the bank first attached.
    a. The bank made a loan on May 1 and, on May 2, took possession from the debtor of promissory notes for collection through the bank collection system.
    b. The bank made a loan on May 1 and, on May 2, took a written security agreement signed by the debtor covering after-acquired inventory. On May 3, the debtor acquired its first shipment of inventory.
    c. The bank made a loan on May 1. On May 2, the debtor signed a security agreement covering equipment then owned or thereafter acquired. On May 3, the debtor identified a machine that it planned to use in its business and agreed to purchase from Seller Co. Seller Co. delivered the machine to Debtor on May 4.
    d. On May 1, the debtor signed a security agreement, and the bank made a binding commitment to make a loan. The security agreement covered after-acquired property. On May 2, the debtor acquired property of the kind described in the security agreement. On May 3, the bank disbursed the loan proceeds.
    e. The facts are the same as in d, but the loan commitment is not binding.
    f. The bank made a loan on May 1. On May 2, the debtor signed a security agreement covering inventory. On May 3, the debtor acquired new inventory.
    g. On May 1, the bank made a loan. On May 2, the debtor signed a security agreement covering all inventory. The debtor, on May 3, sold some inventory and received a promissory note from the purchaser.

32. *§9-106.* On May 1, Debtor granted First Bank a security interest in all of its accounts. In which of the following items of Debtor's property does the bank enjoy a security interest?

    a. Office furniture. §9-109(2).
    b. Word processors. §9-109(2).
    c. Stationery, fuel for vehicles, and unsold merchandise. §9-109(4).

33. *§9-109(4).*   On May 1, Debtor, an aluminum fabricator, granted First Bank a security interest in all of its inventory. In which of the following items of Debtor's personal property does the bank enjoy a security interest?
    a. Aluminum ingots Debtor plans to melt and mold into parts it will sell to its customers.
    b. Partially manufactured aluminum parts.
    c. Finished goods.
    d. Cartons Debtor uses to ship finished goods.
    e. Stationery and fuel for vehicles.

Section 5. Definitions

By now it should be apparent that Article 9 differentiates collateral by type. The distinctions are functional and accommodate different rules that reflect merchant and banking practices. Much of Article 9 study is the study of the rules that rest on these distinctions, rules relating to priorities and the place to file being chief among them. Later, you will see that Code provisions defining parties also play a key role in application of Code rules. For now it is enough to be concerned with definitions that relate to collateral. As you do the following problems, you may find it helpful to consult the comments to §9-102, the scope provision. Comment 5 to that section is a catalogue of the various kinds of collateral and the rules that apply to each kind.

Problems

34. *§9-106.*   Joe Buyer owes Carl Creditor $5,000. In which of the following cases is the debt an account?
    a. When Creditor loaned the money to Buyer.
    b. When the sum is due for goods sold to Buyer on credit.
    c. When the sum is due for services performed by Creditor for Buyer on credit.
    d. In either b or c, if Creditor holds
        i. a promissory note signed by Buyer.
        ii. a written lease under which Buyer grants Creditor an interest in goods and agrees to pay the $5,000 in monthly installments. §9-105(1)(b).
        iii. a non-negotiable promissory note or some other written contract evidencing Buyer's obligation to pay Creditor.

35. *§9-318.*   Seller's customers buy goods periodically from Seller on open account. On May 1, Seller decided to sell these obligations to First Factor Co., which undertook to collect the sums due from the customers. First Factor paid Seller 95 percent of the total amount of the obligations and agreed that the sale was without recourse, that is, Seller does not have to buy back from First any obligation that goes bad by virtue of a customer's default.

    a. Does Article 9 apply to the transaction? If so, what steps must First take in connection with the sale of the accounts?

    b. What are the Article 9 terms in this transaction for
        i. customer's obligation to Seller?
       ii. Seller?
      iii. First Factor?
      iv. the customers?

    c. If First notifies the customers of the sale of the obligations, may the customers pay Seller? Would your answer to this question differ if the terms of the obligation between Seller and the customers forbade Seller to sell the obligation to anyone?

    d. If a customer receives notice of the sale of his obligation to First but pays Seller, is the customer's obligation discharged?

    e. If a customer does not receive any notice of the sale of his obligation to First, will the customer's payment to Seller discharge the obligation?

36. Dealer sells pipe and pipe fittings to plumbing contractors on 60-day terms. Dealer's accounts from these customers aggregate $2.5 million. In addition, Dealer has inventory, a warehouse, and equipment, all of which are valued at about $650,000. Dealer is retiring and plans to sell his assets to X for cash. Must X comply with the attachment and perfection rules of Article 9? Must X worry about the rules of §9-318?

Section 6. *Defining Proceeds*

In a simpler age, commerce was rather static; debtors' collateral did not move. In the modern day, however, collateral moves with alarming celerity. Secured parties protect themselves by policing the activity of their borrowers. The Code provides further help for the secured party by fashioning a proceeds rule that is rather generous. To accommodate commercial practices, the proceeds section's rules often differentiate among the kinds of collateral involved.

Problems

37. *§9-306(1).* On May 1, Dealer granted First Bank a security interest in all of Dealer's new cars, then owned or thereafter acquired, including all accessories and additions thereto. To which of the following items received by Dealer during the week of May 1, will the bank's security interest attach?

    a. Three used cars and a used truck that customers traded to Dealer as down payments on new vehicles.

    b. Ten retail installment sales contracts signed by customers that purchased new vehicles and that contained a security interest granted by the purchaser to Dealer.

c. Nine checks that customers used as down payments on new cars.

d. A check that was a down payment on a used car. (Would it matter that the used car was not a trade-in for the sale of a new car?)

e. Two hundred dollars in the cash drawer that includes some cash down payments and some payments for work done by the service department. (Would it matter that some of the cash, no one knowing how much, had been used during the week to buy lunches for employees of Dealer?)

f. Insurance proceeds from damage done to a new car when a customer test-drove it.

g. A customer's obligation to pay for parts and service.

h. A deposit account that contains $500 from a check received that day from the sale of a new car. (Would it matter that non-proceeds had been deposited in the account that week? Would it matter that the proceeds were deposited on Monday and the non-proceeds later in the week?)

i. A deposit account segregated for proceeds from the sale of new vehicles.

38. In the preceding question, who bears the burden of showing that the items are proceeds?

Section 7. *Commingling*

The following two problems deal with the commingling of collateral.

Problems

39. *§9-315.* Copper Co. sells copper ingots to Brass Co. for $60,000. Zinc Co. sells zinc to Brass for $60,000. Both sellers sell on credit and retain a security interest in the metal they sell. Brass has made brass (60 percent copper and 40 percent zinc) parts out of the shipments from Copper and Zinc and sold them to customers on open account for $75,000. Brass is now insolvent. Copper and Zinc both claim the accounts. What part of the accounts will go to Copper and what part to Zinc?

40. After granting each of the sellers a security interest in the product they sell, Bakery Co. purchased on credit flour from *F*, butter from *B*, and leaven from *L*. Bakery has turned all of the ingredients into bread. Under §9-315, what must each of the sellers show to claim a security interest in the bread?

41. On May 1, *F* granted First Bank a security interest in *F*'s sorghum crop. On May 2, *F*, who is a member of a local farm cooperative, sold the sorghum to the cooperative in return for the right to draw up to $40,000 in feed, fertilizer, seed, and other products the cooperative sells to its members. Does First Bank have any interest in the drawing rights?

42. In May, *F* granted First Bank a security interest in all of his grain or legume crops then growing or thereafter to be grown on his 1,000 acre farm in Princeville, Illinois. The following winter, *F* entered into a government program under which he agreed not to plant any cash or feed crop on his farm, but only clover or prairie grasses. Under the program, at the end of the growing season, *F* will be entitled to the market price on the day he cashes his entitlement of 40,000 bushels of corn and 30,000 bushels of soybeans. Does the bank have any interest in the entitlements?

43. In the preceding problem, *F* also granted the bank a security interest in all of his livestock, then owned or thereafter acquired. *F* owned 100 head of dairy cattle, 15 of which calved the following spring. Does the bank have any interest in the calves?

Section 8. *Tracing*

Tracing rules are customarily the concern of accountants, but in proceeds cases tracing becomes a problem for the lawyer. The lowest intermediate balance method of tracing funds commingled in an account comes to secured transactions law from trust law. Note that the courts — for this is judge-made commercial law, not Code law — eschewed tracing rules (e.g., LIFO or FIFO) that they might have used. The lowest intermediate balance rule can be thought of as treating proceeds as heavy water that sinks to the bottom of the bucket. The debtor takes water from the top of the bucket and may never dip into the proceeds that have sunk to the bottom. If he does dip into the proceeds, however, the proceeds are lost to the secured party. Non-proceeds water poured into the bucket thereafter will replenish the bucket but not the proceeds that remain depleted at the lowest intermediate balance level.

Problems

44. The following chart shows the deposits and end-of-day balances of a checking account of Dealer, which has granted a security interest in all of its inventory to First Bank. Each deposit is comprised of checks received from customers as down payments for the purchase of new cars out of Dealer's inventory. What is the amount of proceeds in the account on each day? (Bear in mind that the chart does not show debits, only credits and the balance on each day.)

Date	Deposit	Balance
May 1	$10,000	$20,000
May 2	— 0 —	5,000
May 3	— 0 —	1,000
May 4	5,000	6,000
May 5	— 0 —	1,000
May 6	— 0 —	100,000

45. *§9-110.* If Debtor grants First Bank a security interest in "all of debtor's property no matter where situated, now owned or hereafter acquired," will the bank have a security interest in any of Debtor's property?

46. *§9-105(1)(b) and (i).* Debtor, a commodities broker, granted First Bank a security interest in all of Debtor's "instruments and chattel paper." Debtor has in its safe a negotiable bill of lading covering 200,000 barrels of West Texas crude oil. Debtor and the bank orally agreed that the bank would have an interest in the bill. Thereafter Debtor delivered the bill to the bank. Does First Bank have any interest in the bill? In the oil?

Section 9. *More on Classifying Collateral*

Definitions are the subject of the next 14 problems. One purpose of the problems is to make the definitions second nature. You cannot understand class discussion without a working understanding of the definitions. It simply will not do for you to refer back to the definition section or your notes as the instructor and fellow students talk about purchase money security interests, accounts, chattel paper, and equipment. To be literate in commercial law (the primary object of your commercial law study in law school), you must move these definitions from your passive to your active vocabulary. The problems help.

Problems

47. *§9-109.* Rockford, Inc. manufactures steel door locks, hinges, fasteners, and other hardware for the construction industry. Rockford owns rolled steel sheets, steel wire, and steel rods, all of which it uses in the manufacture of its products. For purposes of Article 9, what kind of collateral would the steel sheets, wire, and rods be? What kind of collateral would partially manufactured products be? Finished goods?

48. *§9-109.* Wausau Co., a modular home builder, owns hinges and door hardware it acquired from Rockford. Wausau also owns electric saws and drills, trucks, and heating oil for the plant it uses to manufacture its products. For purposes of Article 9, how would you classify the hinges and door hardware, the electric saws and drills, the trucks, and the heating oil?

49. Contractor, a sole proprietorship, does small home improvement jobs, driveway repaving, and snow removal work. Over the years customers have paid him by
     a.   cash, §9-304(1),
     b.   promissory note, §9-105(1)(j),
     c.   agreeing in writing to pay him 30 days after he completes the work, §9-106, and
     d.   trading an oriental rug that he took home and put in his living room, §9-109(1).

How would you classify the various assets for Article 9 purposes?

50. *§§9-105(1)(f), 9-109(4).*   Dealer sells personal computers. He has 20 pc's on his showroom floor and a negotiable bill of lading covering 10 more that are en route to his establishment from a manufacturer. How would you classify Dealer's assets?

51. *§9-109.*   Cincinnati sells new and used grand pianos. On May 1, he sold a Steinway to *A* for use in the music studio where she teaches her students. On May 2, Cincinnati sold a Mason & Hamlin to *B* who took the piano home for use by her children. On May 3, Cincinnati sold a Baldwin to *C* to use in her piano bar. How do you classify the three pianos?

52. In the preceding problem, Cincinnati sold the Mason & Hamlin under a written contract that obligated *B* to pay Cincinnati in 60 equal monthly installments and granted Cincinnati a security interest in the piano to secure the payments.
    a. What special character does Article 9 give to this security interest? §9-107.
    b. In what kind of property does Cincinnati have a security interest? §9-109(1).
    c. If First Bank takes a security interest in the retail installment contract, in what kinds of collateral will the bank have a security interest? §§9-109(1), 9-105(1)(b).
    d. Does Cincinnati have to file a financing statement to perfect its security interest in the piano? Would it have to file if it had taken similar retail installment sales contracts from *A* and *C*? §9-302(1)(d).
    e. Does the bank have to file a financing statement to perfect its security interest in the chattel paper? §§9-304(1), 9-305.
    f. Does the bank have to file a financing statement to perfect its security interest in the piano? §9-302(2).
    g. Would any of your analysis in this question change if Cincinnati had sold the retail installment sales contract to the bank? §9-102.

53. *§9-305 and comment 1.*   On May 1, Investor subscribed and paid for 4,000 shares of preferred stock in ABC Co. The company could not issue the stock certificate to Investor until the Securities and Exchange Commission issued a letter to the company validating the company's opinion that the stock was not covered by regulations requiring registration of the offering. On May 2, Investor granted First Bank a security interest in her rights to the stock. How do you classify Investor's interest? How would you perfect the bank's security interest? Can Investor pledge her stock to the bank on May 2? What other kind of collateral cannot be the subject of a pledge?

54. *§9-304(1).*   Syndicator sells limited partnership interests in aircraft that the partnership leases to airlines. Under the syndication, the limited partners invest $500,000, of which $50,000 is to be in cash, with the balance to be evidenced by a negotiable promissory note. Syndicator intends to borrow money to complete the acquisition of the aircraft. What will he have to offer the bank as security? How will the bank perfect its security interest? May it file a financing statement?

55. Jones, a lawyer, enjoyed watching motion pictures made in the 1930s. Jones bought a VCR from Chicago, a retailer, that sold the equipment to Jones under a retail installment sales contract. Under the terms of the contract, Jones granted Chicago a security interest in the VCR to secure payment of the purchase price, which Jones agreed to pay over 24 months.

    a. Must Chicago file a financing statement to perfect its security interest? §9-302(1)(d).

    b. Would your answer differ if Jones had acquired the VCR to show clients films on estate planning?

    c. What should Chicago do if Jones plans to use the VCR 25 percent of the time to watch the films and 75 percent for his clients? §9-109(1) and comment 2.

    d. What should Chicago do if Jones buys the VCR for use in the home and a month later takes it to the office? §9-401(3).

56. *§9-109.* Hennery has 100 gross of eggs. It sells them to Farm Distributor Co, which sells them to Ace Food Markets, Inc., which sells one dozen of them to Smith, who takes them home and puts them in the kitchen refrigerator. For Article 9 purposes, how do you classify the eggs in the hands of each of the parties?

57. *§9-109(3).* Dillon operates a feedlot on which he fattens 10,000 head of cattle. Dillon owns 50 percent of the cattle. The other 5,000 head are owned by a consortium of schoolteachers, ophthalmologists, and attorneys. How would you classify the cattle for Article 9 purposes? Are the cattle in the possession of one engaged in farming operations?

58. *§9-106.* How would you classify for Article 9 purposes the following assets?

    a. Drawing rights under an investment cooperative.

    b. Capital investment of a partner available to the partner upon withdrawal from the firm.

    c. Royalties due from a publisher to an author.

    d. Right to return of membership fees due country club member upon death.

    e. Alimony payments.

    f. Bequests due from an estate under administration.

59. *§9-107.* Which of the following secured parties has a purchase money security interest?

    a. Chicago, which sells a snowmobile to Jones on credit for use on weekends (late September through early May) in Michigan's northern peninsula and takes a security interest from Jones.

    b. First Credit Union that takes a security interest from Jones and lends her the money to pay Chicago cash at the time she acquires the snowmobile from Chicago. Would your answer to this question differ if Jones used the money from the credit union to pay tuition and borrowed the purchase price from her mother to pay Chicago?

    c. If the credit union is a purchase money secured party, does it need to file a financing statement to perfect its security interest? §9-302(1)(d). How might the credit union protect its assumption that it is a purchase money secured party?

60. Dealer sells personal computers to farmers and other small businesses on credit. Under the arrangement, the purchasers execute installment contracts granting Dealer a security interest in the computers and reflecting the purchasers' obligation to pay Dealer the purchase price over a fixed period of time, usually 24 months. Dealer also takes a financing statement from the purchaser and files the statement with the office of the register of deeds or of the secretary of state, all in proper fashion.

    a.   What is the nature of Dealer's collateral? §9-109(2).

    b.   If Dealer discounts its paper with First Bank, what is the nature of First Bank's collateral? Does First Bank have two kinds of collateral? §9-105(1)(b).

    c.   What must First Bank do to become a perfected secured creditor with respect to the personal computers? §9-302(2).

    d.   With respect to the paper? §9-302.

Section 10.   *The Financing Statement*

Part 4 of Article 9 deals with the financing statement. Section 9-402 sets out the requirements for the statement; section 9-401 indicates the office or offices where the secured party must file the statement in order to be perfected.

You will note that there are three choices for the state legislatures under the official text of Article 9. The problems in this book assume that the legislature has chosen "second alternative subsection (1)." That section is the most commonly adopted section, and it has sufficient variation to allow the problems to capture the flavor of filing problems in general. Of course, in practice, you will consult your state's version of §9-401 or the version of the state whose law governs the perfection of the assets in question.

It will not surprise you to learn that these two sections, 9-401 and 9-402, prompt a considerable amount of trouble for the careless lender. When a trustee in bankruptcy succeeds to the assets of a debtor's estate, the trustee takes free of unperfected security interests. Filing in the incorrect office or filing an inadequate financing statement are two common mistakes that leave a secured party unperfected. Trustees are aware of that fact and comb through the financing statements carefully to see whether they can upset a secured creditor's claim of perfection. The following problems deal with technical rules, the observance of which is often critical to the secured lender.

Problems

61.   *§9-401(1).*   Where should First Bank file to perfect a security interest in the following items of collateral?

    a.   A combine owned by a farmer residing in Lake County, Michigan and farming in Mason County, Michigan. Would your answer differ if the owner were a feed store operator who combined for farmers on a contract basis?

    b.   A sum due from a Lake County dairy to a Mason County farmer.

    c.   A Cleveland, Ohio doctor's cattle located on a Mason County feedlot.

    d.   A boiler in an apartment building.

    e. Inventory of a Detroit hydraulic lift manufacturer.

    f. Accounts held by a tool and die manufacturer in Chicago.

    g. Equipment leases held by the subsidiary of a bank.

    h. Cash.

    i. A negotiable bill of lading covering
       i. cattle;
      ii. plastic pellets.

    j. Cattle at a slaughterhouse.

    k. Trotters at Northville Downs race track in Northville, Michigan.

62. *§9-402.* Which of the following defects in a financing statement would render the filing defective?

    a. "A.B. Jones Mfg. Co." for a debtor whose name is "A.B. Jones Manufacturing Co., Inc."

    b. Description of collateral as "farm products" for
       i. a dairy herd;
      ii. a race horse.

    c. Secured party listed as "Joe" Smith for "Joseph" Smith. Would your answer differ if Smith were the debtor?

    d. Debtor listed as Benjamin Smith, when
       i. debtor is J. Benjamin Smith;
      ii. debtor is JBS, Ltd., a corporation of which Smith is sole shareholder.
      iii. Does it matter in either of the foregoing cases that no creditor is misled? In i, that everyone knows that Benjamin Smith is J. Benjamin Smith?

63. *§9-402(7).* On May 1, Ace Heating & Supply Co. sold all of its assets to ABC Co., which granted a security interest in the assets to Ace. Ace immediately filed a financing statement designating ABC as the debtor and Ace as the secured party. On May 2, Ace changed its name to XYZ Co., and ABC changed its name to Ace Heating & Supply Co. (This is a not uncommon way for a new corporation (ABC) to acquire the assets, including the goodwill of an existing company (Ace).) What are the risks here? Has XYZ (the original Ace and the secured party) behaved in bad faith? Is its filing misleading? Does Article 9 require it to make a new filing? If Ace had owned substantial inventory and if the security agreement covered that inventory and after-acquired inventory, does XYZ have a problem? When a bank takes a loan application from a customer, do you suppose the application asks the customer whether it has changed its name within the last five years?

64. *§9-402(1), (7).* If First Bank is about to make a secured loan to Hartford Inns, a division of Old Colony Hotel Corp., under what name should it search for previous filings? Under what name should First Bank designate the debtor on its financing statement?

65. *§9-403(1).* On May 1, First Bank perfected its security interest in Dealer's inventory by filing a proper financing statement in the office of the secretary of state. The filing officer, however, indexed the filing improperly. On May 2, Second Bank searched for filings against Dealer and, finding none, took a security interest in Dealer's inventory. Dealer has now defaulted on both loans. Which bank should have priority?

66. *§§9-402(1), 9-110.*   Would a financing statement listing the debtor as "Joe Smith, Maplewood, Maine" be sufficient? Would a filing listing the debtor as "Joe Smith, Los Angeles, California" be sufficient? Would a crop description listing the real estate as "80 acres farmed by Joseph Smith in Antrim County" be sufficient if the debtor farmed only one 80-acre tract? If he farmed two different farms, one of 80 and the other of 160 acres?

67. *§9-402(7).*   On May 1, Wholesaler, Inc. granted First Bank a security interest in all of Wholesaler's inventory, including after-acquired inventory. On the same day, First filed a financing statement listing the debtor as "Wholesaler, Inc." On May 2, ABC Co. acquired all of the stock of Wholesaler and merged the two companies under the name ABC Wholesalers, Inc. On July 2, the merged company received a shipment of inventory. On October 1, the company acquired another shipment of inventory. If ABC Wholesalers, the merged company, filed in bankruptcy on October 20, will First Bank be able to claim the July inventory? The October inventory? Would your answer differ if First Bank filed a financing statement on September 30 indicating the name change? If it filed such a statement on October 5?

Section 11.   *Introduction to Fixtures*

Fixtures are a problem for two reasons. First, they fall into two categories, real estate and personal property, with different legal regimes. Second, there are times when no one can be sure that a piece of equipment, say, or a consumer appliance is a fixture or not. The Code responds to these confusing features of the fixture with an array of rules that ultimately make quite good sense but can be a little confusing.

We begin the study of fixtures with problems concerning the definition and the proper place to file. Note that there are two possible filings: a regular financing statement or a fixture filing, which is a financing statement with some additional information. The issues of priority among claims to fixtures are illustrated in Problems 151 through 160.

Problems

68. *§9-313.*   Where should a secured party file a financing statement to cover the following collateral? Must the filing be a fixture filing? What are the consequences in each case if it isn't?
   a. Pella windows incorporated into a new house. §9-313(2).
   b. A photocopy machine. §9-313(4)(c).
   c. A four-color, high-speed printing press bolted to the floor of a manufacturing facility that was installed by tearing down a wall, which was later rebuilt.
   d. A boiler used as part of a central heating system in an apartment house.
   e. A Tiffany chandelier in a residence owned and occupied by the debtor.

  f. A radio tower bolted to a concrete platform and held in place by guy wires fastened by hooks imbedded in the concrete.

  g. A two-ton sign that is held in place by bolts and that can be removed in one hour by one person with a crescent wrench and a hydraulic hoist mounted on the bed of a truck.

  h. Would your answers to any of the foregoing problems differ if the owner of the real estate and the secured party agreed that the equipment would not become part of the real estate?

69. *§9-313(4)(d).* In the foregoing question, if the equipment mentioned is owned by a corporation and if the secured lender filed in the office of the secretary of state,

  a. Would the lender defeat the debtor's trustee in bankruptcy? Bankruptcy Code §544(a)(3).

  b. Would your answer differ if the secured lender filed a regular financing statement (as opposed to a fixture filing) in the office of the register of deeds?

  c. Would your answer to problem a differ if the secured lender were contesting with a purchaser of the real estate?

70. On May 1, Debtor granted First Bank a mortgage on a lot in the city. Thereafter Debtor built a house on the lot, installed a boiler in the house, added a sound system, and moved office equipment into a room of the house that Debtor uses as an office. In which of the foregoing items does the bank have an interest?

71. On May 1, Debtor granted a security interest in a wire strapping machine to Minneapolis Machines, Inc. The machine was installed in a building. The secured party filed centrally.

  a. If the machine is a fixture under the law of the jurisdiction, will the company defeat the trustee in bankruptcy of Debtor?

  b. Assume that the company made a fixture filing locally but did not file centrally. If the court finds the machine to be a fixture, will the trustee defeat the company? Will the trustee defeat the company if the court finds the machine not to be a fixture?

  c. Would your answers to any of the foregoing questions differ if the company were competing with a lien creditor instead of the trustee in bankruptcy? A mortgagee of the premises that obtained its mortgage after the machine was installed?

72. *§§9-313(1)(b), 9-402(3) and (5).* What information must be included in a fixture filing that need not be included in a regular filing? In which of the following sources would you look for that information?

  a. A copy of the deed that the person your client tells you is the owner has in his records.

  b. A real estate tax bill.

  c. Your client.

  d. The county real estate records.

73. If you as counsel for a tenant who is granting a security interest to a secured party are called on by the secured lender to give an opinion that the secured party's security interest in equipment installed in a building is

superior to all other security interests, which of the following steps would be sufficient?
   a. File centrally.
   b. File a fixture filing locally.
   c. Obtain the legal description and the identity of the owner of record by getting a title search from a title company.
   d. Obtain a disclaimer from the mortgagee.
   e. Rely on the readily removable equipment exception.

74. An equipment lessor suspects that some of its leases are going to be construed by the courts as security agreements. If it files centrally, it will
   a. always defeat the trustee; Bankruptcy Code §544(a)(3).
   b. defeat a subsequent purchaser of the real estate.

Section 12. *More on the Place to File*

Filing the financing statement can be a nuisance, but it is the statutory means for effecting the stated purpose of Article 9: to give notice to the world that the secured party is claiming an interest in the collateral.

In the best of all possible worlds, there would be one office for all UCC filings. But because we do not live in that world, we must analyze a secured transaction to determine which office is the appropriate office for filing.

These problems are exercises in that analysis. They assume, for pedagogical purposes, that §9-401, second alternative subsection (1), is in effect.

Problems

75. *§9-401(1).* Indicate the proper office for filing a financing statement to perfect a security interest in the following collateral:
   a. A plastic extrusion machine used by a tool and die company to make plastic parts for the toy industry.
   b. Plastic pellets used by the tool and die company to make the parts.
   c. A riding mower that Joe Smith uses to mow lawns for a living. If Smith bought the mower for personal uses while living in Adams County, where should the secured lender file? Must it re-file if Smith thereafter moves to Washington County?
   d. Payments due Weaver, a dairy farmer, from Hood Milk Co. for milk Weaver delivered to Hood last month.
   e. Weaver's herd of cows.
   f. Sums due Weaver under an oral lease of his prize breeding bull.
   g. Sums due from supermarkets for bread that International Baking Co. delivered last week.
   h. Equipment leases.
   i. Income tax refund due Weaver.
   j. Income tax refund due Smith.

76. *§9-401(1)(a).*   On May 1, Weaver purchased a tractor from Ace Tractor Co. and granted Ace a security interest in the tractor to secure payment of the purchase price. At the time Weaver was living in Adams County, but he planned to use the tractor in Washington County where he had just purchased a farm. On that day, Ace filed in Washington County. Was Ace perfected on May 1? If Weaver moved to Washington County on May 2, was Ace perfected on May 2?

Section 13.   Perfection Without Filing (Pledges and the Like)

There are three ways to perfect: (1) file, (2) take possession, and (3) do nothing. The following problems deal with the second category (the pledge) and the third (the case of automatic perfection).

Historians think that the oldest secured transaction was a pledge. Pledges figured prominently in societies without juridical institutions to enforce promises. In those days, the pledge looked much like a hostage arrangement. It still does, but we do not pledge our youngsters anymore; we pledge only our property.

There is some property that cannot be pledged: intangible property. There is other property that is so negotiable, so readily passed from one hand to another that it must be pledged if it is going to be the subject of a security interest. Finally, there is property that falls between the two categories. In those cases, the Code allows a secured party to perfect itself by filing but makes so many exceptions to protect third parties who deal with the collateral that the secured party with any risk will hold the collateral, that is, will insist on a pledge.

The Code allows automatic perfection when the costs of filing outweigh the benefits.

Problems

77. *§9-305.*   If Debtor grants Bank a security interest in Debtor's jewelry, may Bank perfect its security interest by appointing Debtor its agent to hold the jewelry?

78. *§9-305.*   If Debtor has securities in a safety deposit box, can Debtor pledge the securities to Finance Co. by giving the finance company the key to the box?

79. How do you take possession of an account? Of a general intangible? Of a letter of credit issued by SWIFT in electronic data interchange format? Of an unissued security?

80. *§§8-313(1)(a) and (h)(i), 8-321.*   On May 1, Debtor granted Broker a security interest in 100 shares of ABC Co. common stock to secure a loan of $50,000. The stock is worth $200,000, and Debtor would like to grant a second security interest in the stock to Uncle to secure a loan that Uncle is now making to Debtor.

    a.   How should Broker perfect its security interest?

    b.   How should Uncle perfect his?

81.   *§9-207.* On May 1, Debtor pledged shares of XYZ Co. common stock and ABC Co. convertible debentures with First Bank as security for a loan. On May 2, ABC Co. called the debentures, but the bank failed to act and missed the deadline for converting the shares. Had the bank effected the conversion, the common shares of ABC would be worth $100,000. Today, the debentures are worth $15,000. Over the period that First Bank held the XYZ stock, its value has diminished by 50 percent.

    a.   Is First Bank liable to Debtor for any of these losses?

    b.   Would First Bank be liable to Debtor if it repledged the securities with Second Bank as security for a loan from Second to First? Would the amount of the loan or the ability of Debtor to redeem the stock from Second matter? (Would your answer differ if Second sold the debenture after First defaulted on its loan? *See* §9-207(2)(e).)

82.   *§§3-503(a) and (c) (previously §3-502(1)(a) and (2)(b)), 9-207(1).* Debtor pledged a promissory note in the amount $100,000 to First Bank. The note was drawn by *D* and endorsed by *I*. The note came due on May 1, 1993. The bank did nothing about the note until May 1, 1994, when it presented it and learned that *D* had become insolvent. *D* duly dishonored. Is the bank liable to Debtor?

83.   *§8-313(1)(a).* *D* owns a certificate covering 1,000 shares of ABC Co., which *B*, a broker, is holding for *D* in a securities account. How does *D* grant a security interest in the certificate to First Bank? Would it be sufficient for *D* to cause the broker to deliver a certificate for the shares to the bank or its broker?

84.   *§8-313(1)(h)(i).* *D* owns 1,000 shares of ABC Co., which are reflected on the books of Broker and are covered by a jumbo certificate held by Depository Trust Co., whose books reflect the ownership interest of Broker. How does *D* grant a security interest in the ABC Co. stock to First Bank? Would it be sufficient for *D* to execute a security agreement granting the bank a security interest in the stock and to notify the broker of the security interest?

85.   *§8-313(1)(j).* Broker holds a certificate covering 1,000 shares of ABC Co., which *D* purchased for cash through Broker. *D* now wishes to borrow 50 percent of the value of the stock from Broker to cover another transaction. How can Broker obtain a perfected security interest in the ABC certificate? Would it be sufficient for the broker to take a signed security agreement from *D*?

86.   *§9-302(1)(d).* On May 1, *C* purchased for cash a refrigerator from *S*, a retailer. On May 2, *C* purchased from *S* a video recorder on credit and granted *S* a security interest in the refrigerator and the recorder. *S* did not file a financing statement.

    a.   Does *S* have a perfected security interest in the refrigerator?

    b.   Does *S* have a perfected security interest in the recorder?

    c. If *C* sells the recorder to neighbor *X* on June 1, is *C*'s security interest good against *X*? Would the security interest be good against *X* if *X* were a merchant who took the recorder in trade? §9-307(2).

87. On May 1, *S* sold *C* on credit $50,000 worth of antiques for *C*'s home and retained a security interest in the goods.

    a. How does *S* perfect its security interest?

    b. If the security agreement stipulates that any antiques *C* acquires thereafter for his home will serve as security for *S*'s debt, will *S* have a security interest in antiques *C* subsequently acquires? §9-204(2).

88. *§9-304(4); cf. §§8-313(1)(i), 8-321(2) (fashioning similar 21-day rule for securities).* On May 1, Broker granted First Bank a security interest in all of Broker's instruments and documents. On the morning of May 2, Broker acquired a batch of documents (negotiable warehouse receipts) and instruments (negotiable promissory notes). That afternoon, the bank covered Broker's overdraft. Bank did not file any financing statement and has not taken possession of the receipts or the notes. On May 3, Broker acquired a second batch of instruments and documents, but the bank made no further advances. On May 31, Broker was still in possession of the paper.

    a. Was the bank perfected on May 3?

    b. Was the bank perfected on May 31?

Section 14. *Multistate Transactions: Section 9-103*

Just as you start to get a grip on the filing and perfection rules of Article 9, the real world intrudes and reminds you that in commercial transactions often the parties or the collateral are not in one state. In that case, the perfection rules become sensitive to the reasonable expectations of third parties.

The rules of §9-103 reflect concern that a third party dealing with collateral or with a debtor not be required to look for filings in unexpected places. To some extent, the Code cannot protect everyone. Generally, the situs of the collateral, if the collateral has a situs, determines the place of filing and, correspondingly, the place in which the third party should search. Because some goods are intangible or mobile by nature, situs cannot determine the place to file for those goods. Also, some debtors move goods from one jurisdiction to another or move themselves from one jurisdiction to another.

The Code rules must take account of these perfectly normal but troublesome facts of commercial life.

Problems

89. *§9-103(1)(b).* In each of the following questions, assume that on May 1, the debtor and the secured party (Bank) are located in State A and that on that date the debtor signed a proper security agreement covering debtor's equipment then owned or thereafter acquired. Is the filing proper in the following cases?

    a.   On May 2, while the goods are in State A, Bank made an advance to Debtor. On May 3, Debtor moved the equipment to State B, and Bank filed in State A.

    b.   On April 10, Bank filed in State A. On May 2, Bank made an advance just after the goods were moved to State B.

    c.   Same facts as in b. On May 3, Debtor moved the goods back into State A.

    d.   Bank filed in State A on May 10. Bank made advance on May 15. On May 20, Debtor acquired an interest in goods by taking delivery of them in and keeping them in State B.

90.   *§9-103(1)(c).*   On May 1, Debtor entered into a contract with Chicago, a specialty manufacturer in State B, for the manufacture of four rotary dryers for use in preparing corn by Debtor in its distillery operation in State A. Debtor granted Chicago a security interest in the dryers, and Chicago filed a financing statement in the office of the secretary of state in State A, the state where Debtor maintained its chief executive office and where Debtor intended to use the dryers. The purchase price of the dryers was $1 million. On February 1 of the following year, Chicago notified Debtor that the dryers were complete and that Debtor, pursuant to the sales contract, should send its flatbed trucks to Chicago's plant to pick up the dryers. Debtor paid Chicago half of the purchase price, and Debtor's workers loaded the dryers onto the trucks on February 2. At that point, a transport union strike resulted in the establishment of pickets at Chicago's loading dock. As a consequence, Debtor left the trucks, waiting for the strike to settle.

    a.   Is Chicago perfected during the times it was manufacturing the dryers? Is it perfected on February 2?

    b.   If the strike prevents removal of the trucks for a period of five weeks, will Chicago be perfected at the end of that period? What should Chicago do to avoid becoming unperfected if the goods remain in State B that long?

    c.   Would your answer to any of these questions differ if Debtor originally intended to keep the dryers at a facility in State B but changed its mind on February 3 and decided to move them to State A?

    d.   If Debtor intended from the start to move the goods to State A, would Chicago be perfected on March 15 if Debtor moved the dryers into that state on that day?

91.   *§9-103(1)(d).*   On May 1, First Bank took a security interest in Ace Printing Co.'s printing presses and filed a financing statement in the office of the secretary of state in State A where the presses were located. On May 2, Debtor removed the presses to State B. On October 1, First Bank refiled in State B. In a contest between First Bank and the following parties, who prevails?

    a.   A buyer of one of the presses who took delivery of the press on June 1 for value and without knowledge of First Bank's security interest. Would your answer change if the buyer failed to take delivery of the press until after the Bank filed in State B?

    b.   A creditor of Ace that obtained a judgment against Ace and levied on one of the presses on June 5.

    c.   Second Bank that took a security interest from Ace in the presses on June 10 and filed a financing statement in the office of the secretary of state of State B on the same day. Would your answer to this question differ if Second Bank failed to file or filed in the wrong office in State B?

    d.   The trustee in bankruptcy of debtor if debtor files his bankruptcy petition on June 1. §9-403(2). Would your answer to this question differ if Bank did not file in State B at all and if the bankruptcy filing occurred on September 25?

92.   *§9-103(2).*   First Bank obtained a perfected security interest in Debtor's automobile on May 1 by noting its interest on the automobile's certificate of title pursuant to the law of State A, the state in which the bank was located and in which the debtor lived. The bank, pursuant to sound lending practices, retained possession of the certificate. On June 1, Debtor moved to State B.

    a.   If nothing else happened with respect to the automobile, is the bank perfected on July 1? December 1?

    b.   If Debtor reregistered the vehicle in State B on June 15, is the bank perfected on that date?

    c.   If Debtor obtained possession of the certificate of title from the bank and surrendered the title to the State B authorities, is the bank perfected if

       i.   the State B official noted the lien on the new title?

      ii.   the State B official failed to note the lien on the new title?

     iii.   Would your answer to either of the foregoing questions differ depending on whether the surrender of the State A title occurred within the four months or outside the four months?

    d.   If the debtor fraudulently obtains a clean title in State B on June 15, and if Buyer buys the vehicle on the 16th of June, will Buyer defeat the bank? Would your answer differ if Buyer were a used car dealer?

93.   *§9-103(3).*   Debtor is a freight forwarder in Oakland, California that owns 40-foot containers that it delivers via rail and truck to customers throughout that state. The customers "stuff" the containers and notify Debtor when they are ready to be picked up, returned to Oakland, and transshipped by ocean-going vessel to other parts of the world or by rail to other parts of the United States. Debtor has granted First Bank a security interest in the containers.

    a.   Where should the bank file?

    b.   Would any of your answers differ if Debtor maintained two classes of containers: (i) 20-foot containers that it used only to transport produce from farms in central California to California's coastal cities, and (ii) 40-foot containers that it used in the fashion described earlier in this problem?

    c.   Would your answer differ if Debtor's chief executive office were located in New York?

94. *§9-103(3) and (4).* Tridelt Co., which manufactures computers, maintains its chief executive office in State A. Tridelt borrowed from First Bank and granted First Bank a security interest in all of its accounts. First Bank filed with the office of the secretary of state in State A.

    a. Does the bank have a perfected security interest in accounts arising from the sale of computers by Tridelt's warehouse and sales office in State B?

    b. If Tridelt leases hardware to customers throughout the country and files centrally in the states where the lessees are located, will the bank if it takes an assignment of those security interests have a perfected security interest
       i. in the hardware?
       ii. in the leases?

    c. How should the bank perfect its security interest in the leases described in the preceding question?

    d. How should the bank perfect a security interest in Tridelt's inventory?

    e. Are there any acts the bank should take in this financing in the event Tridelt moves its chief executive office from State A to State B?

95. *§9-103(3).* B, a custom farmer (a party who provides services to other farmers), who lives in State A, owns a combine that he uses to harvest corn in State A, State B, and State C. Combines, you may assume, are not subject to the certificate of title laws of those states. If B grants a security interest to First Bank in the combine while the combine is in State B, where should First Bank file?

96. *§9-302(1)(d).* On May 1, while she lived in State A, C purchased a grand piano for use in her home and granted First Bank a security interest in the piano to secure the purchase price that the bank loaned to C to enable her to acquire it. On May 2, C moved to State B. Is the bank perfected on September 10?

97. *§§9-201, 9-301(1)(b).* On May 1, S sold a printing press to B on credit, retained a security interest, and filed in State A, where B conducted its printing operations. On June 1, B moved its enterprise to State B. On November 1, S filed in State B.

    a. If B becomes bankrupt on November 2, and assuming no preference problem, will the trustee defeat S?

    b. If L obtained a lien on the press in State B on June 10, would L's lien have priority over S's security interest? Would your answer differ if S refiled in State B on August 1?

Section 15. *Perfecting the Security Interest in Proceeds: More on Section 9-306(3)*

Often, secured parties are unconcerned about proceeds. Some proceeds (cash proceeds) have a tendency to disappear rapidly; others (accounts and chattel paper) may be the subject of another lender's security interest. The working capital lender is well advised, however, to position itself in such a way that if the debtor defaults, the lender can effectively claim the proceeds of the collateral. The lender, then, must be concerned about the perfection rules of §9-306. They are moderately tricky; and while the tricky parts have little operational scope, you need to know how they work in order to understand the section.

Problems

98.   First Bank has a security interest in all of the inventory, now owned or after-acquired, of Bell Furniture, a retailer. First filed in the office of the secretary of state a financing statement describing the collateral as "all inventory." On May 1, Bell sold some furniture on open account and some in return for chattel paper and cash.

    a.   Does the bank have a perfected security interest in the accounts, the chattel paper, and the cash on May 1?

    b.   Does the perfection continue after May 10?

    c.   Does the security interest in the cash remain perfected if Bell commingles the cash?

    d.   Would your answers to any of the foregoing questions differ if Bell were the local branch of a national enterprise with its chief executive office in a different state?

99.   On May 2, Bell Furniture (referred to in the preceding problem) used cash it received from customers who bought furniture to purchase a word processor to use in the office. Does the bank have a perfected security interest in the word processor on May 13? Would your answer differ if the filing described the collateral as "inventory and equipment"?

100.   Assume that the bank's filing referred to in the two preceding problems covers only inventory manufactured by "Maple Wood Products, Inc." Does the bank have a perfected security interest in chattel paper Bell receives upon the sale of Grand Rapids Furniture Co. furniture? If Bell receives cash from the sale of inventory manufactured by Grand Rapids and deposits that cash in an account designated "Maple Wood Products Proceeds Account," does the bank have any interest in that cash?

101.   On May 1, Bell received $100,000 in cash proceeds, $25,000 in cash and $75,000 in checks. Later that day Bell used the cash to purchase a certificate of deposit from Second National Bank. Does First Bank have any interest in the certificate and the checks on May 1? On May 12? Would your answer differ if Bell had deposited the cash into a checking account?

Section 16.   *Introduction to Priorities: Sections 9-301 and 9-312*

Claims to collateral drive secured transactions disputes. Article 9 fashions a regime for dealing with most of them. That regime distinguishes claimants on the basis of policy concerns that may not be readily apparent to you and that are properly the scope of class discussion.

For the purposes of these problems, it is enough to know that the Article 9 priority rules rest on three schemes. The first is a hierarchy that distinguishes among the following creditors: the unsecured creditor, the secured creditor (that is, the creditor whose security interest has attached), the perfected secured creditor (that is, the creditor whose security interest has attached and is perfected), and the lien creditor.

The second scheme involves buyers. That category includes, among others, (1) buyers in bulk or buyers who otherwise are not buyers in ordinary course, and (2) buyers in ordinary course.

The third scheme is a timing rule that essentially favors the first perfected secured party to file or perfect.

In the following eight problems, assume that the security interests are created in equipment. In each problem, indicate the priorities of the various creditors.

Problems

102. *§§9-201, 9-301.*

May 1   Bank took security interest in after-acquired equipment.
May 2   *S* sold equipment to Debtor on credit.
May 3   Bank filed.
May 4   *S* obtained judgment lien against Debtor's equipment.

§9-301(1)(c) and (d).   Alter the facts by assuming that the actor that intervened on May 2 was *B*, a buyer not in ordinary course from Debtor who took possession on that date. What result? If *B* does not take possession until May 4, what result? Why treat the buyer differently depending on the day it takes delivery? Is a buyer that prepays different from a buyer that does not?

Would your answer to the original problem differ if the bank filed on May 1 and took its security interest on May 5? Would your answer differ if *B* bought not in the ordinary course from Debtor on May 2 and took delivery on that date? Took delivery on May 5? If the bank filed on May 1 and took a security interest on May 5? (Do you see why *B* loses if he takes delivery on May 5 but wins if he takes delivery on May 2?)

103. *§9-305.*

May 1   *S* sells to Buyer on credit and retains possession of the goods.
May 2   Sub-buyer gives value to Buyer without knowledge that *S* is holding the goods.

104.

May 1   First Bank takes perfected security interest in all equipment, including after-acquired equipment.
May 2   *S* sells equipment on open account and obtains judicial lien.
May 3   Debtor acquires more equipment.

105. *§9-301(2).*

May 1   *S* sells on credit and retains a security interest.
May 2   *L*, who sold services on credit, obtains judgment lien.
May 3   *S* files.

Would your answer to this question differ if the party intervening on May 2 were a buyer not in ordinary course that took delivery without knowledge of the security interest? A bulk buyer?

106. *§9-301(1)(b).*

May 1	First Bank lends $50,000 to Debtor and takes security interest.
May 2	Utility Co. obtains judgment and levies.
May 3	First Bank files.

107. *§9-301(2).*

May 1	First Bank takes purchase money security interest.
May 2	Utility Co. obtains judgment and levies.
May 3	First Bank files.

108. *§9-312(5)(a).*

May 1	First Bank takes possession per agreement with Debtor.
May 2	Second Bank takes security interest and files.
May 3	First Bank lends $50,000.

109. *§9-312(5)(a).*

May 1	First Bank files.
May 2	Second Bank takes security agreement, lends, and files.
May 3	First Bank takes security agreement and lends.

110. *§9-312(7).*

May 1	First Bank lends $25 and takes possession per agreement.
May 2	Second Bank takes security agreement, lends $50, and files.
May 3	First Bank lends an additional $10.
May 4	Collateral sold for $35.

111.

May 1	First Bank lends $25.
May 2	Second Bank lends $25.
May 3	Second Bank takes security interest and files.
May 4	First Bank takes security interest and files.

112. *§9-312(4).*

May 1	Bank takes security interest.
May 2	*S* sells to Debtor on credit and retains security interest.
May 3	Bank files.
May 4	*S* files.

Would *S* prevail if it filed on May 13?

113.

May 1	Bank lends 10 percent down payment for purchase of press.
May 2	*S* sells press to debtor on 90 percent credit.
May 3	*S* files.
May 4	Bank files.

Assume that the collateral sold for 50 percent of the purchase price and that neither creditor had been paid. Would your answer differ if the bank filed first?

114. *§9-312(4).*

> May 1 First Bank takes perfected security interest in all equipment then owned or thereafter acquired.
> May 2 S sells Debtor drill press on credit, retaining a security interest.
> May 3 S files.
> May 4 Debtor sells press and holds a check from Sub-buyer after Sub-buyer took delivery of the press.

115. *§9-312(3).* Assume in the preceding problem that the collateral was beer held by a beer wholesaler and that S filed and gave notice to the bank on April 29 and filed prior to its delivery of a shipment of beer to the wholesaler. Would S get the check? Would S get the check if the wholesaler received the check as a down payment from a retailer to whom it had resold the beer S had delivered on May 2? Would S get any accounts due from retail sub-buyers of S's beer if the wholesaler sold S's beer to them on open account? Would S have priority over the bank as to the beer S delivered to the wholesaler?

116. *§9-312(4).* Assume that the collateral in the prior problem was 1,000 steers held by S, a cattle feed lot operator, and that S sold steers on credit to the debtor, another feed lot operator, on May 2 under a security agreement granting S a security interest in the steers. Would S defeat First Bank if S filed on May 3? Is it necessary for S to notify the bank before it delivers steers to the debtor?

117. *§9-401(2).* On May 1, First Bank took a security interest in all of Debtor's equipment, which Debtor used in farming operations. First Bank filed the same day in the office of the secretary of state and loaned Debtor $100,000. On May 2, Debtor went to Second Bank and borrowed another $100,000. Second Bank ran a check of filings in the recorder of deeds office in the county where Debtor lived and found no filings. Debtor told Second, however, that he had granted First a security interest in all of his farm equipment. Second filed its financing statement in the office of the recorder on May 2. On May 3, Debtor defaulted on both loans. First and Second claim the equipment. Which has priority?

Would your answer to the preceding question differ if Second had run a search of the filings in the office of the secretary of state and seen First's financing statement? Would your answer differ if Second knew nothing of First's filing, that is, if Debtor had not told Second of First's interest?

Section 17. *Future Advances: Sections 9-301(4), 9-307(3), 9-312(7)*

In the old days, as they say, bank loans were made against discrete items of collateral and were self-liquidating. The residential real estate mortgage is a classic case of lending against a discrete asset. The bank that lends to a commodities broker that borrows to purchase a given shipment and repays the loan when he sells that shipment has made a classic self-liquidating loan.

Commercial lending sometimes works that way, but most of the time the middle market that borrows against assets is interested in a working capital loan. Under that kind of loan, the borrower typically grants the lender a security interest in all of its assets, or nearly all of them, and receives in return a commitment from the lender giving the borrower a line of credit. The borrower makes draws on that line when he needs cash and makes payments against the outstanding balance when he has a positive cash flow. At any given time the loan balance can be zero or the maximum amount of the line.

The working capital loan makes the floating lien and the future advance essential components of Article 9. You have already confronted the floating lien in the after-acquired property illustrations that appear frequently in these problems. The following problems deal with the future (sometimes called "after") advance.

Note that the future advance sections deal with three parties with whom the secured party is competing for the collateral: (1) lien creditors, (2) buyers, and (3) other secured parties.

Problems

118. *§9-301(4).*

May 1   First Bank obtains perfected security interest in Debtor's equipment and lends $25.
May 2   L obtains judicial lien for $25.
May 3   Bank lends additional $25.

How should the court divide the proceeds of the sale of the equipment if it yields $50? Would your answer be the same if the bank advanced the second $25 on May 15 without knowledge of the lien? On June 20 without knowledge of the lien? What should L do to prevent the bank and the debtor from squeezing L out? Should he notify the bank on May 2? On June 17? Is there anything L can do to prevent the squeeze-out if the bank enters into a commitment to make future advances on May 1? On May 20 without knowledge of the lien?

119. *§9-307(3).*

May 1   Bank obtains perfected security interest in Debtor's equipment and lends $10.
May 2   B, a buyer in bulk, buys the equipment.
May 3   Bank makes an additional advance of $5.

Will the bank defeat B if the equipment is worth only $15? Would your answer differ if the bank had made its advance on May 20 without knowledge of B's interest? On June 17 with or without knowledge of B's interest? Would your answer to the last question differ if the bank had on May 1 made a commitment to lend the $5? If it had made the commitment to lend on May 1? On May 20 with (or without) knowledge of the sale?

120. *§9-312(7).*

> May 1   First Bank takes security interest in Debtor's equipment, lends $25, and files.
>
> May 2   Second Bank takes security interest in equipment, lends $25, and files.
>
> May 3   First Bank lends an additional $10.

    a. If the equipment is sold on May 3 for $35, how should the court allocate the sales price?

    b. Would your answer to the preceding question differ if First knew of Second's May 2 filing when, on May 3, First Bank made the second advance? Would First Bank enjoy priority over Second Bank if First had made no loan until May 3? If Debtor had paid the balance on the loan with First down to zero on the morning of May 2? Would your answer to this question differ if First Bank perfected its security interest on May 1 by taking possession of the equipment? If First Bank's security interest was perfected not by filing and not by possession but temporarily under §9-304(4)?

    c. Would your answers to any of the questions in b differ if the security agreement between First and Debtor granted First a security interest to cover only the May 1 loan? If the security agreement is so limited, would the security interest secure the renewal of the loan on May 1 of the next calendar year?

    d. If the security agreement Debtor executed on May 1 covered only the May 1 advance, is there anything First Bank can do on May 3 to make a loan to Debtor that is prior to Second Bank's security interest?

    e. If, on May 1, Debtor and First Bank were thinking only of equipment loans but drafted the documents to cover all loans, would First's priority over Second be affected by the fact that the May 3 advance was made to permit Debtor to acquire inventory?

Section 18.   *Purchaser Priorities: Sections 9-306(2) and 9-307*

The following questions deal with sections that protect purchasers that are usually buyers. A secured party, of course, is a purchaser. *See* §1-201(32) and (33). Secured parties customarily must guard against prior filings. There are exceptions to that rule when the collateral is of a type that moves without inquiry, but usually that is the rule for secured lenders even though they are purchasers. Buyers, on the other hand, are often not the kind of enterprise that can pause to determine the state of the seller's interest in goods. Certainly most ordinary course purchasers are not. Buyers in bulk, the buyer of a company's assets, for example, usually are concerned with that state, however. The following problems illustrate the way Article 9 deals with the reasonable commercial expectations in these transactions.

Problems

121. *§§1-201(9), 9-307(1).*   On May 1, *D* granted First Bank a security interest in all of *D*'s inventory of earth moving equipment. In the security agreement First forbade *D* to sell any earth movers without obtaining the bank's prior written authorization. Which of the following parties will defeat the bank?

    a.   *A*, an ordinary course buyer of an earth mover that knows of the bank's security interest. Would your answer differ if *A* had agreed to buy the equipment but had not paid for it? Had agreed to buy it but had not taken delivery?

    b.   *B*, a buyer of an earth mover that knows of the security agreement provision forbidding *D* to sell without the bank's prior written approval. Would your answer to this question differ if the bank had not enforced the prohibition of sale over a period of two years during which period *D* made many sales?

    c.   *C*, a pawnbroker.

    d.   *D-2*, a dealer in earth moving equipment that competes with *D*, that often buys from *D* when its own inventory is inadequate to satisfy its customers, and that sells to *D* when *D*'s inventory is not adequate to satisfy *D*'s customers.

    e.   *E*, who is buying *D*'s business and all of *D*'s inventory.

    f.   *F*, a finance company that wanted to lend to *D* but declined to do so after finding First Bank's filing; *F* instead bought two earth movers from *D*.

    g.   *G*, a buyer that prepaid the purchase price for one earth mover that is identified but has yet to be shipped. (How might a prepaying buyer protect itself from *D*'s creditors?)

122. *§1-201(9).*   On May 1, *D*, an appliance dealer, granted First Bank a security interest in all of *D*'s inventory of white goods. First duly perfected its security interest by filing on the same day. On May 2, *D* sold three washers and three dryers to *B*, who bought them for his apartment building. *B* purchased the goods on credit and executed a retail installment sales agreement that granted *D* a security interest in the goods and included a promise to pay for them over a period of 36 months. *D* made a proper filing in the proper office.

    a.   Does *B* take free of the bank's security interest? If *B* sells the washers and dryers to *C*, does *C* take free of the bank's security interest?

    b.   Does *B* take the goods free of all security interests?

    c.   If *D* assigns the retail installment sales agreement to the bank, does *B* defeat the bank?

123. On May 1, *F*, a farm producer, granted First Production Credit Association a perfected security interest in all of *F*'s corn growing on *F*'s farm. The security agreement stipulated that *F* could not sell without the PCA's prior approval. On May 2, *F* sold his corn to *B*, a broker. On May 3, *B* sold the corn to *K*, a cereal manufacturer. On May 4, *K* sold cereal made out of the corn to *S*, a retail food chain; and on May 5, *S* sold the cereal to *T*, a consumer. (In answering the following questions, assume that the state whose law governs did not enact any change in its statutes as a result of the Food Security Act of 1985.)

    a.   Does *B* defeat the PCA's security interest?

    b.   Does *K* defeat it?

    c.   Does *T*?

    d.   Absent protective legislation such as the Food Security Act, which parties are liable to the PCA in conversion?

124. *§§9-306(2), 9-307(1).* On May 1, *D*, a hardware store, granted a perfected security interest to First Bank in all of *D*'s inventory. Assume that the security agreement contains a clause allowing *D* to sell inventory in the ordinary course. Which of the following purchasers will defeat the bank's security interest.

    a.   *B*, a buyer in ordinary course.

    b.   *C*, a lender that takes a perfected security interest in the same inventory. §9-312(5)(a).

    c.   *E*, *D*'s son to whom *D* makes a gift of a lawn mower.

    e.   *F*, an investor that buys the hardware store and all of the inventory.

125. On May 1, *R*, a mobile home dealer, granted a perfected security interest in all of its inventory to First Bank. On May 2, *R* sold a mobile home to *B* on credit and took back a retail installment sales contract in which *B* granted *R* a security interest in the mobile home and agreed to pay for the home over a 60-month period. Assume that under governing law mobile homes are not subject to any certificate of title law.

    a.   Does *B* take free of the bank's security interest?

    b.   Does *B* take free of all security interests?

    c.   If *B* sells the mobile home to his neighbor *C*, will *C* take free of the bank's security interest? Of *R*'s security interest? §9-307(2).

    d.   Would your answer to the last question differ if *R* had filed a financing statement? §9-302(1)(d).

126. *§9-307(1)("his seller").* Assume in the foregoing problem that *B* decided to sell the home and sold it to *X*, a used mobile home dealer, and that *Y* purchased the home from *X* in the ordinary course.

    a.   Does *Y* defeat *R*'s security interest?

    b.   If *R* assigns its security interest to the bank, would *Y* defeat the bank's security interest?

127. On May 1, *M*, a carpet mill, sold 100,000 yards of greige goods to *B* on a bill-and-hold basis. Under the bill-and-hold contract familiar to all parties, *M* retained possession of the goods until *B* desired to take delivery. The sale was on credit, and *B* granted *M* a security interest in the goods to secure payment of the purchase price. On May 2, *B* sold the goods to *C*, who bought in the ordinary course. *B* has never paid for the goods. *C* has paid *B*, who is now insolvent. Does *C* cut off *M*'s security interest?

128. On May 1, *D* granted a perfected security interest to First Bank in all of *D*'s inventory of computer parts. On May 2, *D* defaulted on the loan by the bank, and the bank repossessed the inventory. On May 3, *B* bought a carload of computer parts in the ordinary course. Does *B* cut off the bank's security interest?

129. On May 1, *M*, a lumber mill, sold lumber to *R*, a lumber yard, on credit. *R* granted *M* a security interest in the lumber. *M* perfected its security interest by designating an agent, a field warehouse, to take possession of the lumber by placing it in an area of the yard that was secure and to which *R* did not have access. On May 2, *B*, a contractor, purchased 20,000 feet of lumber for a construction job in the ordinary course of business and paid *R*. Does *B* cut off *M*'s security interest? Should the law be that no one is a buyer in ordinary course when the seller is not in possession of the goods?

130. *§9-306(2)*. Debtor granted Bank a perfected security interest in all of Debtor's equipment. The security agreement forbade Debtor to dispose of the equipment without Bank's prior written consent. Subsequently, Debtor sold a piece of the equipment to *B*.

   a. Does Bank's security interest follow the goods into *B*'s hands?
   b. How does Bank enforce its security interest against *B*?
   c. Would your answers to the prior questions differ if *B* were a donee?
   d. If *B* gives value to Debtor, does Bank have any claim to the value?

Section 19. *Chattel Paper and Account Problems*

Chattel paper and accounts are similar types of collateral in that they often arise on the sale of collateral. They are also mildly problematic because they involve three parties instead of two and, therefore, create some conceptual complications. Commercial transactions are like children —the complications with three parties are exponentially more than with two.

Problems

131. On May 1, Smith purchased a snowblower from Retailer on credit and executed a retail installment sales contract granting Retailer a security interest in the equipment. Retailer did not file any financing statement. On May 2, Retailer "sold" the contract along with other such contracts to First Bank, which took possession of them.

   a. Did Retailer have a security interest in the equipment on May 1? Did First Bank have a security interest in the equipment on May 2?
   b. Did First Bank have a perfected security interest in the contract on May 2? §9-304(1).
   c. If First Bank had chosen not to take possession of the contract, would it have a perfected security interest in the equipment? Would it have a perfected security interest in the contract? Where should First Bank file its financing statement covering the contract? Who should sign that financing statement as debtor? §§9-302(1)(d), 9-302(2).

132. Computers, Inc. manufactures computer hardware, which it leases to its customers nationwide. Most of the leases are disguised security agreements, but some are true leases. Computers assigned "all of its leases" to

First Bank as security for loans that First made to Computers. First filed a financing statement signed by Computers covering "chattel paper" in the office of the secretary of state in the state where Computers is located. Computers is now bankrupt.

    a.   Describe First's interest, if any, in the computers subject to true leases.

    b.   Describe First's interest, if any, in the lease payments under the true leases. §9-105(1)(b).

    c.   Describe First's interest, if any, in the leases that are credit sales disguised as lease arrangements. Is First protected against the possibility of the bankruptcy of a purchaser-lessee under one of these arrangements? §2-401(1)(2d sentence).

133. *§1-201(37).* On May 1, Leasing Co., a New York company, entered into a lease of 10 earth movers with Construction Co., which does business in New Jersey. The lease provided that Construction Co. could use the earth movers, which had a projected life of 8 years, for 48 months at a monthly rental of $10,000. At the end of the 48 months, the contractor was to return the equipment in the condition it was in at the beginning of the lease, normal wear and tear excepted. On May 2, Leasing Co. assigned the lease to First Bank as security for a loan. The security agreement between the bank and the leasing company provided that the bank would also have a security interest in the equipment.

    a.   If Construction Co. executes a security agreement granting Second Bank a security interest in the equipment, what interest will Second Bank have? How does Second Bank's interest relate to the interests of Leasing Co. and First Bank in the equipment? How would Second Bank perfect its security interest? If it takes a financing statement, who should sign it as debtor, and where should Second file?

    b.   How should First Bank perfect its security interest in the lease? §9-304(1). If it takes a financing statement, who should sign as debtor, and where should First file? How should First describe its collateral in that filing? How should it perfect its security interest in the equipment? Who should sign the financing statement as debtor? Where should First file? How should the filing describe the collateral?

    c.   On May 1, First properly perfected its security interest in the lease and in Leasing Co.'s reversionary interest in the equipment. On May 2, Construction Co. filed in bankruptcy. What rights does the bankruptcy trustee have against First? On May 3, Leasing Co. filed in bankruptcy. May Leasing Co.'s trustee defeat First's rights to the equipment? What would Leasing's trustee's rights be if First took possession of the lease and filed as to the equipment in New Jersey?

134. *§9-318(3).* On May 1, Debtor "sold" all of its accounts, then owned or thereafter arising, to First Bank. First duly perfected its security interest. On May 2, Debtor performed services for Buyer under a contract that required Buyer to pay Debtor $10,000 per month for ten months. Over the next ten months Buyer paid Debtor under the contract, and Debtor remitted none of the proceeds to the bank.

a.   May First Bank recover any of the payments from Buyer?

b.   Would your answer differ if First Bank had notified Buyer on May 2 that it was assignee of this account?

c.   If First Bank had notified Buyer of the assignment on May 1 and directed Buyer to make its payments directly to the bank, could Buyer assert against the bank

   i.   a defense it has against Debtor under the contract?

   ii.   a setoff Buyer has against Debtor by virtue of Debtor's breach of another contract it had with Buyer? §2-717, comment 1.

d.   Would your answer to the preceding question differ if the contract between Buyer and Debtor provided that Buyer would not assert against assignees of the contract any defenses it had against the Debtor?

135.   *§9-318(1).*   On May 1, Construction Co. granted First Bank a security interest in all of its accounts to secure its indebtedness to the bank. On May 2, Construction Co. entered into a contract with Owner to construct a building on Owner's real estate. Under the contract, Construction Co. was to receive payments twice a month for work done and materials delivered to the job. Over a period of months, Construction Co. falsely certified that it had done work and paid for materials. On the basis of these false applications, Owner made payments directly to First Bank, and the bank reduced the construction company's loan balance. Owner has now discovered the construction company's fraud and seeks recovery of the payments from the bank. Did First Bank take those payments subject to the Owner's "claim"?

Section 20.   *More on Purchasers, This Time of Paper*

Previously we have considered the Article 9 rules that apply when purchasers take goods from a debtor who has already granted a security interest in them to a lender. Here we consider the rules that apply when the purchaser is taking paper: chattel paper, negotiable documents, and negotiable instruments.

In these and the prior problems, the Code is fashioning rules that protect buyers from having to inquire into the state of the seller's or transferor's title to the subject of the transfer. Security of property may be the first rule of transfer law, but in commercial law it admits of many exceptions.

A transaction in goods is the unlikeliest candidate for the second rule of conveyancing law, good faith purchase; and yet we find that there are instances in which goods enjoy some measure of "negotiability," if we can murder that term for a moment. Goods held in inventory travel without baggage when the merchant sells them to a buyer in ordinary course. Paper is a much likelier candidate for such treatment. Even with paper, however, we find that there are degrees of protection, with the highest degree accorded the favored purchasers of the three kinds of negotiable paper: negotiable instruments, negotiable documents, and negotiable securities. Chattel paper falls in between.

As you do these problems, remember that a lender can be a purchaser and that the priority rule of §9-312 may fall before the purchaser protections these problems invoke.

Problems

136. *§9-308.*   On May 1, Dealer granted First Bank a perfected security interest in all of Dealer's inventory of golf carts. On May 2, Dealer leased a cart to *B* for the summer. On May 3, Dealer took the lease to Finance Co., which took possession of it and gave Dealer value.
    a. If it did not know of First Bank's interest, does Finance Co. defeat the bank?
    b. If it did know of First Bank's interest, does Finance Co. defeat the bank?
    c. If it did not know of First Bank's security interest, does Finance Co. defeat the bank if Finance Co. loaned money to Dealer on April 1 and is taking the lease as further security for its loan?
    d. Would your answers to any of these questions differ if First Bank's security agreement covered all inventory, accounts, and chattel paper? If the evidence showed that the bank relied in fact on the proceeds from the sale of inventory?
    e. Would any of your answers differ if *B* purchased the cart and gave Dealer a promissory note rather than a lease?
    f. What might First Bank have done to prevent losing to Finance Co.?

137. *§9-306(5).*   On May 1, Dealer granted First Bank a perfected security interest in all of Dealer's inventory of sailboats. On May 2, Dealer sold a sailboat to *B* under an agreement in which *B* agreed to pay for the boat in equal monthly installments over a period of 36 months and to grant Dealer a security interest in the boat. On May 3, Dealer sold the contract to Ace Finance Co. Ace took possession of the contract and gave Dealer value. On May 4, *B* defaulted on the contract, and Dealer repossessed the boat. Dealer and *B* are now bankrupt.
    a. Does First Bank have a security interest in the boat on May 2?
    b. Does First Bank have a security interest in the boat on May 4?
    c. Does Ace have a security interest in the boat on May 3?
    d. Between Ace and First, who has the prior claim to the boat?

138. On May 1, Broker granted Bank a security interest for new value in a stock certificate covering 10,000 shares of IBM. Bank perfected under the temporary perfection rule of §§8-313(1)(i) and 8-321(2). On May 2, Broker entered into a repurchase agreement with *R*. Under the repurchase agreement, or "repo," *R* bought the stock from Broker, and Broker agreed to repurchase it 30 days later for an amount equal to the purchase price and interest for 30 days. (Not surprisingly, courts treat repurchase agreements as secured transactions.) *R* protected itself by taking possession of the certificate. On May 3, Broker became insolvent.
    a. Does Bank have a perfected security interest? §§8-313(1)(i), 8-321(2).
    b. Does *R* have a perfected security interest? §8-313(1)(a).
    c. If it applies, who would prevail under §9-312? §§9-312(5)(a), 9-309.

    d. Does §9-309 interdict the application of §9-312? §8-302(1)(a), 8-302(3).

    e. If under §8-302 *R* is a bona fide purchaser that cuts off the claims of prior parties, can *R* use §8-302 to defeat the bank?

139. On May 1, Bank loaned money to Broker to cover Broker's overdrafts and took a security interest in all of Broker's negotiable instruments and negotiable documents. Bank perfected by doing nothing under the terms of §9-304(4). On May 2, Broker took a negotiable promissory note in the face amount of $100,000 and a negotiable warehouse receipt covering 10,000 bushels of soybeans to Ace Finance Co. and asked Ace to lend it money. Ace took the note and the receipt, both properly endorsed, and made the loan. On May 3, Broker became insolvent.

    a. Does the bank on May 1 have a perfected security interest in the note and the receipt? §9-304(4).

    b. Does Ace Finance Co. have a perfected security interest in the note and the receipt on May 2? Does it have title to the receipt as well? *See* §7-502.

    c. If it applies, which of the secured lenders would prevail under §9-312?

    d. Does §9-309 interdict application of §9-312?

    e. If Ace is a holder in due course under Article 3 and if §3-306 [previously §3-305(1)] gives a holder in due course superior rights to a prior claimant, will Ace defeat the bank as to the note?

    f. If Ace is a holder by due negotiation of the warehouse receipt and if §7-502 gives such a holder rights superior to those of a prior claimant, will Ace defeat the bank as to the receipt?

140. On May 1, First Bank paid *S*, a foreign seller, by honoring *S*'s draft drawn under a letter of credit issued by the bank to *S. B*, the bank's customer, is the buyer in the international sale, and *B* has yet to reimburse the bank for the payment the bank made under the letter of credit. The goods which were the subject of the sale are in the North Atlantic on a ship that issued a negotiable bill of lading for them. First Bank took the bill from *S* when it paid *S* and is holding the bill as collateral for *B*'s reimbursement obligation. On May 2, *B* sold the goods in question to *C*, who claims to have bought the goods in the ordinary course of business.

    a. Is First Bank a perfected secured party, or is it the owner of the goods? §7-502(1)(a). If the goods are worth more than the advance First Bank made in *B*'s behalf, do you think the court would let the bank keep the difference between the advance and the value? (I don't.)

    b. Is First Bank's security interest created by *B*? §4-210(a) [previously §4-208(1)].

    c. If the bank is a perfected secured party and if the security interest is created by *B*, does §9-307(1) apply to cut off the bank's security interest? Does §9-307(1), a rule in Article 9, operate to limit the rights of a holder of a negotiable document of title by due negotiation?

Section 21. *Bailments*

Often, parties will want to finance goods while they are in the possession of a bailee, usually a warehouse or a carrier. In those cases, Article 9 distinguishes, as much of commercial law does, between goods in the possession of a bailee who has issued a negotiable document of title covering them and a bailee who has issued a nonnegotiable document or no document at all.

Section 9-304 details the treatment. Note in that section and in these problems that the negotiable document stands for the goods, and the nonnegotiable document does not.

(For further problems dealing with Article 7, see Problems 253 through 274 in Part II, Payments Systems.)

Problems

141. *§9-304(3).* On September 1, Oklahoma Gas Co. (Seller) sold propane to Distributor Co. (Buyer) under a contract that required Seller to deliver the propane to Southwest Pipeline Co. (Carrier). Seller delivered a nonnegotiable delivery order to Carrier, and Carrier accepted it and returned it to Buyer. Buyer will not need the propane until October but must pay Seller on September 30. Buyer has asked First Bank to lend it money to pay Seller and has offered to grant the bank a security interest in the propane. How will the bank take and perfect its security interest?

142. *§9-304(2).* On May 1, Farmer bailed cotton with Gin Co. On May 2, Gin Co. issued Farmer a negotiable warehouse receipt covering the cotton. On May 3, Farmer granted First Bank a security interest in the cotton. First filed a proper financing statement in the proper office on the same day. On May 4, Farmer granted Second Bank a security interest in the warehouse receipt by delivering the receipt to Second as security for a loan. Farmer has defaulted on his loan to both banks.
    a. Is First Bank perfected?
    b. Is Second Bank perfected?
    c. If both banks are perfected, which bank has priority?

143. *§7-501.* Cotton producer *P* delivered cotton to *G*, a gin. *G* issued a warehouse receipt to *P*, who put the receipt in his desk. *T* stole the receipt and delivered it to *B*, a cotton broker.
    a. In order for *B* to rise to the level of a holder by due negotiation, which of the following facts must be true?
        i.   The receipt must be negotiable.
        ii. The receipt must be endorsed by the producer or be in bearer form.
        iii. *T* must negotiate to *B* in the regular course of business or finance and not in satisfaction of a debt.
        iv. *B* must take for value, in good faith, and without notice of the producer's claim.
    b. Is *T* a holder by due negotiation?

144. *§7-501.* In the preceding question, which of the following circumstances would render the transfer to *B* such that *B* would not be a holder by due negotiation?

    a. The producer's endorsement is forged.
    b. *T* is a truck driver, a tramp, or a professor.
    c. The receipt is in order form and is not endorsed to *B*.
    d. *B* takes the receipt as security for an antecedent debt from *T*.
    e. The receipt recites that it is nonnegotiable.
    f. *T* endorses the receipt after *B* takes it and after *B* learns that the receipt was issued fraudulently.
    g. *T* gives the receipt to *B* as a birthday gift.
    h. *B* is a bank.
    i. *T* is a bank.

145. *§7-502(1).* If, in the foregoing transaction, *B* is a holder by due negotiation, does *B* have greater rights than *T* in the receipt? Than the producer in the cotton? Would your answer to this question differ if *B* were a lender taking the receipt as collateral for a contemporaneous loan, rather than a broker buying the cotton for resale?

146. *§7-504.* If *B* would defeat the producer in the foregoing problem and if *B* transfers to *C* not by due negotiation, so that *C* is not a holder by due negotiation, what are the rights of *C*?

147. *§7-504.* In the transaction illustrated in problem 143, if *B* is not a holder by due negotiation, does *B* have greater rights in the cotton than the producer?

148. *§7-503(1) and comment 1 (second sentence).* *T*, a cotton farmer, steals cotton from a producer and bails the cotton with a gin, which issues *T* a negotiable receipt. *T* then negotiates the receipt to *B*, as security for a loan. *B* takes for value, in good faith, and without notice of the theft.

    a. Does *B* defeat the producer?
    b. Does *B* defeat First Bank, to whom the producer granted a perfected security interest in the cotton before *T* stole it?
    c. Would your answer differ if *T* were a truck driver? If he were, what section would govern, and what would be the result? §7-504.

149. *§7-503(1)(a).* Would your answer to the preceding question differ if the producer had entrusted the cotton to *T* with directions to deliver it to the gin?

150. *§7-502(1)(c).* *W*, a trader in metals, anticipated a delivery of copper ore on May 1 that *W* planned to deliver to *S*, a carrier, for shipment to a foreign customer. The delivery of the ore was late, and *W* desperately needed a negotiable bill of lading to present to the foreign buyer's bank under a letter of credit that was about to expire. *S* fraudulently issued a negotiable receipt to *W*, which *W* duly negotiated to Bank on May 1. Two days later, the ore arrived, and *W* delivered it to *S*. *W* is now insolvent, and his trustee in bankruptcy claims that the bill of lading stood for nothing on May 1, the day the bank took it. What argument should the bank make? Could the bank make it if the bill had been a straight bill, that is, if it had been nonnegotiable?

Section 22. *Fixture Priority Rules*

The following problems deal with conflicts between real estate encumbrancers and a lender holding a security interest in a fixture. For our purposes, encumbrancers fall into two categories: owners and mortgagees. We worry about owners when the borrower granting the security interest is a tenant. Often, of course, the debtor granting the security interest will be the owner, and the potential conflict will be with the mortgagee.

The general rule for priorities between a security interest in fixtures and a mortgage of the real estate is in §9-313(7), which provides that the mortgage interest will prevail. That general rule is subject to exception, however, as these problems illustrate.

(In all of these problems, assume that the real estate encumbrancer's interest is perfected under real estate law.)

Problems

151.

May 1   O granted a mortgage in its factory to S&L.
May 2   O granted security interest in a furnace to Heating Co., which perfected by a fixture filing.
May 3   Heating Co. installed the furnace.

    a. Who has priority? §9-313(7).
    b. Would your answer to this question differ if on May 4 S&L transferred its mortgage to Mortgage Investment Co.? §9-313(4)(b).
    c. Would your answer to either question differ if Heating Co.'s security interest were a purchase-money security interest? §9-313(4)(a).

152. *§9-313(4)(a).*

May 1   O granted Heating Co. a purchase-money security interest in a furnace. Heating Co. perfected by an ordinary filing and installed the furnace.
May 2   O granted a mortgage to S&L.

    a. Does Heating Co. defeat S&L?
    b. Would your answer differ if Heating Co. made a fixture filing on or before May 11?

153. *§9-313(4)(a).*

May 1   O granted mortgage to S&L.
May 2   O granted a purchase-money security interest in a furnace to Heating Co.
May 3   Heating Co. installed furnace.
May 4   Heating Co. made fixture filing.

    a. Does Heating Co. defeat S&L?
    b. Would your answer to this question differ if
       i.   the mortgage were a construction mortgage?
      ii. Heating Co. made the fixture filing on May 15?

154. *§9-312(5)(a).*   On May 1, First Bank took from Ace Apartments Co. a security interest in a copying machine that Ace installed in its apartment building office on May 3. First filed centrally on May 1. On May 2, Second Bank took a security interest in the same machine from Ace and filed centrally. Under governing state law, the copying machine is a fixture. Ace defaults on both loans.
  a.   Which bank gets the machine?
  b.   What provision in Article 9 governs?
  c.   Does it matter that neither bank made a fixture filing?
  d.   Would either bank defeat a mortgagee that held a mortgage at the time the machine was affixed? §9-313(4)(c).

155.   Would your answer to the preceding question differ if the goods were a modular home that the owner of the real estate had affixed to a concrete foundation and that would be a fixture under applicable state law? Would it differ if First Bank were a purchase-money secured party?

156. *§9-313(4)(d), Bankruptcy Code §544(a)(3).*   Assume in Problem 154 that the machine is worth enough to pay both banks but that the owner, the debtor, is bankrupt. Who gets the machine?

157. *§9-313(4)(c).*   On May 1, Dealer sold a Tiffany window to consumer C on credit for installation in C's home. Dealer retained a security interest. The home is subject to a mortgage C granted S&L two years earlier. On August 1, C defaulted on both loans. If you assume that the window is a fixture, who gets it? Would your answer differ if there were no mortgage and C's trustee in bankruptcy were claiming the window? Would your answers to any of these questions differ if the collateral were a new refrigerator replacing the refrigerator that was in the home at the time of the mortgage?

158. *§9-313(4)(a).*   On May 1, O granted a mortgage on her apartment building to S&L. On June 1, Heating Co. installed a furnace in the building and retained a security interest to secure the purchase price. On June 9, the heating company filed a financing statement centrally. O is now in default on the mortgage and the sales agreement. Who has prior claim to the furnace? Would your answer differ if the heating company had filed a fixture filing on June 9? On June 19? Does it matter whether the mortgage is a construction mortgage?

159.   On May 1, O granted First Bank a mortgage on its steel plant. On May 2, O granted Second Bank a security interest in a boiler in the plant, and Second perfected by making a fixture filing on the same day.
  a.   If O defaults on the loans to First and Second, which bank will have the prior claim to the boiler? §9-313(7). What section governs?
  b.   Would the result differ if First Bank took its mortgage on May 3? §9-313(4)(b).

160. *§9-313(4)(c).*   St. Paul Co. manufactures minicomputers that it sells on credit throughout the country. St. Paul's buyers typically grant St. Paul a security interest in the computers. St. Paul has followed the policy of taking a financing statement from its customers and filing in the respective states centrally before it delivers the goods. If a customer becomes bankrupt, will St. Paul defeat the trustee? If the customer's premises are subject to a mortgage and the customer defaults on the mortgage, will the mortgagee have superior rights in the computer?

Section 23. Further Scope Questions

Earlier problems 13 through 17 illustrated operation of §§9-102 and 9-104, the scope and excluded transactions sections. That discussion of §§9-102 and 9-104 omitted an important area of controversy, however, namely that involving the definition of "security interest."

The definition becomes problematic in several settings. The first is the lease transaction. For a number of commercial reasons, users may prefer to lease goods rather than buy them. In the simplest case, a traveler will lease an automobile for a few days and return the vehicle at the end of the lease to the leasing company. In other cases, manufacturers lease production equipment for long periods. Sometimes the lease is a disguised sale, but sometimes it is a "true" lease designed to take full advantage of the income tax laws, of bank capital adequacy regulations, and of covenants in loan agreements requiring the manufacturer to maintain certain ratios of assets and liabilities. Leasing is a huge industry, but Article 2A, which governs leasing, is traditionally not included in courses on Secured Transactions or Payments Systems, which are the subject of this book. The following problems, then, deal with leases to the extent that they may be disguised security agreements.

The second transaction that has given rise to scope questions is the consignment. At first blush, the consignment looks like an inventory loan under which the consignor holds title to the goods as security for payment by the party in possession of them, the consignee. In some industries, however, parties market products on the assumption that the consignee will probably not sell some of the merchandise. Jewelry and book stores and art galleries, for example, often assume that they will return a significant portion of inventory to their suppliers. Many courts are not comfortable applying Article 9 to consignments in those cases and in commercially marginal operations such as used goods stores.

Finally, a manufacturer's practice of contracting out certain work to fabricators or other manufacturers that can perform manufacturing services more efficiently than the owner of the work in process has given rise to claims that the fabricators or secondary manufacturers are really engaging in inventory borrowing. The problems involve mildly complicated conceptual problems. They begin here with an easy problem, however: the case of the mechanic's lien.

Problems

161. *§9-310.*   Dealer sold a new automobile to C on May 1. C executed a retail installment sales contract granting dealer a security interest to secure the installment payments that C agreed to make over a three-year period. Dealer assigned the paper to its floor planner, First Bank. On May 2, C was involved in a collision that left the vehicle with extensive body damage. C took the car to G, who repaired the vehicle. C is now bankrupt, and G, who has yet to be paid, is holding the car and refusing to return it to the bank that is claiming it. Must First Bank pay *G* before it can claim possession of the car? Would your answer differ if the garage's lien were based on common law holdings that made the lien subordinate to prior perfected security interests? Would it differ if the garage's lien were statutory and the statute rendered the lien subordinate to prior perfected security interests?

162. *§1-201(37).*   Lessor, Inc. purchases heavy equipment for the oil industry and leases it to oil exploration companies. On May 1, it leased 20 diesel engines to Oil-Ex Co. for a period of four years. In which of the following cases would you as counsel for Lessor recommend to your client that it file a financing statement?

    a. The lessee has an option at the end of the four-year term to purchase the equipment for $1.

    b. At the end of the first four-year term, the lessee has an option to lease the equipment, at a fair rental price, for an additional four years, with the option to purchase the equipment at the end of the second term for $1. Would your answer to this question differ if the rental for the second four-year term were "nominal"? How do you determine whether the rent for the second term is nominal?

    c. The equipment has an estimated useful life of ten years, the lease is for four years, and the lessee must return the goods at the end of the lease term in the original condition, normal wear and tear excepted.

    d. The equipment has a life of ten years, the lease term is for four years, and the lease provides that the lessee must purchase the equipment at the end of the four-year term at a price equal to the then-market value of the equipment.

    e. §1-201(37)(y). The lease is for four years, and the goods have an estimated useful life of three years. (For the purposes of this problem, as of what date does the statute direct the estimate of useful life to be made?)

    f. The lease is for ten years, the estimated useful life of the equipment is twenty years, and the lessee has the option to continue the lease for an additional ten years for

       i. $1.

      ii. $100.

     iii. a sum of money equal to 50 percent of the estimated value of the equipment at the end of the ten-year term.

    g. Would your answer to any of the questions in this problem differ if the lessee had the right to terminate the lease?

163. *§2-326.*   *M*, a bicycle manufacturer, consigned bicycles to *R*, a retailer, for resale at *R*'s bicycle shop. Under the terms of the consignment, any goods that *R* did not resell would be returned to *M*. The consignment agreement stipulated that title to the goods remained in *M* and that *R* was only an agent with power to transfer title to customers of *R*. *R* is now bankrupt, and its trustee in bankruptcy is claiming the goods. In determining whether the trustee or *M* should recover the goods, which of the following facts would be relevant?

    a.   That *R*'s bicycle shop had a sign at the entrance reading "*M* Bicycle Shop."

    b.   That there is a small sign over the door of the shop reading "*R*, authorized dealer."

    c.   That *R* posted a notice in the shop window reading "*M* bicycles in this store are on consignment."

    d.   That *M* filed a financing statement centrally designating *M* as consignor and *R* as consignee. §9-408.

164. *§9-114.* *W*, a wholesaler, has granted First Bank a security interest in all of its inventory of beer and wine. *B*, a brewer that is trying to enter the market, offers to sell 20,000 cases of wine to *W* "on consignment." You are counsel to *B*, who has asked for your opinion on the action it should take to protect itself from First. What do you advise?

165. *§2-326.* *P*, a farm producer, delivered cotton to *G*, a gin, for ginning and baling. Traditionally, *G* has marketed cotton for its customers by distributing samples of the cotton and taking orders. When *G* sells cotton, it subtracts its ginning and baling costs, its storage charges, and its commission, and remits the balance to the customer.

    a.   *G* is now bankrupt, and its trustee claims the cotton that *P* delivered to *G*. Does the trustee defeat *P*? Would your answer differ if *P* could show that the trustee knew of the bailment?

    b.   Prior to its bankruptcy, *G* granted First Bank a security interest in all of its inventory, then owned or thereafter acquired. Does First defeat *P*? Would your answer differ if *P* could show that First knew of the bailment?

166. On May 1, Wool Co., which manufactured woolen textiles at its plant, entered into a sale of fabric with Mill Co. Mill did not want to take delivery of the goods and, after paying for them, asked Wool Co. to hold them pending delivery instructions. In the meantime, Wool was having difficulty with Aussie Co., its wool supplier to whom it owed $1 million. On May 2, Wool conveyed to Aussie, in satisfaction of the debt, all of Wool's textile inventory, including Mill's fabric. Wool delivered the goods to Aussie, which was unaware that it was taking property to which Mill would later make a claim. Wool is now bankrupt. Mill claims that Aussie has converted its property.

    a.   Is Aussie a buyer in ordinary course?

    b.   Is Aussie a secured party that has repossessed its collateral?

    c.   Is Aussie liable in conversion to Mill? §2-402(2).

167. *§2A-307.* A&B Co. sells metal strapping to manufacturers that use the strapping to seal containers in which they ship product. A&B also "leases" wire strapping machines to its customers for use in applying the wire to the containers. The machines are costly, but A&B does not profit from the leases. It profits from the sale of the strapping. If a customer becomes insolvent, will A&B lose the machines to the trustee? To the customer's bank holding a perfected security interest in the customer's equipment? Does your answer to this question depend on the amount of rent that A&B charges the customer? What result if the rent is $1 per year? What result if the rent is a reasonable rental?

Section 24. *The Seller's Right to Reclaim*

In the discussion of the doctrine of voidable title in Problems 9 and 10, we noted that a seller loses something when the fraud with voidable title conveys goods to a good-faith purchaser for value. We never identified, however, what it is that the seller loses. He loses the right to reclaim, and the following problems deal with the attempt of the seller to assert that right against third parties. As we know, he will not be successful when he asserts the right against the good-faith purchaser for value, but we will also see that not every important commercial personage fits the definition of such a good-faith purchaser and that the seller can assert the right against parties that frequently appear in the real commercial world, most notably the trustee in bankruptcy.

This set of problems is an introduction to the bankruptcy issues that are the subject of the problems under the next section.

Problems

168. *S* contracts to sell diesel engine components to *B*, an engine manufacturer, for $75,000. *B* submits a purchase order to *S* calling for payment within ten days of shipment. *S* accepts the purchase order. Under the purchase order, *S* must manufacture the parts to *B*'s specifications and must ship in two installments. *S* has shipped one installment, but *B* failed to pay within the ten-day period. *S* has completed the second shipment and prepared it for delivery in cartons marked with *B*'s name and address.

   a. What is *B*'s interest in the second shipment? §2-501(1).

   b. May *S* cut off that interest? §2-703(a).

   c. Would *B*'s inventory lender have an interest in the shipment? §9-203(1). If so, would *S* be able to cut off that interest?

169. *§§2-702(1), 2-705(1).* If *S* had shipped the second installment, under what circumstances could *S* stop delivery?

170. If *S* had delivered the parts included in the second installment and if *B* did not pay for them, does *S* have any interest in the parts after the delivery? Would *B*'s inventory lender? *B*'s trustee in bankruptcy? What must *S* do to obtain an interest in goods that it delivers on credit to *B* when *B* is guilty of no fraud but does not pay?

171. *§2-702.* If *B* practiced fraud on *S*, does *S* have any interest in the goods after delivery? What must *S* do to "perfect" this interest? Are there circumstances that relieve *S* from its perfection duties? What might *S* do to avoid having to make the demand referred to in §2-702? If *B* gives *S* a check drawn on insufficient funds, is that check a written representation of solvency? What proof of fraud must *S* marshal in these cases? Is common law fraud good enough? Anything else? At common law did *S* have to "perfect" its interest? Is it fraudulent for *B* to receive goods on credit while it is insolvent? Does it matter whether *B* knows it is insolvent? For the definition of "insolvent," *see* §1-201(23).

172. *§2-507(2).* S entered into a sale of lumber with B. Under the terms of the contract, S was to deliver the lumber to B's shed. When S arrived at B's yard, B told S to unload the lumber into the shed and return to the office for payment. After S unloaded the lumber, he drove his truck to the office, which he found locked. When he returned to the shed, it was locked also. B has refused to return the lumber.
    a. Does S have any rights in the lumber?
    b. Is it necessary for S to show that B planned all along to defraud S?
    c. Must S "perfect" his rights?
    d. Would your answers to this question differ if, when S went to the office, B gave S a check drawn on insufficient funds? §2-511, comment 6. Does it matter whether the check was post-dated? Does it matter whether B knew that the check was an overdraft?

173. *§2-507(2).* Which of the following parties does a cash seller with the right to reclaim defeat?
    a. A buyer in ordinary course to which B resells the goods.
    b. A purchaser for value in good faith, such as a lender with a security interest in all of B's after-acquired inventory. Does it matter whether the secured party is perfected?

174. *§2-507, comment 3.* Must a cash seller that is asserting its right to reclaim under §2-507(2) give a notice of demand for return of the goods?

175. *§2-403(1).* Customarily, the seller's right to the goods in §§2-507(2) and 2-702(2) is characterized as the seller's right to reclaim. The rule of §2-703(a) is probably a codification of what the common law called the seller's lien. What other name might we give the seller's right?

176. *§2-403(1) (second sentence).* There are at least four cases of fraud: (1) common law fraud in which B defrauds S with scienter and in a manner that satisfies the traditional definition of fraud; (2) taking delivery of goods on credit under a contract of sale while insolvent; (3) taking delivery under a cash sale in return for a check drawn on insufficient funds; and (4) grabbing the goods in a cash sale and refusing to pay for them. In these four instances, what do we call B's interest in the goods?

177. *§2-403(1) (second sentence).* If B holds voidable title to goods it purchased from S under a contract of sale, what interest relative to S passes to the following parties?
    a. A lender that holds a perfected security interest in B's after-acquired inventory.
    b. C, a customer of B to whom B resells the goods in the ordinary course of business.
    c. D, a buyer in bulk to whom B resells the goods.

178. *§2-702(3).* In voidable title cases, will a lien creditor of B defeat S's right to reclaim? What does §2-403(1) suggest? In some jurisdictions, the Code includes a "lien creditor" in the list of persons in §2-702(3) to whose rights the seller's right to reclaim are "subject." What does that version of §2-702(3) suggest? How should we read the words "subject to" in §2-702(3)?

179. *Bankruptcy Code §546(c)(1).*   Assume that *B*'s lien creditor in the foregoing problems is the trustee in bankruptcy.

a. Does the Bankruptcy Code fashion rules for *S*'s right to reclaim to the extent it is not codified in UCC §2-702? What about UCC §2-507? Is there a negative implication in Bankruptcy Code §546(c)(1) to the effect that it is the sole source of relief for *S*, that is, that *S* may not rely on common law fraud or on UCC §2-507(2)?

b. Must *S* "perfect" to defeat the trustee? How do the perfection requirements of the Bankruptcy Code differ from those in UCC §2-702?

c. Does "subject to" in Bankruptcy Code §546(c)(1) mean what those words mean in UCC §2-702(3)? Where do we look to find the meaning? Does the Bankruptcy Code use the term "subject to" to mean "subordinate to"? If the common law of the jurisdiction gives the lien creditor rights superior to those of the reclaiming seller, does the trustee defeat the reclaiming seller? If Bankruptcy Code §546(c)(1) changes the law in those states, does it change it with respect to the seller's right to reclaim under common law fraud? Under UCC §2-507(2)?

d. Will *B*'s periodic statements of solvency obviate *S*'s need to demand return of the goods under Bankruptcy Code §546(c)(1)?

180. *§§1-201(37), 9-102(1)(a).*   Does Article 9 apply to *S*'s right to reclaim? If *B* resells the goods delivered by *S*, does *S* have a right to the proceeds? If so, does that right defeat third parties (that is, lien creditors, *B*'s trustee in bankruptcy, *B*'s inventory lender, *B*'s account lender)?

181. *§§1-201(37), 2-505(1)(a), 2-711(3).*   Is the seller's right to reclaim a security interest? Can it be a security interest under Article 9? Are there security interests in Article 2? How does the seller's right to reclaim differ from the Article 2 security interest defined in those provisions? If the seller's right to reclaim is not a security interest, what is it?

Section 25.   *Article 9 and the Powers of the Trustee in Bankruptcy*

Article 9 is state law, and it is subject to the provisions of the Bankruptcy Code and of the powers granted under that federal law to the trustee in bankruptcy.

Secured lenders often face the perils of bankruptcy. There are a number of sections in the Bankruptcy Code that traditionally fall within the study of Article 9. Chief among them are (1) the trustee's power to assert the rights of a lien creditor that obtains a lien on all of the debtor's property on the filing of the bankruptcy petition, and (2) the trustee's power to set aside transactions that are preferences. In addition, §362 of the Bankruptcy Code, the automatic stay provision, has impact on the rights of the secured creditor. The rules of §552 also are particularly relevant.

The following problems examine the effect of these Bankruptcy Code sections on the security interest. Notably absent from these problems is discussion of the effects of Chapter 11 on the rights of the secured party. Study of that complex of bankruptcy rules is better left to courses on creditors' rights.

Assume in the following problems that the debtor filed a straight liquidation petition under Chapter 7 of the Bankruptcy Code on December 1, which makes September 2 the 90th day before bankruptcy. Assume further that at all times, unless the problem otherwise states, the secured party is undersecured.

Problems

182. *Bankruptcy Code §§544(a)(1), 552(a); UCC §9-301(1)(b).* On October 1, Debtor executed a security agreement that purported to grant First Bank a security interest in all of Debtor's equipment, then owned or thereafter acquired. The bank filed a proper financing statement in the proper office on October 5. On December 2, Debtor obtained rights in a press that it had paid for in November. Does the trustee as a lien creditor defeat First Bank's interest in the press?

183. *Bankruptcy Code §552(b).* On May 1, Debtor granted First Bank a perfected security interest in all of Debtor's inventory, then owned or thereafter acquired. On December 2, Debtor in possession, who has the rights of a trustee, sold on open account inventory that it had owned on May 1 and immediately before the filing. Does Debtor in possession defeat First Bank's claim to the account?

184. *Bankruptcy Code §§362(b)(3), 546(b); UCC §9-301(2).* On November 18, debtor granted Manufacturing Co. a security interest in kitchen equipment Manufacturing Co. was selling on credit. Manufacturing Co. delivered the equipment on November 27 and filed a proper financing statement in the proper office on December 5. Does the trustee as a lien creditor defeat Manufacturing Co.?

185. *Bankruptcy Code §362(b)(3).* On November 28, Supply Co. delivered a truckload of inventory to Debtor on credit when Debtor was insolvent. May Supply Co. on December 5 successfully demand in writing that the inventory be returned?

186. *Bankruptcy Code §362(a)(5).* On May 1, Debtor granted First Bank a perfected security interest in all of Debtor's equipment. If Debtor is in default on the note secured by the equipment, may First repossess the equipment under UCC §9-503 on December 2? If First repossessed the equipment on November 30, may First sell it under UCC §9-504 on December 2? If First Bank's security interest were unperfected on December 1, could it file a financing statement on December 2?

187. On August 30, Debtor granted First Bank a security interest in all of Debtor's equipment to secure a debt of $10,000. On September 3, Electric Co. obtained a judgment in the amount of $100 against Debtor and levied on Debtor's equipment. On September 4, First filed.

a. May the trustee defeat First under the preference section, or is the transfer deemed to have occurred on August 30? Bankruptcy Code §547(e)(2)(A).

b. May Electric Co. defeat First Bank? UCC §9-301(1)(b). (Bear in mind that this is not a purchase-money security interest.)

c. May the trustee defeat Electric Co. under the preference section? *See* Bankruptcy Code §101(54) (defining "transfer").

d. If it defeats Electric Co., will the trustee step into Electric Co.'s shoes as a lien creditor as of September 3, and will the trustee, therefore, defeat First? Bankruptcy Code §551.

e. If the trustee defeats First under Bankruptcy Code §551, is the trustee's victory limited to Electric Co.'s $100, or may trustee upset First's security interest in its entirety?

Section 26.   Preferences

The following four problems deal with preferences as defined in §547(b) of the Bankruptcy Code, with the exceptions to that definition in subsection (c) of §547 and with the timing rule of subsection (e). The emphasis is not so much on the preference rules as it is on the intersection of those rules with secured lending practices.

Problems

188. *Bankruptcy Code §§101(54) (defining "transfer" for Bankruptcy Code purposes) and 547(b) (listing elements of voidable preference).*   On September 5, Manufacturing Co. became anxious about the security of its claim against Debtor for equipment Manufacturing Co. delivered to Debtor on credit. Manufacturing demanded a payment on that open account. On the next day, Debtor paid $10,000 to Manufacturing Co.

a. May the trustee recover the payment?

b. Would your answer to the preceding question differ if instead of paying cash to Manufacturing Co. on September 6, Debtor had granted Manufacturing Co. a perfected security interest in Debtor's equipment on that date? Could the trustee set the creation of that security interest aside?

c. Would your answer differ if instead of obtaining a cash payment or a security interest, Manufacturing Co. obtained a lien by judicial proceedings against Debtor on September 6? Could the trustee set the lien aside?

189. *Bankruptcy Code §547(b), (c)(3), (c)(4), (e)(2).*   Which of the following transactions is a preference that the trustee in bankruptcy may recover under §547?

a. On November 1, Debtor paid $1,000 to First Bank on First Bank's demand note. §547(b).

b. Would your answer differ if the note were completely secured by a perfected security interest in Debtor's property? §547(b)(5).

    c. On May 2, Debtor gave $100 to its president in satisfaction of a loan the president had made to the company. §547(b).

    d. On October and November 1, Debtor paid $1,000 to First Bank on an installment note that called for payments of that amount on the first day of each month. §547(c)(2).

    e. On November 3, Debtor granted First Bank a security interest in all of its equipment as security for a $100,000 loan made on that date. §547(e)(2). Does it matter whether First files its financing statement before or after November 13?

    f. On August 1, Second Bank made an unsecured loan to Debtor of $50,000. On August 31, Second deemed itself insecure and asked Debtor for a security interest in all of Debtor's inventory. Debtor granted the security interest on that date. Does it matter whether Second files its financing statement before or after September 10? *Id.*

    g. On November 29, Seller Co. sold and delivered inventory to debtor on credit, and debtor granted Seller Co. a security interest in the inventory. Does it matter whether Seller files before or after December 9? §547(c)(3) and (e)(2)(A). Would your answer differ if the security interest were not a purchase money security interest? Is the date of delivery critical?

    h. On August 15, Debtor executed a security agreement purporting to grant Fourth Bank a security interest in all of Debtor's general intangibles. Fourth made a loan to Debtor for the first time on September 10. Fourth filed on September 17. §547(e)(2)(A). Would your answer differ if Fourth had made a commitment to lend on August 15?

    i. On August 15, Fifth Bank loaned Debtor $50,000. On September 15, Debtor granted Fifth a perfected security interest in a piece of Debtor's equipment that was worth, and is still worth, $50,000. On October 15, Fifth made a second unsecured loan to Debtor of $20,000. §547(c)(4).

    j. On August 20, Supply Co. delivered a month's supply of fuel to Debtor on 20 days' open account. On September 9, Debtor paid for the August delivery. On September 20, Supply Co. delivered another month's supply of fuel, for which Debtor made payment on November 10. Supply Co. made a third delivery on November 20. §547(c)(2).

190. On August 15, Debtor granted First Bank a perfected security interest in all of Debtor's accounts, then due or thereafter arising. On the same day, First loaned $100,000 to Debtor.

    a. Under the UCC, when does the bank first obtain an interest in an account that arises out of the sale by Debtor of inventory on September 15?

    b. If the bank first obtains an interest in the account on September 15, is there a transfer by Debtor of that account on that date, and is that transfer not on account of the antecedent debt of August 15? Bankruptcy Code §547(e)(3); UCC §9-108. Can courts rely on UCC §9-108?

    c. Given this analysis, is it correct to say that under the UCC and the Bankruptcy Code revolving account financing would be seriously problematic for lenders?

d. Does the Bankruptcy Code interdict this analysis for revolving account (and revolving inventory) loans? Bankruptcy Code §547(c)(5).

e. Would your answers to any of the foregoing questions differ if the collateral were equipment rather than inventory or accounts?

191. *Bankruptcy Code §547(c)(5).* On May 1, Debtor granted Lender a security interest in all inventory then owned or thereafter acquired. In which of the following examples would the revolving inventory lender have received a preference?

a. On September 2, the value of the inventory was $10,000, and the balance due on the inventory loan was $8,000. On December 1, the value of the inventory was $20,000, and the balance due on the loan was $19,000.

b. Would your answer differ if the value of the inventory on September 2 was $5,000 and the debt $19,000?

c. On September 2, the value of the inventory was $10,000, and the balance due on the loan was $12,000. On the date of bankruptcy, the respective figures were $10,000 and $10,000. $20,000 and $22,000. $4,000 and $6,000.

Section 27. The Trustee as Lien Creditor

More powerful, though less intellectually challenging, than the trustee's power to recover preferences is the trustee's power under Bankruptcy Code §544(a)(1) to set aside security interests that fall before the lien creditor. This provision coupled with the rule of UCC §9-301(1)(b) permits the trustee to defeat the unperfected secured party and makes the Code's perfection rules critical. Assume, again, that the debtor filed in bankruptcy on December 1.

Problems

192. *Bankruptcy Code §§544(a)(1), 547(e)(2)(C).* On April 1, Debtor granted First Bank a security interest in return for a loan, and the bank filed a proper financing statement in the proper office on December 5. Does the trustee have the right to set the secured transaction aside as a preference?

193. *Bankruptcy Code §§544(a)(1), 547(e)(2)(C); UCC §9-301(2).*

a. In the preceding question, if the bank had loaned and taken the security interest on November 30, would your answer differ?

b. Would it matter whether the bank's security interest was a purchase-money security interest?

194. *Bankruptcy Code §547(c)(1).* On the morning of November 20, First Bank loaned Debtor $20,000. That afternoon, Debtor granted the bank a perfected security interest in Debtor's chattel paper. May the trustee recover the chattel paper?

Section 28. Proceeds in Bankruptcy

Section 9-306(4) is an attempt to deal with proceeds in the insolvency setting. Subsections (a) through (c) are straightforward. Subsection (d) is a resourceful response to the real world impracticalities of tracing proceeds that have been commingled in a deposit account. Pre-Code law was theoretically pure, but practical nonsense; and the Code drafters used a measure of imagination and compromise to fashion a fine, rational rule. Unfortunately the drafters were fashioning state law, and most insolvency law is federal. It does not take a great deal of effort to make an argument that subsection (d) runs afoul of bankruptcy rules against statutory liens or preferences. It does take effort to overcome those arguments.

Presumably, Grant Gilmore, Homer Kripke, and Karl Llewellyn were aware that they were arguably trespassing on federal ground when they drew subsection (d). They probably assumed that commercial lawyers would be resourceful and imaginative enough to protect their resourceful and imaginative solution to the proceeds tracing problem. We may be disappointing them.

Solution to the Bankruptcy Code-UCC conflict must abide, however, a proper understanding of the rules of UCC §9-306(4). The following problems aim to foster that understanding.

Problems

195. On May 1, Appliance Co. (AC) entered into an arrangement with *R*, a retailer, under which *R* purchased the AC line of appliances on credit and granted AC a perfected security interest to secure the unpaid purchase price. In which of the following will AC have a perfected security interest in the event of *R*'s bankruptcy?

    a. Trade-in appliances received by *R* for credit toward the purchase of a new AC appliance and the balance in a deposit account named "AC Account" in which *R* deposited only those checks it received from the sale of AC appliances. §9-306(4)(a).

    b. An envelope containing cash that *R* had received from a customer in payment of a portion of the purchase price of an AC appliance. §9-306(4)(b).

    c. Three checks that *R* had not deposited when it became insolvent, all of which *R* had received from customers in payment of all or a portion of the purchase price of an AC appliance. §9-306(4)(c).

196. *§9-306(4)(d).*   On September 1, *R* filed a petition in bankruptcy. At the time, *R*'s general checking account contained $35,000, due in large part to a tax refund check that the company deposited two days before bankruptcy. *R*'s president will testify that from time to time the company also deposited checks from customers who purchased goods from *R*, including some goods that were AC appliances. It is not clear from the company's records, however, how many of the checks that were deposited were from the sale of such appliances. The records do indicate that the company received $25,000 in cash proceeds from the sale of AC appliances during the ten-day period preceding bankruptcy, though none of that money went into the account.

a.   If AC can show that $10 of the proceeds from the sale of its appliances were deposited in the general account, how much will AC be able to claim as a perfected secured party? Does it matter whether the $10 was deposited during the ten days? A year ago? Would your answer differ if during the ten-day period *R* paid over $10,000 in proceeds to AC? Would your answer differ if *R* received proceeds from the sale of products other than AC products during the ten-day period?

b.   If AC cannot show that any proceeds from the sale of its inventory were deposited in the account, how much of the account is subject to AC's security interest?

c.   If AC can show that (1) $50,000 of proceeds from the sale of its collateral went into the account on the 11th day prior to bankruptcy, and (2) under the lowest intermediate balance rule $20,000 of that amount remains in the account, but it cannot show that *R* received any proceeds from the sale of AC products during the ten days preceding bankruptcy, how much does AC receive under §9-306(4)?

d.   If AC cannot show under the lowest intermediate balance method or under some other state rule for tracing proceeds that there are proceeds from the sale of its collateral in the deposit account, and if the rule of §9-306(4)(d) gives some or all of the account to AC, does the operation of the rule offend the Bankruptcy Code's provision against liens that arise upon insolvency? Bankruptcy Code §545(1)(A). Would the result under the application of the Code to such facts constitute a preference in favor of AC?

Section 29.   Part 5: Default

In the event the debtor defaults on the underlying obligation that the security agreement supports, the secured party may want to enforce the rights it enjoys under the provisions of the security agreement and under Part 5 of Article 9.

There has been some litigation here, fostered for the most part by disputes over debtor protection provisions that turn on factual determinations. As you will see, some of the rules of Part 5 require reasonable conduct. Often, parties will disagree on the question of reasonableness.

Even if they do not agree, they know they can usually get to a jury with a reasonableness issue, being as it is one of fact rather than law.

The purpose of these problems is not to deal, however, with those issues but only to provide you with an understanding of the sections themselves.

Problems

197. On May 1, Seller sold and delivered goods to Debtor, and Debtor agreed to pay Seller $10,000 on June 1. On May 2, Bank loaned Debtor $10,000 and took a security interest in the goods that Seller had delivered. Debtor executed and delivered to the bank a promissory note for the $10,000. There was a provision in the security agreement under which Debtor covenanted that she would not allow judgments or allow liens to attach to the collateral. Bank perfected its security interest in the goods on the same day. On June 1, Debtor defaulted on both debts, and Seller obtained a judgment against Debtor. The bank has obtained no judgment.
   a. Does Bank have the right to take possession of the goods? §§9-501(2), 9-503.
   b. Would your answer differ if Seller had obtained a lien on the goods by having the sheriff levy on them? §9-301(1)(b).
   c. Would your answer differ if Debtor was not in default on the promissory note that she signed when she borrowed the money from the bank? §9-501(1).

198. *§9-503.* Assume the same facts as in the foregoing problem. Under which of the following circumstances has the bank exercised its rights properly under Part 5 of Article 9?
   a. Bank called Debtor's employee and told the employee that a truck would be arriving that afternoon to pick up the goods. The employee, without speaking to Debtor, allowed the bank's agents to take the goods.
   b. Banker arrived at Debtor's place of business, told the employee of Debtor that he was there to pick up the collateral, walked into the premises, and took the goods.
   c. The goods were inside Debtor's plant, and Banker broke a lock, went into the premises at night, and took the goods. Does it matter whether Bank has offered to repair the lock? Does it matter whether the security agreement gave Bank the right to enter the premises and remove the collateral?
   d. The goods included a truck that Debtor had parked on the street in front of Debtor's plant. During the night, Banker forced the lock on the truck, hot wired it, and drove it away.
   e. The goods were sitting on public property when Banker arrived to pick them up. Debtor was present, and when she saw the banker, she told him not to take the goods. Banker took them anyway. Would your answer differ if Debtor had told Banker that if he tried to remove the goods that there would be trouble? Would your answer differ if the banker used vulgar language?

199. *§§9-504(3), 9-507.* Assume the following problem, that the bank repossessed the goods properly and took the following actions in connection with them. In which of the following cases has the bank acted improperly? In all cases assume, unless the facts state otherwise, that the bank gave the debtor timely notice of the proposed dispositions. (In answering these questions, ask yourself how the bank would prove the reasonableness of its conduct.)

    a.   The bank sold a drill press to one of its best customers at a price below the market price for a used drill press.

    b.   The bank sold a second drill press through a used equipment dealer at the fair market price and paid the dealer a commission.

    c.   The bank sold a third drill press six months later at the market price for used drill presses but at a price substantially below the market price on the day it repossessed the press.

    d.   The bank kept for itself a personal computer and credited the debtor with the fair market value of the computer.

200. *§9-504(4).* If the bank sold the defaulting debtor's collateral to an innocent third party and made the sale in violation of the debtor's rights under the security agreement or under Part 5 of Article 9, will the third party take good title to the goods?

201. *§§9-504(2), 9-507.* A secured party sold collateral of its debtor and received $9,000 as proceeds after deducting the costs of the sale. The debt that the collateral secured was for $10,000. In which of the following cases may the secured party obtain a judgment against the debtor for the deficiency?

    a.   The secured party sold the collateral without giving the debtor notice of the sale, but the sale was reasonable, and the evidence indicates that the secured party received a fair price.

    b.   The secured party disposed of the collateral without giving notice to the debtor, but the security agreement contained a provision under which the debtor waived its statutory right of notice. §9-501(3).

202. *§9-506.* A debtor borrowed $10,000 and granted secured party a security interest in goods. The promissory note that the debtor executed stipulated that in the event of a default on a payment of principal or interest, the full amount of the note would come due. The security agreement provided that a default under the note would be a default under the security agreement. After the debtor defaulted on an interest payment, the secured party repossessed the collateral. The debtor now seeks to reclaim the collateral and offers to pay the secured party the full amount of interest due. The secured party proposes to sell the collateral, apply the proceeds of the sale to the note, and seek a deficiency judgment against the debtor for the balance.

    a.   May the secured party pursue that course of action?

    b.   Would your answer differ if the debtor proposed to pay the secured party the interest and the full principal balance due on the note?

Secured Transactions: Answers

Section 1. *Transferring Property Interests: Security of Property, Good-Faith Purchase and Fraudulent Conveyance*

1. Dealer has no interest in the equipment, which it sold to Mine Co. Dealer's "repossession" of the equipment would be tortious and, perhaps, larcenous. Dealer and Mine Co. could have structured the transaction differently (of course) by reserving a security interest in Dealer, but they did not. Dealer, moreover, has no common law right to repossess the equipment. Title, the location of which is normally not dispositive in Code matters, is in Mine Co. *See* §9-202.

2. This transaction does not resemble a "true" consignment, *see* §2-326, but looks like an attempt by a seller of goods to retain title after delivering the goods to the buyer. Section 2-401(1) renders this attempt by seller to reserve title a security interest. This security interest is not an Article 2 security interest. It is a consensual security interest that falls within the definition of "security interest" in §1-201(37) and is subject to Article 9 rules. *See* §9-102.

   Under various good faith purchase rules in Article 9, buyers from Distributor Co. will defeat Woolen Co.'s claim to the wool, as will Distributor Co.'s creditors. The notion that Distributor Co. can act in these circumstances as an agent for Woolen Co. is a subterfuge that should not fool anyone in this day and age, though American Woolen Co. fooled the U.S. Supreme Court in an earlier day. This arrangement is one of inventory financing, whether the parties dub Distributor Co. "agent" or anything else.

3. The analysis here is the same as that in the preceding "consignment" question. Article 9 will not work if parties can avoid its scope by characterizing their arrangements in archaic terms. Both this reservation of title and the earlier "consignment" were truly secured transactions, and Arti-

cle 9's scope rule, §9-102, correctly commands that all such arrangements fall within the purview of that Article. The seller's interest is a security interest and no more. *See also* §1-201(37).

4. The first sentence of §2-403(1) codifies the *nemo dat* and umbrella (or "shelter") principles of conveyancing law. This is the first rule of conveyancing, a security-of-property principle to the effect that the transferee gets what the transferor had and what he conveyed. Under *nemo dat*, the transferor cannot convey greater interests than he has; under the umbrella principle, the transferee gets everything the transferor has, provided the transferor conveys what he has. If he conveys only a one-half interest, the transferee only gets the one-half interest, even though the transferor has a full interest.

    Using this first rule of conveyancing, the starting point in any conveyancing analysis, the answers to the questions follow.

    a. *B* gets absolute ownership.
    b. *B* takes subject to the security interest. (Note that the rules of Article 9 may alter this conclusion by invoking either the second or the third conveyancing rules. Under the first rule of conveyancing, however, *B* cannot take more than *A* has; and after the conveyance to *C*, *A* has title subject to a security interest. *B*, therefore, takes subject to the interest.)
    c. *A* has already conveyed all of his interest to *B*; *B* takes all, and *C* takes nothing. (If *B* had left the toluene with *A*, *B* may have permitted *A* to defraud *C*.)
    d. The first rule of conveyancing serves the free transferability of goods and the security of property principle. To say that *A* owns goods but may not transfer them is to say that ownership does not mean much. In commerce, the ability to transfer ownership, to convey, is essential. The law's recognition of the right to convey title to goods doomed feudalism, for it permitted the lowly merchant to create wealth and make himself and his contemporaries wealthier than the lords and to reduce the lords to the point of having to rent out their estates on the weekend for the merchants' employee picnic. (The merchants' struggle to have the law recognize the right to own goods and convey them was not an easy one; it took centuries for the merchants to prevail. Lords do not surrender privilege easily. They knew what the merchants were about. The lords may have been lazy, but they were not stupid. Modern society has lords. Some of them sit in the Congress or in state legislatures. Most of them, however, teach law.)

5. Under the first sentence of §2-403(1), the first rule of conveyancing (*nemo dat*), Buyer Co. takes subject to the security interest of First Bank. *Nemo dat* also dictates that Second Bank takes subject to the security interest. Buyer Co. cannot give Second Bank what Buyer Co. does not have.

    If for some reason First Bank's security interest is not good against Buyer Co. (under one of the good-faith purchase exceptions to the *nemo dat* principle), Second Bank will come under Buyer Co.'s umbrella, take what Buyer Co. has (title free of First Bank's security interest), and defeat First Bank.

6. In the case of loss, *C* may retain the watch as against the whole world, except for *A*. In the case of theft, *C* has nothing. The different results reflect in the first case the romance of a young chimney sweep named Armory, in the latter the law's animus toward theft.

7. Owner and Auctioneer may think of themselves as clever chaps. The law regards them as odious creeps. Buyers such as Collector should be able to rely on Auctioneer's apparent authority and should be able to bind Owner. Thus agency law may estop Owner from asserting his title. This is the beginning of the second conveyancing rule, the notion that a transferee takes something extra, more than he would get under the first rule of *nemo dat*.

8. In this problem, the two contenders are innocent, but Jones is more innocent than Smith, who permitted Dealer to mislead Jones. Efficiency analysis helps here. While some goods, such as yachts, are subject to certificate of title laws, which permit a buyer to check on a seller's title, most goods are not subject to such laws, and this problem does not tell you that the yacht was titled. It would be grossly inefficient in sale-of-goods transactions to insist that buyers check on the seller's title. To put the loss on Jones would have that effect. Smith can avoid the loss by entrusting his yacht to an honest dealer or by taking dealer's bond or other security. It is easier for him to protect himself than it is for Jones to protect herself.

   Whether the result should differ if Smith took the yacht to Dealer for storage is a matter of some dispute. Those who would protect buyers think it makes no difference. The efficiency analysis holds. At least one court disagrees. Note that there is tension here between the first rule of conveyancing, a security-of-property rule, and the good-faith purchase doctrine, which is a security-of-purchase rule. You will not be surprised to learn that the lords often prefer security of property while merchants usually prefer security of purchase.

9. Taking delivery of goods using a check drawn on insufficient funds is fraud at common law. Under the voidable title rule, which is only partly codified in §2-403(1) (second sentence), a fraud feasor has power to transfer good title to a good-faith purchaser for value. Dealer is such a purchaser even if she has not paid for the goods. The law protects her expectation interest — an important interest, evidently more important than Manufacturer's security-of-property interest. Note again that efficiency analysis helps explain the rule. Manufacturer could protect itself by checking on Middle's credit rating, by insisting on cash or other security before payment, or by refusing to do business with Middle. In fact, merchant sellers do all of these things, while buyers such as Dealer do exactly what Dealer did. They rely on Middle's "ostensible ownership" of the goods. Dealer has behaved in commercially reasonable fashion. Manufacturer has made a mistake. It is not a bad rule that lets people who make mistakes pay for them.

10. The retailers should prevail under the same economic analysis that we used in the preceding answer. Some of the early voidable title cases used intent to hold that a seller such as Owner should lose. Because Owner intended to vest Reed with title, Jones took voidable title, they reasoned. The intent rationale fails in the imposter case, however. There, Owner intended to vest the imposter, whatever her name, with title. The efficiency analysis prevails under the Code's version of voidable title, as subsection (1)(a) of §2-403 indicates.

11. This problem illustrates the operation of the oldest fraudulent conveyance rule. Fraudulent conveyance law comprises the third conveyancing principle, the second exception to the notion that the transferee receives that which the transferor had. In good-faith purchase, the taker receives more than the transferor had. Under fraudulent conveyance, the taker receives less. Here, Ace and his company have defrauded the bank. The law regards the transfer as not having occurred, and First Bank will be able to levy on the equipment.

12. Under the rule of *Twyne's Case*, it is fraud at law for a buyer to pay for goods and leave them with the seller, unless the buyer can provide a good-faith reason for his conduct. To leave a truck with a seller to have it undercoated is such a reason. Edison would prevail over First Bank. Note that §2-402(2) does not codify *Tywne*. It merely refers to *Twyne*. Section 2-402(2) codifies only the good-faith reason proviso of *Twyne*.

Section 2. Scope

13. Finance Co. must comply with Article 9, with or without recourse. It matters not that the transfer of accounts is by sale or by creation of a security interest. Both characterizations fall within the scope section. For scope purposes, there is no difference between the sale of accounts and the assignment of accounts as security. (Note that there are exceptions for the assignment of accounts for collection purposes or as part of the sale of a business. *See* §9-104(f). The exceptions are not commercially significant. For now it is enough to know that the sale of accounts to a factor, the name we give the buyer of accounts, is an Article 9 transaction that requires the factor to obtain a security agreement and to file a financing statement. There is an exception to the filing requirement in the event of the "occasional" transfer of an account. *See* §9-302(1)(e). This exception can be mischievous.)

14. Bank must comply with Article 9. It does not matter whether Dealer and Bank characterize their transaction as a sale or as a transfer for security. The Code treats both transactions (which are pretty hard to distinguish anyway) as secured transactions that fall within the scope of Article 9. Section 9-104(f) excludes the sale of chattel paper as part of the sale of the business out of which it arose.

15. Most authorities take the position that when the secured party takes a security interest in the note and perfects it, it has a perfected security inter-

est in the mortgage if it is conveyed to the secured party, as it always should be. In most jurisdictions, then, Article 9 applies to the transaction between Mortgage Co. and National Bank. A minority of courts arguably read §9-104(j) as requiring the bank to follow real estate law to perfect its interest in the mortgage. (Bank's interest in the note, as a matter of negotiable instruments law, is probably not a security interest but outright ownership. The note by itself is an instrument. *See* §9-105(1)(i). As we will see later, possession of an instrument is essential to the perfection of the bank's security interest and to protection against subsequent takers. In these transactions, commercially sophisticated parties take possession of the note if they have any question about the financial integrity of their borrower. That possession satisfies negotiable instrument concerns and Article 9 concerns. Trouble arises in the commercially infrequent cases in which the borrower, the mortgage company in this problem, gets into financial trouble or if the transaction is a homemade one, say, between a small construction company and an unsophisticated lender.)

16. Section 9-104(a) excludes from Article 9 any transaction governed by federal law, to the extent that federal law governs it. Federal statutes do govern the perfection of security interests in aircraft and in federally registered water craft. Federal law also governs the creation and perfection of security interests in patents.

17. The challenge of this question is the basic challenge in most secured transactions — classifying the collateral. Lenders will often take a security interest in anything of value, and the listed items all have value. Not all of them, however, are subject to Article 9. The sums due from the recording company for services rendered are probably accounts. *See* §9-106. The tort and the insurance claims and the transfer of the sum deposited in the Dublin bank are excluded from Article 9. *See* §9-104(g), (k), and (*l*). (The Code leaves to non-Code law questions concerning the transfer of these valuable assets as security. Most of those questions are matters for assignment law. Under assignment law, transfer of a chose in action is not good against third parties unless they have notice of it or, in some cases, unless they acknowledge the assignment. It is not unusual for a bank taking such assets to ask the obligor (the record company, the defendant in the tort action, or the Irish bank) to acknowledge the assignment by "attorning," that is, by expressly agreeing to pay whatever is due to the lender rather than to Andy Swinger. That attornment is easier to obtain in some cases than it is in others.)

Section 3. *The Concept of Security*

18. By now you know that Seller may not sneak the press away. Seller's remedies are the common law remedies: suit for the balance due, levying on the property, judicial sale. These remedies are notoriously time-consuming and therefore inefficient. In collections, delay is deadly. During the time that Seller is waiting for Debtor to file an answer to Seller's complaint, Debtor is usually doing one of the following: letting the drill

press rust in the rain, letting insurance coverage lapse, failing to maintain the drill press, selling the drill press and skipping town with the proceeds, filing in bankruptcy.

19. If Seller has a security interest, it may repossess the press without notice, as long as Seller does not breach the peace. Taking the press in the middle of the night from a vacant lot is probably not breaching the peace. Taking it from the lot in broad daylight is probably not breaching the peace, unless Buyer resists the repossession. Repossession involving trespass or any threats of violence (by Seller or Buyer) is probably a breach of the peace. If Buyer will not let Seller repossess the press peaceably, Seller may maintain an action in replevin. In theory, that relief is summary and should not entail the kind of judicial delays that characterize an action for debt.

Once Seller repossesses the press, it may sell it in accordance with Part 5 of Article 9. That sale is quicker and less costly than the judicial sale. See Problems 197 to 200.

Buyer's bankruptcy invokes the automatic stay provision of the Bankruptcy Code. Bankruptcy Code §362. It suffices to say now that the stay prevents Seller from acting against Buyer in any way. The Bankruptcy Code protects Seller, however, by requiring Buyer's trustee to take possession of all assets and to conserve them for Buyer's creditors. Generally under bankruptcy law, Seller will be preferred as a perfected secured creditor.

20. In fact, Article 9 often protects purchasers in good faith. Here, if Buyer was in the business of selling drill presses, §9-307, a provision that is the subject of Problems 121 through 129, would protect Sub-Buyer. As we see there, buyers in ordinary course should not have to check the title of their sellers. The policy that protected the buyer in ordinary course of the watch from the watch merchant in Problem 6 applies here.

Section 4. Creating the Security Interest: The Security Agreement

21. As a general rule, all of them are bound. Once Debtor has conveyed an interest in the molding machines to Secured Party, all subsequent transferees take subject to that conveyance. This conclusion follows from the first rule of conveyancing law, which §9-201 codifies. Note, however, that §9-201 provides that it controls only to the extent that the Code does not otherwise provide. The exceptions to §9-201 comprise the bulk of Article 9 study.

22. The location of title is immaterial. See §9-202. Debtor's failure to execute a security agreement could be fatal under §9-203, and the failure to perfect the security interest will be fatal when Secured Party comes into conflict with a later secured party that does perfect. Parts a and b of this question illustrate two of the many exceptions in the Act to the general rule of §9-201 that the security agreement binds the whole world.

23. The security agreement describes the collateral as "inventory, equipment, and accounts, now owned or hereafter acquired or arising." The snow

shovels are inventory. *See* §9-109(4). The sums due from the retailers are accounts. *See* §9-106. Both, then, are covered by the security agreement. (The bank cannot have a security interest in the accounts as of May 1, however, because they have yet to come into existence.) The forklift trucks are equipment and therefore also come within the security agreement. *See* §9-109(2). The money due under the copyright license is a general intangible and, therefore, is not covered by the security agreement. *See* §9-106. The checks are proceeds from the sale of inventory. Unless the security agreement otherwise provides, a secured party automatically has a security interest in the proceeds of its collateral. *See* §9-203(3). Because the hinges, door knobs, and other items were inventory and because the bank had a security interest in the inventory, it has a security interest in the checks as well.

The bank cannot have an interest in any property acquired after May 1 until the debtor has an interest in that property. On August 1 the bank will have a security interest in the after-acquired inventory and equipment and in the after-arising accounts.

(Note that the proceeds section, §9-306, defines proceeds in the broadest terms. The burden of proof in proceeds cases, however, can limit the secured party's interest. If the secured party cannot prove that the proceeds are from the sale, exchange, or other disposition of *its* collateral, generally the secured party has no rights in the proceeds. That proof burden is often heavy. Cash proceeds such as the 13 checks in the problem, of course, rarely arise. If the debtor is in trouble, it tends to spend those cash proceeds in a flash.)

24. Joe's failure to sign the security agreement may prove fatal, though some courts have been generous with the secured party regarding as done that which ought to have been done or looking to the intent of the parties. (Tough bankruptcy judges, of which there are plenty, will not provide comfort for this secured party.)

    Late signing of the security agreement is better than no signing, but the late signing may have the effect of rendering the date of the transfer August 1 instead of May 1. That change in the facts will have significance in bankruptcy, as later study of Bankruptcy Code §547 illustrates. (*See* Problems 188-191.)

25. The question here is whether the secured party has an interest in the computer equipment or only in Debtor's leasehold in the equipment. If the lease is a true lease, Debtor's only interest in the equipment is a leasehold, and Debtor cannot transfer more than the leasehold to First Bank. If the lease is not a true lease but a disguised sales agreement wherein the lessor's retention of title operates as retention of a security interest, then First Bank has a security interest in the equipment, and the priority will depend on the rules of §9-312, which sorts out disputes of this kind.

    Often it is not easy to determine whether an equipment lease is a true lease or a disguised sale. Section 1-201(37) attempts to answer the question. Under that section, the lease in this problem is probably a true lease. First Bank's interest is in the leasehold, that is, the bank has the right to retain the equipment if the bank pays the rent to the lessor. At the end of the lease term, First Bank would have to return the equipment to the lessor.

26. This problem, taken from a rather famous case, illustrates the operation of the after-acquired property clause found so often in security agreements taken by banks or finance companies in connection with working capital loans. In fact, the notion that inventory and accounts "revolve" is indispensable to the classic working capital loan that is so important to small enterprises.

    Commercial is a purchaser; it has given value; and it has acted in good faith. It will defeat the farmers, then, unless a state or federal statute interdicts application of the Code.

    The purchase-money priority rule of section 9-312(3) does support the Article 2 analysis that gives Commercial, as a good faith purchaser for value, good title as against the farmers. Had the farmers complied with that section, they could have obtained priority over Commercial. Federal law and some state statutes alter the result here when the sellers to the debtor are farmers. Farmers, the legislatures apparently believe, are not sophisticated enough to comply with §9-312(3). The non-Code statutes are limited to farm sellers; non-farm sellers must comply with the section to avail themselves of the priority against Commercial.

27. The language of the security agreement governs the result. If the security agreement recites that the conveyance is to secure the loan for the equipment, as many equipment security agreements would, the later advance to cover payroll would not be covered. "Dragnet clauses" in security agreements provide that the collateral will secure all indebtedness of any kind whatsoever. That clause would protect the bank in this problem.

28. In this modified example, CNC is a secured party and may avail itself of the remedies afforded a secured party under Part 5 of Article 9. Repossession is one of those remedies. *See* §9-503. The parties do not have to describe the agreement as a security agreement. Article 9 applies to any transaction intended to create a security interest. The CNC-ABC transaction reflects that intent. *See* §§2-401(1) (second sentence), 9-102.

29. This kind of loan is critical to the small enterprise that typically borrows on secured credit. First Bank does have a security interest in the after-acquired inventory, and it does not matter that the bank left the inventory with Beer and let Beer sell it. The Code rejects pre-Code law to the contrary. *See* §9-205. Many courts consider inventory and accounts as such fleeting collateral that they automatically give the secured party a security interest in after-acquired collateral of that nature unless the security agreement indicates the contrary. The careful lawyer, however, will include language in the security agreement that grants the secured party an interest in not only the inventory and accounts on hand at the time but all after-acquired inventory and after-arising accounts.

    Note that the rule in favor of the lender here is not one of favoring banks over other creditors. It is a rule designed to permit certain borrowers to obtain credit.

30. Probably not. After-acquired equipment is generally not covered by a security agreement covering "equipment." Only inventory and accounts, both of which turn over quickly, benefit from the presumption that after-

acquired collateral is covered. A security agreement that is supposed to include after-acquired equipment should recite that it includes after-acquired equipment.

31. The three elements of attachment are set out in §9-203(1): (1) a signed security agreement describing the collateral or possession pursuant to agreement; (2) value; and (3) debtor's rights in the collateral. In the following problems, the three events occur on the date indicated.
    a. Under Article 9, the bank has no security interest unless it is clear that the borrower delivered the notes for security and not for safekeeping. If, however, the bank satisfies the requirements of §4-210(a) [previously §4-208(1)], it will have an Article 4 security interest, a security interest that arises by operation of law.
    b. May 3.
    c. May 3. *See* §2-501(1). Some authority suggests that the debtor does not have sufficient interest until it has the right to possession of the after-acquired property as against the seller.
    d. May 2. (The binding commitment constitutes value.)
    e. May 3.
    f. May 2, if Debtor has inventory on that date; if not, May 3.
    g. The problem obviously assumes that the debtor has inventory at all times. In that case, the security interest in the inventory first arises on May 2. The security interest in the promissory note, which is proceeds from the sale of inventory, cannot arise until the debtor has an interest in it. For the note, the security interest attaches on May 3.

32. None of these items fit the definition of "account." *See* §9-106. It is remotely possible, but unlikely, that the bank can show that one or more of these items were purchased with proceeds from the accounts. In that case, the item would be proceeds of proceeds, and the bank would have a security interest in it. *See* §9-306(1), (2).

33. All of these items fit the "inventory" definition.

Section 5.   *Definitions*

34. Only Problems b, c, and d(iii) are accounts. The debt in Problem a should be represented by a promissory note, which would be an instrument. *See* §9-105(1)(i). If it is not represented by a negotiable note, the right is a general intangible. *See* §9-106. The lease is chattel paper. *See* §9-105(1)(b).

35. (You should not have trouble finding the section that describes the assignment of an account and the rights of the various parties. If you look at Comment 5 to §9-102, you will see the special reference to §9-318.)
    a. Yes, Article 9 applies, and First should obtain a written assignment signed by the debtor. That document will be a security agreement. (As we see later, First must also perfect its security interest.)

    b. i. An account.
      ii. Assignor (debtor). §9-105(1)(d).
      iii. Assignee (secured party). §9-105(1)(m).
      iv. Account debtors.
    c. The customers *may* pay Seller, but if Seller does not remit the money to First, the customers will have to pay First and will end up paying twice. The clause is not enforceable. (The struggle to convince the common law courts to render choses in action, such as accounts, assignable was arduous. The law merchant had recognized that need for centuries when the King's courts began exercising jurisdiction over merchant matters. The story is a part of the downfall of the feudal notion that property is personal to its owner — a concept the merchants, of course, found wholly unacceptable. The greater concern of the judges at Guildhall, however, was with multiplicity of lawsuits and uncontrollable increases in litigation. Those fears have only now been realized but largely not in the merchant context, where filing a lawsuit is courting a reputation as (1) a sore loser or (2) one who cannot plan transactions properly.)

    d. No. (A young lawyer (me) once delivered to a leading member of the bar a notice of assignment of a chose in action. The curmudgeonly lawyer in the well-appointed office gave the youngster a frosty reception. "We'll look into this and see whether we will comply. We agreed to pay [*A*], and I don't see why we should have to do business with your firm's client who is a stranger to us" (and a competitor of his client, he might have added). The neophyte resisted the temptation to tell the old so and so he had no choice and that if he paid the assignor, his client would be the poorer. To his credit, the lawyer called later to say that his client would comply with the assignment. He was, after all, a good lawyer — nasty, but good.)

    e. Yes. Any other rule would be grossly unfair.

  36. No and yes. This is not an Article 9 secured transaction, but the law of assignment codified in §9-318 requires the buyer to notify the account debtors or run the risk that they will pay the seller and thereby be discharged on their account obligations.

Section 6. Defining Proceeds

  37. The items in Questions a, b, c, f, h, and i are proceeds. The check for the down payment on the used car in example d would be proceeds only if the used car is a trade on a new car. In that case, the $500 is proceeds of proceeds — something received on the sale of a car that was proceeds. Proceeds of proceeds are proceeds for purposes of §9-306(1). The $200 is not proceeds because we do not know how much is from the sale of new cars and how much is from repair work. If the bank can establish that $150 in the account is from new car deposits, the bank would be entitled to that money as proceeds. If some of the money has been spent, under the lowest intermediate balance rule discussed below, the $150 would remain in the account. Similarly, the $500 in the deposit account is protected under the lowest intermediate balance rule. That rule sounds very pro-creditor, but the fact is that creditors rarely can show where their cash proceeds went. Generally, the creditor loses the cash proceeds not as a matter of law but under the facts. He cannot prove that the account contains proceeds or he cannot prove how much is proceeds. See Problem 44.

38. The only fair rule requires the secured party to establish the fact that property is proceeds of the creditor's collateral. There is a presumption, a compromise of sorts, in §9-306(4). That presumption raises other questions. See Problems 195 and 196.

Section 7. Commingling

39. The sellers will divide the proceeds according to the ratio established by §9-315(2). Note that it is the *cost* of the metals, not their proportion, that determines the ratio. If the cost of the brass is $150,000, strict observance of the section's language gives $60,000 to Copper and $60,000 to Zinc. The balance is not subject to the parties' security interests.

40. They must show first that they had a security interest in the ingredients they supplied. Then they need to show the respective costs: the costs of each ingredient and the cost of the bread.

41. Yes. Section 9-306(1) says that "whatever" is received on the sale of collateral is proceeds.

42. The issue here is whether the entitlements are proceeds. There being no crops, the bank had no collateral, and the entitlements were not received on the sale, exchange, or other disposition of the crops. On the other hand, the decision of the farmer not to plant in return for the entitlements was a disposition of his right to plant the crops and an exchange of the potential crop for the entitlements. A modicum of violence to the language will render these entitlements proceeds. Some courts have considered that violence a proper price to pay for what would appear to be the essential purpose of the section. Some view them as general intangibles.

(Note that the Code's policy section not only authorizes but *commands* liberal implementation of the Code. Section 1-102 commands the courts to construe Code provisions liberally. "This Act shall be liberally construed and applied to promote its underlying purposes and policies." Comment 1 makes it clear that it is consistent with that command for courts to apply a provision even when its language appears to interdict application and to apply a provision beyond its literal terms. This "case-code" approach makes practice of commercial law a lot more challenging than literal application of the Code would do. Judges and lawyers who use the Code must discern the Code's underlying policies, that is, they must characterize facts and transactions in a way that makes sense out of the Code and their intended use of it. To some extent, all modern American law is an exercise in this form of realism and its implicit rejection of formalism. Yet, that conclusion is facile. Formalism survives too in the Code. Knowing when to invoke realism and when to invoke formalism is part of the challenge and renders the practice of commercial law more than reading cases and applying statutory language.)

43. The calves are not proceeds in the view of the courts that have considered the matter. The entitlements in the preceding section came into being after many banks took their security interests. It was a little unfair to deprive them of the entitlements when they came into being after the date of the security agreement. Bankers know, however, where baby cows come from. (In rural areas, bankers know more about animal husbandry and agronomy than law professors. They know more about banking too and often more about Article 9.) If the banker wanted a security interest in the calves, she should have included a reference to them in the security agreement ("now owned or hereafter owned" or "and any natural increase thereof"). Calves are not received on the sale, exchange, or other disposition of the cow.

Section 8. Tracing

44. This problem introduces the lowest intermediate balance rule of trust law. We could use last-in, first-out or first-in, last-out or some other accounting rule for determining what happens to commingled funds, but the courts have generally used trust law and its lowest intermediate balance rule. The rule is easier to apply than it is to state.

May 1	$10,000	
May 2	5,000	
May 3	1,000	Note that the lowest intermediate balance rule assumes that the proceeds sink to the bottom of the account and do not come out until all non-proceeds are exhausted. On May 1, only 50 percent of the account is proceeds, but on May 2 and 3, the account is 100 percent proceeds. The withdrawals were initially of non-proceeds. When the non-proceeds were gone, the withdrawals began to deplete the proceeds to $5,000 on May 2 and $1,000 on May 3.
May 4	6,000	Because there has been a deposit of proceeds of $5,000, that deposit and the previous lowest intermediate balance of $1,000 yield a total proceeds figure on May 4 of $6,000.
May 5	1,000	
May 6	1,000	The deposits that yield the high account balance on this date were not deposits of proceeds. They cannot, therefore, augment the amount of proceeds in the account. The proceeds balance remains $1,000, the lowest intermediate balance from May 5.

45. Probably not. Grant Gilmore, the chief drafter of Article 9, opined early on that such a description did not satisfy the requirements of §9-110. Careful drafters use Article 9 categories. The broad form financing statement and security agreement from a corporate debtor list the collateral as "all inventory, equipment, other goods, instruments, chattel paper, general intangibles, accounts, documents, now owned or hereafter acquired or arising, and all accessions thereto and products thereof," or similarly all-inclusive language. This rule is perhaps an instance of lingering formalism, but most authorities feel comfortable with it. "All property" generally will not work. Note that if the debtor is an individual, the description should also include reference to consumer goods, and, if a farmer, to farm products.

46. First Bank does not get the bill or the oil for which it stands. The security agreement does not cover documents. The bill is a document. It is not clear that the bank took possession of the bill pursuant to agreement, and that action is necessary to satisfy §9-203(1) and cause the security interest to attach.

Section 9. More on Classifying Collateral

47. They all satisfy the "inventory" definition in §9-109(4).

48. The hinges, door hardware, and heating oil are inventory. The rest is equipment.

49.   a. Cash is money, and Article 9 applies to money but has no separate category for money. *See* §9-304(1).
        b. A promissory note is an instrument. *See* §9-105(1)(i).
        c. This agreement is an account because the obligation is not evidenced by chattel paper or by an instrument. *See* §9-106. (You should know that this agreement is not an instrument because it is not negotiable in form. The agreement is not chattel paper because it does not include an interest in goods. Leases and installment sales agreements with security agreements are chattel paper. *See* §9-105(1)(b). An account is an intangible. It differs from a general intangible in that it arises from the sale or lease of goods or the sale of services. *See* §9-106.)
        d. The oriental rug is consumer goods.

    (If you are having trouble finding the definitional sections, go to §9-102, comment 5.)

50. He has inventory, the 20 computers on the floor, and a document of title, the bill of lading. *See* §§9-105(1)(f), 9-109(4).

51. The Steinway and Baldwin are equipment; the Mason & Hamlin is consumer goods. *See* §9-109(1), (2).

52.   a. This is a purchase money security interest. *See* §9-107.
        b. Cincinnati has a security interest in consumer goods. *See* §9-109(1).

c. The bank will have two security interests. First, as assignee of Cincinnati, it will get what Cincinnati had, namely, a security interest in consumer goods, the piano. Second, it will have a security interest in the paper that Cincinnati assigned to the bank. That paper is chattel paper, and the assignment of chattel paper is a secured transaction under Article 9. *See* §9-102(1)(b).

d. Cincinnati does not need to file to perfect its security interest in B's piano. Section 9-302(1)(d) creates for purchase money security interests in consumer goods an exception to the general filing requirement. Cincinnati must file as to the other two pianos, however, because they are not consumer goods; and even though Cincinnati has a purchase money security interest, it is not in consumer goods.

(It is best to think of this rule as an exception for the department store or national retailer that formerly more than now used to sell "big ticket" items (consumer durables such as refrigerators and washing machines) on secured credit. The customer made a 10 percent down payment and paid the balance over time. The customer granted the seller a security interest by executing a retail installment sales agreement at the time of the purchase. Because the transactions were relatively small and because the goods normally left commerce after the consumer took possession of them, the Code drafters agreed with the national retailers and the department stores that it would only clutter the filing system to require a filing in these transactions. Retailers use the retail installment sales agreement far less frequently today than they did in the 50s when the Code was drafted.)

e. The bank may either file or take possession of the chattel paper. See §§9-304(1), 9-305.

f. No. The bank is the assignee of a perfected security interest. Thus there will be no filing as to the piano. Cincinnati does not need to file because it holds a purchase money security interest in consumer goods. The bank does not need to file because it is assignee of a perfected security interest. *See* §9-302(2).

g. No. The Code does not distinguish sales of chattel paper from assignments of chattel paper as security for a debt.

53. Investor's interest is not a security under Article 8 or Article 9 and is probably a general intangible. Filing is the only proper mode of perfection for a general intangible. Because the secured party cannot take possession of an intangible, one cannot pledge an intangible. Accounts cannot be pledged either. They are intangible too. (You have to arrive at this conclusion by negative implication. Section 9-305 lists everything except accounts and general intangibles. *See also* §9-305, comment 1 (5th sentence).)

(Later problems deal with the perfection rules in more detail. Reference to perfection is helpful here to illustrate the need to discern the type of collateral early in the analysis of a secured transaction. The perfection rules are the locus of some of the important differences in the Code's treatment of various kinds of collateral.)

54. The bank can take a security interest in the aircraft and in the partners' notes. It will have to take possession of the notes, because they are instru-

ments. *See* §9-304(1). It will not be able to take possession of the aircraft it-self but might designate the lessee (some airline) as its agent. At least one court has accepted this theory. It is probably easiest to file as to the air-craft under the federal statute that governs such filings.

55. There is no need to file if Jones uses the VCR more than 50 percent of the time as consumer goods. *See* §9-302(1)(d). There is probably no need to file if the VCR starts out as consumer goods and then is used in Jones' of-fice. *See* §9-401(3). The section is not strictly apposite but is pretty close. If Jones' initial use of the VCR is as equipment, the retailer must file because there is no exception in the filing requirements of §9-302 for purchase money security interests in equipment.

56. In the hands of the hennery, the eggs are farm products. *See* §9-109(3). The eggs are inventory in the hands of the wholesaler and the market, *see* §9-109(4), and consumer goods while in Smith's refrigerator, *see* §9-109(1).

57. I think they are farm products no matter who owns them. All of the live-stock is in the hands of the feed lot operator, who is engaged in farming operations. *See* §9-109(3).

58. These are all probably general intangibles. *See* §9-106.

59. Chicago surely has a purchase money security interest. First Credit has one too, if it can trace the funds and show that they went to Chicago. *See* §9-107(b). The credit union does not need to file a financing statement be-cause it holds a purchase money security interest in consumer goods. *See* §9-302(1)(d). The credit union can protect itself by making the loan pro-ceeds check payable to Jones and Chicago jointly. In some large purchase money transactions, the lender will hold the closing at its own offices to ensure that it can satisfy the tracing requirement. The credit union would not satisfy the tracing requirement and would not be a purchase money secured party if Jones used the credit union's loan proceeds to pay tu-ition. Money may be fungible as a general rule but not for purposes of §9-107(b).

60. a. The dealer has a security interest in equipment. *See* §9-109(2).
     b. First Bank has a security interest in two kinds of collateral. It takes Dealer's security interest in the equipment under the law of assignment. By virtue of §9-102(1)(b) it also has a security in-terest in the chattel paper that the dealer took from its customers.
     c. The bank is automatically perfected as to the equipment. Dealer has filed and is perfected. The assignment of a perfected security interest does not require the assignee (the bank) to file again. *See* §9-302(2).
     d. The bank must file as to the chattel paper, however, or must take possession of it.

(Note that there is no purchase money exception from the filing re-quirement as to the personal computers. It is true that the dealer had a purchase money security interest in the computers, but the computers are not consumer goods in the hands of the farmers and other small busi-nesses. They are equipment, and there is no exception from the filing re-quirements for purchase money security interests in equipment.)

Section 10.   The Financing Statement

61.

a. File in Lake County. If the owner is a feed store operator, the equipment is probably still equipment used in farming operations, and the filing should be local, that is, in the county where the feed store operator lives. If the feed store is a corporation, file in the county where it has its place of business if it has only one. If it has more than one place of business, file in the county where its chief executive office is located. *See* §9-401(6). (The court might decide that the combine is mobile goods under §9-103(3). In that case, the location of the debtor in another state will have an impact on the selection of the place to file. *See* §9-103(3)(b).)

b. File in Mason County.

c. File in Mason County.

d. The boiler may be a fixture. In that case, the filing should be local (in the county where the building is situated), and the filing must be a special kind of filing, a fixture filing. *See* §9-402(3).

e. File centrally in the state or states where the inventory is located. *See* §9-103(1). (We study §9-103, the multiple state transaction filing rules, later. See Problems 89 through 97.)

f. File for accounts in the state where the borrower maintains its chief executive office, here, centrally in Illinois. *See* §9-103(3).

g. File centrally for chattel paper or take possession. *See* §§9-304(1), 9-305.

h. You cannot file as to cash but must take possession. *See* §9-304(1).

i. The bill is a document, and the rules for documents govern, the nature of the property covered by the document notwithstanding. *See* §9-105(1)(f). It is permissible but risky to file as to negotiable documents. *See* §9-304(1). The filing must be central in the state where the document is located.

j. This cattle is inventory. *See* §9-109(4). File centrally.

k. The trotters are probably equipment if the owner is racing them. *See* §9-109(2). If the owner is leasing them, the horses are inventory. *See* §9-109(4). The filing is still central. If the owner is breeding them, of course, they would be farm products, and the filing should be local.

(The filing rules are complex. You cannot apply them without first identifying the nature of the collateral. The rules of §9-401 and other provisions depend on the nature of the collateral. Note, moreover, that there are often multiple state transactions considerations. The lender must know a good deal about the debtor: its name, whether it is a corporation, where it is located, the nature of its business, the use to which it will put the collateral. Commercial lenders are usually quite sophisticated in this analysis. Loan application forms ask the questions that elicit the information the lender needs to make the filing decision, and commercial credit departments check on critical facts that determine filing location.

Often, you will be able to rely on your client. But beware. There is a widespread practice among banks and commercial finance companies to take an opinion from the debtor's lawyer that the lender is perfected. You may think of yourself as a general practitioner unconcerned with the rules a bank needs to follow when it makes a secured loan. When that bank lends working capital to your hardware store client, however, you find that the bank makes one condition of the loan your opinion that the bank is fully secured with a first priority. The business planner that helps closely held companies structure their corporate and family affairs and helps them avoid unnecessary taxes may find a similar condition in the lease of a million dollar machine from a bank subsidiary.)

62.   a.   The result may depend on the practices of the agency that holds the financing statement. If it is clear that a computer search of filings against A.B. Jones Manufacturing Co., Inc. would reveal the filing in the name of A.B. Jones Mfg. Co., many courts would find the error not seriously misleading and the filing good. If the filing agency's practices do not reveal the filing, however, the filing is probably bad. No lawyer worth her salt would take the risk.

Note.   This is harsh, but you may as well learn it now as later. One of the most important parts of your practice as a lawyer is not going to be saving orphans from villains. It will be getting little facts right, facts like the name of a debtor or the description of collateral. Incredibly, you will find that sometimes a client does not know his legal name. Businesses may use letterheads and the President of the United States may run for office under pseudonyms. The law, of course, could not care less that Charles R. Hansen has been called "Skipper" by his friends for 70 years. As far as the law is concerned, he is Charles R. Hansen. When your secretary types his name on the form as "Charles R. Hanson," moreover, the mistake is yours, not the secretary's. Lawyers are not people who have a license to practice law. Lawyers are people who know that Hansen can be spelled with an "o" or an "e" and watch for the error every time. They know that Jimmy Carter is not James Carter's name until he changes it by legal proceedings.

When a merchant changes its name, the credit agencies send out an all points bulletin. Name changes are big news in the credit industry. Only in the Old Testament do names receive more attention than in commerce. Of course, the law, especially as applied by some judges who never practiced commercial law and who never read the Old Testament, may not always have much respect for names and the clarity they bring to matters, especially matters of responsibility. But, you will not rely in advance on such law. You will structure the transaction properly and avoid the potential problem. In some cases, of course, you will receive the file after someone else has messed the transaction up. Then you will have no choice but to rely on such law.

It is with only a modicum of hyperbole that I suggest to you that this little note is the best bit of concentrated learning you will get in law school. This diatribe is a consequence of the fact that as a brand new associate I drafted a complaint (for a bank, of all clients) and got our client's name wrong in the caption. A partner in the firm caught it before we filed, and he launched into such a tirade (in the elevator, the hall, the reception area, and his office, in that order) that it never occurred to me to interrupt with the explanation that I had followed the Harvard Citator. (He would have thought that really funny.) With colorful language that I omit here for the sake of euphony, he asked rhetorically, "How do you expect to practice law when you can't get your client's name straight?" Best law teacher I ever had.

This bit of concentrated learning is not to say, however, that good lawyers never make mistakes. They do, and you will too. There are some scoundrels that never admit they make mistakes and try to blame others for the mistakes they make. The real lawyer owns up to them and pays the costs. (Some lawyers make so many mistakes they have to give up the practice and become judges or law teachers.)

b.   The herd surely falls within the farm products category. The race horse, as I suggest above, may be equipment or inventory or farm products. You need more information. (If that information is unavailable and time is growing short, you would not be the first lawyer to use a broad description and a filing in more than one office as a precaution. Filing fees are typically $10 or thereabouts.)

c.   Accuracy in the name of the secured party is less critical than is accuracy in the debtor's name. The filing system indexes use the debtor's name. Probably this type of error in the secured party's name will not render the filing seriously misleading.

d.   i.   Probably this filing is bad.
ii.   Surely this filing is bad.
iii.   It does not matter in bankruptcy court and should not matter elsewhere.

63.   The secured party (the original Ace and now XYZ) has a problem if it is looking to after-acquired inventory or equipment as collateral for the buyer's debt. Usually in the sale of a business, the seller must be satisfied with a security interest in the inventory and equipment it sells and does not get a security interest in after-acquired property.

Subsequent lenders may be confused here. When Ace Heating (the buyer with the new name) seeks credit, the creditor will search for filings under that name as debtor and will find nothing, the filing being under the prior name, ABC Co. Commercial lenders, of course, are well aware of this risk and always ask borrowers whether they have done business under any other name within the last five years. Filings are good for five years. *See* §9-403(2). The unsophisticated lender may suffer from the confusion inherent in this arrangement. At least one court has found that the seller, knowing in advance that there would be a misleading name change, acted in bad faith by not refiling under the new name after the change.

64.   This is from a real case decided by a judge who did not share your author's respect for certainty and who held the filing good. The name of this debtor is Old Colony Hotel Corp. Corporations have names that are spelled out, usually in the first article of the corporate charter. The secretary of state will not issue a charter to a company under a name that is al-

ready taken, that is likely to cause confusion because of its similarity to an already chartered enterprise, or that otherwise does not comport with the state's version of the Business Corporation Act. States maintain registers of corporations chartered in the state or licensed to do business there and usually have telephone services for those checking on the corporate name. Divisions are not corporations; they are profit centers or marketing entities created unilaterally by the corporation and do not constitute a separate person under the law. Subsidiaries, of course, are separate corporations and are incorporated as such. If a subsidiary borrows and grants a security interest, the subsidiary will be the debtor on the financing statement and must sign it and the security agreement. Often related companies assist each other's borrowing. A parent's subsidiary may grant a security interest to secure the parent's debt. Lawyers structuring the transaction must be certain that the party that owns the collateral is designated as the debtor. Making the ownership determination can be problematic and may call for certified audits or opinions, or both, from the attorney for the borrower.

65. First Bank prevails under the rule of §9-312 that gives the first secured party to file priority. Second Bank, not First, pays for the filing officer's error. *See* §9-403(1) and comment 1.

66. Less than 100 people live in Maplewood, Maine. The requirement in §9-110 that a description of a person or real estate need only reasonably identify the person or property should apply by analogy here. "Joe Smith, Los Angeles, CA" does not constitute a reasonable address for the debtor. The farm description in the problem is probably good enough if the debtor only farms one tract. If he farms two, it may be sufficient, the difference in the size of the tracts being sufficient to differentiate the two.

67. Corporate changes can create problems for secured lenders. A merger might consist of the debtor's sale of its assets to the new company followed by dissolution of the debtor. It might consist of the acquiring company's purchasing the shares of the debtor and then dissolving it. It might even consist of the debtor's acquisition of the shares of the purchaser and the dissolution of the purchaser. Cautious and watchful secured parties spot these mergers, acquisitions, spin-offs, and other corporate transmogrifications and act promptly. The security agreement can forbid them without the lender's prior approval. The lender can then take additional documentation, including new financing statements, to protect itself. Credit agencies will report this kind of activity. Lenders that adequately monitor their borrowers' activity will spot it.

   Cases in which the lender is unaware of the corporate change are rare. When they arise, courts will usually attempt to resolve the matter by literal application of the Code — an unsatisfactory resolution. Thus a lender may win if the merger takes one form and lose if it takes another, the result being adventitious.

   Note that the after-acquired collateral will not accrue to the lender if the collateral is acquired more than four months after the name change. *See* §9-402(7).

Section 11.   Introduction to Fixtures

68.   a.   It may not be possible to take a security interest in the windows that will survive their incorporation into a building, because windows sound like ordinary building materials today. That result might not obtain in the case of a Tiffany window taken from an old building and incorporated into a new one. *See* §9-313(2).

b.   In most jurisdictions, a photocopy machine is not a fixture. If the debtor is a business, the machine is equipment, and the filing should be central under §9-401, second alternative subsection 1, which these problems follow. Some lawyers instinctively fear giving opinions on whether something might constitute a fixture. They view the opinion in the first sentence of this answer as folly. To them, courts are unpredictable and might hold that the copier is a fixture, say, under the "institutional" approach or perhaps because the machine takes special wiring or because there was modification of the building to house the copier. To cover these remote possibilities, the ever-cautious lawyer will not assume that the copier is not a fixture.

If the copier is a fixture, it must surely be a readily removable office machine that falls within the rule of §9-313(4)(c). The central filing would be sufficient, then, to perfect whether the machine is equipment or a fixture.

You could run across a transaction in which the secured party financed a number of fixtures and used a fixture filing (that is, a filing designated as a fixture filing) filed in the real estate records and containing the additional information required by §9-402(3) and (5). That filing is good as to the copier only if the court decides that the copier is a fixture. (Note that the readily removable office equipment rule of §9-313(4)(c) applies only if the court finds that the equipment is a fixture. If it is not a fixture, that subsection does not apply, and only a centrally filed financing statement will suffice.)

In short, when in doubt, the transactional lawyer may be best advised to file centrally if the equipment is readily removable. That filing will be good if the court finds that the equipment is a fixture, and it will be good if the court finds that the equipment is not a fixture. If the lawyer is uncertain that the court will find that the equipment is readily removable, she must file centrally and must also make a fixture filing.

c.   This is probably a fixture and will require a fixture filing filed locally. If the court finds it is equipment and not a fixture, the local filing will not be sufficient.

d.   This sounds like a fixture. Make a fixture filing.

e.   This is consumer goods. If it is consumer goods, file locally, as §9-401(1) (2d alternative subsection 1) requires. If it is consumer goods and a fixture, the filing must be a fixture filing. If the owner is conducting a business on the premises, the chandelier is equipment. File centrally to cover the possibility that the court finds that it is not a fixture and make a fixture filing to cover the possibility the court finds that it is a fixture. (These rules may sound hopelessly inefficient. They are less so in practice because this kind of collateral is not commercially important. The problems are illustrative only.)

    f.   This is a fixture in the view of at least one court and requires a fixture filing.

    g.   Professors White and Summers would classify as not a fixture any item that can be removed in one hour by one person with a crescent wrench. Under that rule, equipment that also requires for its removal the use of a flatbed truck and a hydraulic lift is a fixture.

    h.   That agreement cannot alter the nature of the collateral as a fixture.

69.   a.   Yes, whether or not the court finds the property is a fixture. Section 9-313(4)(d) protects the secured party against the trustee in bankruptcy. Section 544(a)(3) reflects Congress' concern that the rule be the same.

    b.   If the court applies the subsection literally, the regular filing is no good. A local filing other than a fixture filing is never "permitted" by the Act for equipment. It may be, however, that the policy of the subsection is to protect people who file against the claim of the trustee. The careful lawyer would probably hold the regular local filing insufficient.

    c.   Unless the goods are readily removable office machines, yes. A good-faith purchaser of the real estate will defeat the secured lender if the goods are fixtures and if there is no fixture filing.

70. As a matter of real estate law, the bank has an interest in anything that becomes part of the real estate. By definition, a fixture becomes part of the real estate. The house, the boiler, and the sound system are probably fixtures. The office equipment probably is not.

71. The company will defeat the trustee in bankruptcy if the company filed centrally. If the company made a fixture filing, it will defeat the trustee only if the equipment is a fixture. The answers are the same if the competing claimant is a lien creditor. The mortgagee will be a good-faith purchaser of the real estate. If the equipment is not a fixture, the mortgagee has no interest in it, and the company wins. If the equipment is a fixture, the mortgagee will defeat the company unless the company makes a fixture filing or unless the equipment is readily removable.

72. This question illustrates the nuisance of having to make a fixture filing. It is easy enough to designate the filing as a fixture filing for filing in the real estate records. It is not easy to determine a legal description or the record owner or whether the debtor's interest is a matter of record. The careful lawyer will never opine on the basis of what the parties think or, worse yet, what they say. Sometimes the owner of a closely held business thinks he owns the property when in fact his real estate alter ego company owns it. When you copy a real estate description from a deed prepared by another lawyer, you run the risk of copying someone else's mistakes. Do you order a title search that is moderately expensive and will cause delays in getting the transaction buttoned up?

(This question also illustrates the wisdom of subsection (4)(c). A computer manufacturer that markets its equipment under a lease that may be a disguised sale will file centrally. If the computer is equipment, the filing is good. If the equipment is a fixture, the filing is good. The lessor, then, in this commercially important transaction will prevail without hiring an attorney in each state or city to find legal descriptions and the identity of record owners.)

73. All of these steps may be necessary and more.

74. The correct answer is (a).

Section 12. *More on the Place to File*

75. (Remember that we are using §9-401, second alternative subsection 1, throughout these problems.)
     a. Secretary of state.
     b. Same.
     c. Same. In the second case; file in Adams County. There is no need to refile when Smith moves. *See* §9-401(3). (Why do you suppose loan application forms ask potential borrowers to list their addresses for the last five years?)
     d. Local office in county where the farmer lives.
     e. Same.
     f. Same.
     g. Secretary of state.
     h. Same.
     i. Same. Weaver is a farmer, but it is difficult to argue that this general intangible arises from or is related to the sale of farm products. This general intangible arises from the over payment of income taxes. Cautious lawyers might disagree. They could file centrally and locally.
     j. Same.

76. Clearly Ace was not perfected on May 1 because the filing is not in the county where Weaver resided. Arguably, however, Ace was perfected on May 2, a time at which the filing would mislead no one and when the literal requirements of §9-401 are satisfied. At least one court disagrees.

Section 13. *Perfection Without Filing (Pledges and the Like)*

77. No. Generally a pledge must deprive the debtor of possession. There are two exceptions. *See* §9-304(4) and (5).

78. No. The bank will drill the box for Debtor if Debtor signs an affidavit certifying that he has lost the key. Given that policy of safe deposit compa-

nies, Finance Co. cannot argue successfully that it has deprived Debtor of possession of the contents of the box.

79. The account, the general intangible, and the unissued security are intangibles. The concept of possession and the concept of a general intangible are dissonant. One cannot take possession of or deprive another of possession of an intangible. I do not know what the electronic letter of credit is, but until the parties issue the credit in hard copy and designate it in some fashion as the original and operative copy, creditors would be well advised not to consider it the proper subject of a pledge.

80.   a. Delivery of the certificate to Broker is sufficient. *See* §8-313(1)(a). Broker, however, may be in possession of the certificate, holding it in a securities account for Debtor. In that case, Broker is a financial intermediary. *See* §8-313(4). The pledge concept does not fit if the broker is maintaining a securities account, and Article 8 requires Broker to obtain a written security agreement from the debtor. *See* §8-313(1)(j).
        b. Similarly, the pledge concept does not work well for Uncle. He also must obtain a written security agreement and must send broker a written notice of his interest. The notice must be signed by Debtor. *See* §8-313(1)(h)(i).

81.   a. There is authority, misguided it would seem, holding that the bank is under a duty to manage the debtor's portfolio if the bank is in possession of that portfolio. That burden is heavy and fraught with peril, as this problem illustrates. The debtor should decide when or whether to convert debentures or to sell declining stocks or bonds. It is difficult to reconcile the language of §9-207 with the notion that the pledgee becomes an investment counsellor. The references to chattel paper and instruments in subsection (1) probably refer to factors who undertake to collect the sums due. Note that the section permits the parties to vary this obligation, and traditional language in bank pledge agreements takes advantage of that permission.
        b. The secured party may and often does repledge the collateral. Brokers take a pledge from their customers as security for margin purchases and then repledge the securities to a bank that finances the brokerage operation. Section 9-207(2)(e) sanctions this practice only if the repledge does not impair the customer's right to redeem her shares by paying the broker the margin loan. If Second, the bank, sold the stock, as it probably has the right to do as a bona fide purchaser under Article 8, First Bank would be liable to the debtor.

82. Unless the pledge agreement absolves the bank of any duty to collect the note, as some agreements will, yes. The note was dishonored on May 1, 1993. The delay in giving the indorser notice of the dishonor caused Debtor loss because, under the law of negotiable instruments, the indorser is discharged if the notice of dishonor is late. *See* §§3-415(c), 3-503(a) and (c) (previously §§3-502(1)(a), 3-503(2)(b)).

83. Yes.

84. Yes.

85. Yes. (This is a reasonable exception to the customary rule that a written security agreement is not necessary when a pledgee takes possession of collateral. In practice, many financial institutions obtain a written security agreement to cover pledges for the same reason that the Code requires one here. Many financial institutions are depositories for items of value. When default occurs, there may be a dispute over the nature of the bailment, that is, a question whether it is one of safe keeping or is in fact a pledge. The presence of a written security agreement resolves the problem.)

86.
   a. No. The security interest in the refrigerator is not a purchase money security interest, and *S* must file a financing statement. *S* does not qualify for the purchase money exception of §9-302(1)(d).

   b. Yes, under §9-302(1)(d).

   c. The security interest is not good against X. This is the case governed by §9-307(2). Note that the proper way to read this section is to understand that the goods must be consumer goods in the hands of both the seller and the buyer. If X is a merchant, the security interest follows the goods into his hands.

87.
   a. *S* is automatically perfected.

   b. The after-acquired antiques would not be subject to a perfected security interest because *S*'s security interest in them is not purchase money in nature. *S* must file a financing statement. Note also the limits imposed by §9-204.

88.
   a. On May 3, First Bank held a perfected security interest in the documents and notes Broker received on May 2 because the bank gave new value and was automatically perfected under the rule of §9-304(4). First Bank did not have a perfected security interest in the May 3 documents and instruments, however, because it took only under the security agreement's after-acquired property clause. The bank never gave new value for the May 3 documents and instruments, as §9-304(4) requires.

   b. First Bank has no perfected security interest in any of the documents or instruments on May 31. The security interest remained perfected only for 21 days. *See* §9-304(4).

Section 14. *Multistate Transactions: Section 9-103*

89.
   a. No. The filing is the last event, and the goods are in State B when the secured party filed in State A. The filing should have been in State B.

   b. In this question the last event is the loan, value under §9-203(1)(b). Until there is value, there is no attachment. *See* §9-203(2). There cannot be perfection until there is attachment. *See* §9-303(1). The goods were in State B when the last event occurred. The filing in State A, then, is not good.

c.   Arguably, the movement of the goods into State A from State B is a "last event." A holding to that effect is consistent with the policy of the filing system. Searchers would expect to search in the state where the goods are located. The goods are in State A; the filing is in State A. The better rule holds that the secured party is perfected once the goods return to State A.

d.   The last event in this question is the debtor's acquisition of the goods, which occurred while the goods were in State B. At that time, the secured party is filed in the wrong state. The goods remain in State B, and the secured party is unperfected.

90.   a.   The general rule of §9-103(1)(b) requires the secured party to file in the state where the goods are located. The goods were located in State B and the filing is in State A. Unless an exception applies, then, Chicago is unperfected. Chicago is a purchase money lender on these dryers, however, and §9-103(1)(c) applies. Under that section, the filing in State A is good if the parties intended to bring the goods into State A and if the goods actually are moved into State A within 30 days of their delivery to the debtor. Chicago was perfected from the start and is perfected on February 2.

b.   No. Chicago must file in State B if the goods are not removed to State A within 30 days of delivery to the buyer.

c.   Yes. The rule of §9-103(1)(c) applies only if the parties intended at the time the security interest attached to move the goods from the seller's place of business to the buyer's facility in State A. If the buyer decides after the security interest attaches to move the goods into State A, the rule of the section does not apply. In that case, §9-103(1)(b) and its last-event test would apply. Under that provision, the filing in State A would not be good until the buyer moved the goods into State A.

d.   Arguably it would, not under §9-103(1)(c) but under §9-103(1)(b). Subsection (1)(c) does not apply here because the buyer did not move the goods within 30 days of delivery. Yet under the analysis described above to the effect that the removal of the goods to State A would be the last event under the rule of §9-103(1)(b), Chicago would be perfected only for 30 days after delivery while the goods are in State B and would not be perfected on March 14 while the goods are still in State B but would be perfected once they were moved to State A on the 15th.

91.   a.   The failure of the bank to refile within the four-month period renders its security interest unperfected against a purchaser. A buyer is a purchaser and under §9-301(1)(c) will defeat the unperfected secured party if the purchaser takes delivery before the secured party perfects.

b.   A creditor that levies on the presses during the four-month period does not defeat the secured party. A lien creditor is not a purchaser. *See* §1-201(32) and (33).

c.   Second Bank is a purchaser and can defeat First Bank if First Bank fails to file within the four months. If, however, Second Bank does not file or files in the wrong office, it is an unperfected se-

cured party and will lose to First Bank, another unperfected secured party but the party that obtained its security interest first.
Priority of unperfected secured parties dates from the time of attachment. *See* §9-312(5)(b).

    d.   The trustee in bankruptcy has the rights of a lien creditor, *see* §9-
301(3), Bankruptcy Code §544(a)(1); but he is not a purchaser and
will not defeat the bank if the bankruptcy occurs during the four-
month period when the bank is still perfected. It does not matter
whether the bank files. The party's rights are fixed on the date of
bankruptcy. *See* §9-403(2).

92.   a.   The bank remains perfected on both dates if the debtor does not
reregister or obtain a new certificate of title.

    b.   Because the bank retained the certificate of title, this reregistra-
tion arguably is not the kind of registration contemplated by the
statute. If, for example, the registration in State B is pursuant to a
scheme that requires temporary registration or registration in
more than one state, there is authority that the bank is still perfected.

    c.   i.   By noting the lien on the new certificate, as they should, the
authorities in State B have continued the bank's perfection.

        ii.   The failure to note the lien may give rise to liability on the
part of the State B officials, but buyers from the debtor will
defeat the bank. *See* §9-103(2)(d).

        iii.   No.

    d.   Buyer will defeat the bank under §9-103(2)(d). Under the same
section, however, the used car dealer would not.

93.   a.   These containers are mobile goods, and the filing should be in
the state where the debtor's chief executive office is located.

    b.   No. The fact that the 20-foot containers are used only intrastate
should not change the result. The section says that mobile goods
are those of a *type* that are used in more than one jurisdiction,
as containers surely are. The fact that in this case the 20-foot
containers are used only in California should not change the
result.

    c.   If the debtor's chief executive office is in New York, the filing
covering the 20-foot containers and the filing covering the 40-
foot containers should be in New York.

94.   a.   Yes. Accounts are intangibles and have no situs. The correct place
to file is in the state where the debtor is located.

    b.   i.   If we assume that all states have adopted §9-401 second al-
ternative subsection 1, central filing will perfect Tridelt, and
the assignment to the bank of a perfected security interest
will be free of any filing requirement. *See* §9-302(2).

        ii.   The filings in the states where the hardware is located will
not be sufficient to protect the bank against Tridelt's trustee.
To secure an interest in Tridelt's chattel paper (the leases), the
bank must file in the state where Tridelt is located.

    c.   It should file a financing statement describing the collateral as "chattel paper" and the debtor as Tridelt and should file where Tridelt is located; or it should take possession of the leases pursuant to agreement with Tridelt.

d. It should file in the states where the inventory is located. The computers are Tridelt's inventory. The definition of inventory includes equipment held for lease. *See* §9-109(4).

e. The bank must refile in State B because the law of State B now controls. *See* §9-103(3)(e). *But cf.* §9-401(3) (filing "in this state" continues effective notwithstanding change of debtor's location).

95. The combine is probably custom harvesting machinery — that is, mobile goods — and the filing should be in the state where the debtor is located, State A.

96. Yes, if we assume that both states have adopted §9-302(1)(d). Because no action is required in either state to perfect the security interest, the interest is perfected in State A and also in State B.

97. (This is a review question.)
   a. No. The seller is perfected on November 2 and will defeat the trustee under the negative implication of §9-301(1)(b) or under §9-201.
   b. *L*, a non-purchaser, obtained its lien at a time when the seller was perfected. *S* will defeat *L*. It does not matter that *S* failed to refile in State B. If *S* failed to refile and if *L* had obtained its lien after the four months, *L* would prevail.

Section 15. Perfecting the Security Interest in Proceeds: More on Section 9-306(3)

98.
   a. Yes, it does on May 1 by virtue of the automatic ten-day perfection rule of §9-306(3).
   b. Yes, the central filing is good for the accounts and the chattel paper. It is in the office where a filing for those two kinds of collateral would be filed. It is not necessary to mention chattel paper and accounts in the financing statement. The security interest in the cash continues indefinitely. This sounds too good to be true. It is. Cash disappears quickly, and the tracing requirements render cash proceeds problematic for the secured party. The secured party only has a security interest in cash proceeds that it can identify, and it is hard to identify cash as coming from the sale of collateral. In any event, the cash is almost always gone when the debtor defaults or becomes insolvent.
   c. Commingling will not per se destroy the cash as proceeds because the secured party may be able to trace under some tracing theory. Most courts and writers assume that the lowest intermediate balance method is the preferred method for tracing. In insolvency proceedings, §9-306(4) interdicts the application of that method, however. See Problems 195 and 196.

d. Yes. If the debtor is located in a state different from the state where the inventory is located, the filing mentioned in the problem will not be sufficient to keep the security interest in the accounts and the chattel paper perfected after the ten days have expired. Filing for accounts, under §9-103(3), and filing for chattel paper, under §9-103(4), must be in the state where the debtor is located.

99. The word processor is equipment in the hands of Bell, and the filing in the central office is insufficient to continue the perfection beyond the ten days by virtue of the fact that Bell acquired the word processor with cash proceeds. Had Bell taken the word processor in trade, however — that is, in trade for inventory — the central filing would be sufficient. If the central filing described the collateral as "inventory and equipment," it would be sufficient to keep the bank perfected beyond the ten days.

100. The bank has no claim to proceeds from the sale of inventory that is not its collateral. The name on the account should not be dispositive. If the cash is from the sale of the bank's collateral, the cash is proceeds in which the bank has a security interest. Here, the Grand Rapids furniture inventory is not the collateral of the bank, and the proceeds would not go to the bank.

101. On May 1, First Bank has a security interest in the certificate of deposit and in the checks. The security interest remains perfected in the checks, which are cash proceeds, beyond the ten days; but there seems to be agreement that a certificate of deposit is not cash proceeds. Thus, as to the certificate, the security interest becomes unperfected after the ten days. A negotiable certificate of deposit is an instrument, and the only way to perfect a security interest in it is to take possession of it. *See* §9-304(1). If Bell had deposited the cash and the checks into a bank account, First Bank would remain perfected but would have a tracing problem.

Section 16.   *Introduction to Priorities: Sections 9-301 and 9-312*

102. Bank defeats *S*, who is a lien creditor that levied on the equipment after Bank perfected. Under the negative implication of §9-301(1)(b), or under the rule of §9-201, Bank defeats lien creditor. A buyer not in ordinary course, which is any buyer that does not qualify for the super protection afforded by §9-307(1), can defeat an unperfected secured party under §9-301(1)(c) only if the buyer takes for value and takes delivery before the secured party perfects. Bank perfected on May 3; and if buyer takes delivery after that date, buyer loses to Bank. If, on the other hand, buyer takes delivery before Bank perfects, buyer will prevail. Note that, in any event, buyer must buy without knowledge of Bank's security interest in order to defeat Bank.

Buyer must take delivery. Otherwise, the theory goes, Bank might be deceived by the seller/debtor's possession of the equipment. Seeing the equipment on Debtor's premises would lead Bank to think that Debtor had an interest in the equipment. The prepaying buyer, furthermore, creates suspicion. Is he buying or is he lending? Commercial buyers customarily do not prepay unless they are trying to help their seller out of a financial bind. That sounds like lending. Note that §9-301(1)(c) and (d) do not help lenders but buyers.

It does not matter whether the bank files early. B will defeat Bank if Bank fails to perfect. Bank cannot perfect until its security interest attaches. If B takes delivery before Bank obtains its security interest, B should prevail.

103.   Although there is some authority in New York to the contrary, most commentators agree that S, a secured party that has perfected by possession, should win here. Sub-buyer, having prepaid, does not merit much protection. If Sub-buyer is making a loan, it should comply with Article 9's rules of attachment and perfection and should not be able to resort to a buyer protection provision.

This answer assumes, of course, that S has an understanding with Buyer that S is holding the goods to secure payment. The pledge section, §9-305, permits a pledgee to rise to the level of a perfected secured party only if the possession is pursuant to agreement. *See* §9-203(1)(a).

104.   Bank should prevail as to the original equipment and as to the after-acquired equipment. In most jurisdictions, a lien creditor such as S cannot attach after-acquired property without levying on the property after the debtor obtains an interest in it. Because Bank is perfected throughout, there is no way that S can have priority over Bank.

105.   The 10-day grace period protects this purchase money seller. Section 9-301(2) gives the purchase money lender 10 days after the debtor receives possession of the goods to file. S has filed in time. Buyers not in ordinary course win, but bulk buyers lose to S. (Check your state's version of §9-301(2). Many jurisdictions have lengthened the time period to 20 days.)

106.   Here, the secured party is not a purchase money lender, and the lien creditor has obtained a lien before the secured party perfects. The clear language of §9-301(1)(b) dictates that lien creditor prevail. The same rule applies for bulk buyers or other buyers not in ordinary course that take delivery and for value before the secured party perfects. *See* §9-301(1)(c) and (d).

107.   Lenders that are purchase money secured parties have the same benefits under §9-301(2) that purchase money sellers have. The bank has a ten-day grace period within which to file. Here the bank will win.

108.   Second Bank prevails here because it filed before First Bank perfected. Under §9-312(5)(a), the first secured party to file or perfect will have priority. First Bank could have priority if it had given value on May 1. But because it did not give value until May 3, it cannot be perfected until May 3. A secured party is not perfected until its security interest attaches. The security interest cannot attach until value is given. *See* §9-203(1)(b).

109.   Here, Second Bank has perfected first, but First Bank has filed first. Under §9-312(5)(a), the first to file or perfect wins. First Bank wins. This result is

not unfair, because the May 1 filing is theoretically there for Second Bank to see. It should be forewarned, then, not to take a security interest without investigating the circumstances of the First Bank filing.

110.   First Bank gets all of the money. Even without looking at §9-312(7), which expressly so provides, we should know that First Bank prevails. First Bank perfected first, and §9-312(5)(a) says that the first to perfect has priority. By depriving the debtor of possession, First Bank put the world on notice that the debtor may have sold or encumbered the equipment. Unless it receives a satisfactory explanation, what bank in its right mind would lend against an asset that the debtor does not have in its possession?

111.   The order of lending does not determine priority. The order of filing or perfection determines it. *See* §9-312(5)(a). Second Bank perfected first and filed first. Second Bank prevails.

112.   Under §9-312(4), a purchase money secured party with a security interest in equipment has ten days after the debtor receives the equipment to file; and if it does so, it defeats any prior filed secured party. *S*, then, will defeat Bank. *S* would not prevail if it filed on May 13 because the ten-day grace period expired on May 12.

113.   Under a literal reading of §9-312(5)(a), *S* wins here. Arguably, however, the policy of the purchase money priority rules is best satisfied by prorating the funds received upon the sale of the equipment: 10 percent for the bank, 90 percent for *S*. The proration approach, which yields the same result no matter who files first, seems preferable. Literal application of the provision yields one result if Bank files first, another if *S* files first. Note, moreover, that literal application can squeeze a purchase money party out entirely even though that party files within the ten-day period. Under the literal application, the first to file within that period will prevail.

114.   *S* benefits from the purchase money priority afforded by §9-312(4). That priority extends to all proceeds. *S*, therefore, gets the check and defeats the bank.

115.   If the collateral had been beer, which would be the wholesaler's inventory, §9-312(3) would apply; and *S* would not get the check. Although §9-312(3) gives the purchase money secured party with a security interest in inventory priority, that priority becomes quite narrow when the debtor sells the collateral and holds proceeds. In fact, the only proceeds that the purchase money seller of inventory will get are cash proceeds received on or before the resale of the inventory. Unless, then, the debtor sells the purchase money seller's collateral for cash or receives a cash down payment, *S* will not receive any proceeds. *S* will have priority as to the beer *S* sells, but *S* will have no priority in accounts.

116.   This problem illustrates the curious fact that a farmer's "inventory" is not "inventory" for Code purposes. Animals are farm products. *See* §9-109(3). The purchase money priority rule for inventory, §9-312(3), with its protection for inventory lenders, therefore, does not protect agricultural lenders that take a security interest in a farm debtor's livestock, grain, and the like. A purchase money seller of steers would not have to notify the prior filed bank to avail itself of purchase money priority. The seller could rely

on §9-312(4), which applies to collateral other than inventory. Farm products is a category other than inventory.

117. There is authority that Second will take subject to the badly perfected security interest of First, if Debtor told Second that he had granted First a security interest. Some of the writers emphasize that §9-401(2) uses odd terminology: "knowledge of the contents of such financing statement." Because the priority rules of §9-312 generally apply without regard to notice or knowledge, those authorities would limit the application of the subsection to cases in which Second had actually seen the filing. The reason for such a restrictive application is to avoid having to litigate the knowledge issue in every case.

Certainly if Second has seen the filing, the subsection gives First priority. If Second has no notice whatsoever of First's interest, Second will prevail under §9-312(5)(a) because Second filed and perfected first.

Section 17.   Future Advances: Sections 9-301(4), 9-307(3), 9-312(7)

118. The bank is able to squeeze the lien creditor out of the picture. Because the bank's later advance is within the 45-day period, it is protected against the lien creditor. Advances on May 15 and June 20 without knowledge of the lien would also beat the lien creditor. The June 20 advance is beyond the 45th day, but it is without knowledge. If the lien creditor notifies the bank on May 2, the bank and the debtor may still squeeze the lien creditor out, if they desire to do so. Notice on the 45th day would take that option away from the bank because it no longer has the 45 days' absolute protection and now cannot make an advance without knowledge.

Advances made pursuant to commitments incurred by the bank date back to the time of the commitment. Thus if the commitment is during the 45 days or is made without knowledge (either within or without the 45 days), the advance pursuant to the commitment is prior to the rights of the lien creditor.

119. Yes, the bank will defeat the buyer. Either of two events will cut off the ability of the bank to squeeze out this buyer: notice to the bank of the sale to the buyer or running of the 45 days. Unlike §9-301(4), §9-307(3) is solicitous of the buyer's rights.

An advance on May 20 without knowledge of the sale would defeat the buyer. An advance on June 17 with or without knowledge would lose to the buyer. Advances pursuant to commitment date from the time of the commitment and stand or fall on the lender's state of knowledge at the time it makes the commitment. A commitment on May 1 will protect advances pursuant to that commitment because it is within the 45 days and is without knowledge of the sale. A commitment on May 20 would protect advances pursuant to it only if the commitment is made without knowledge.

120.   a.   All of the money goes to First Bank, which filed first and therefore defeats Second Bank under the rule of §9-312(5)(a) and under the clear language of §9-312(7).

b. It does not matter that First knew of Second's entry into the picture. Second was forewarned that First had priority. First and Debtor can squeeze Second out. It should not matter that First does not lend until May 3 or even later. Once First files, Second is on notice. None of the altered facts in this question b should alter First's priority except for the case in which First is perfected without filing and without possession. In that case, §9-312(7) protects Second Bank as to the later advance. The subsection limits First's protection by the language at its beginning: "If future advances are made while a security interest is perfected by filing, the taking of possession, or under Section 8-321 on securities. . . ."

c. Quite apart from any priority issue, no collateral stands as security for a debt unless the debtor has granted the creditor a security interest in the collateral to secure that debt. If the security agreement that Debtor executed in favor of First Bank only secures advances on May 1, the later advances are not secured. Whether the security agreement would secure the loan once it is renewed is a question on which authorities do not agree. The majority probably favors the view that the security agreement covers the renewal. Note, however, that this is not a question of determining which of two secured parties has priority. The question here is whether First Bank is a secured party.

d. Yes. On May 3, First Bank can take a new security agreement from Debtor and obtain security for a new advance. Once First Bank makes that advance, it will have a perfected security interest, and it will defeat Second Bank because First Bank filed first. There is some authority to the contrary, but the plain language of the statute indicates that the first to file wins.

e. Again, there is some authority to the effect that the May 3 advance, not being contemplated by the debtor and the bank on May 1, is subordinate to Second Bank's security interest. That holding would be correct if the language of the loan documents did not cover inventory loans. The problem indicates, however, that the security agreement and the financing statement did cover inventory loans. The majority of cases, and most of the commentators, would protect First Bank. Remember, Second Bank can see the filing and is warned that First Bank is in the picture. No second lender paying attention will lend in those circumstances without obtaining a subordination agreement or a termination statement from First.

Section 18. Purchaser Priorities: Sections 9-306(2) and 9-307

121.   a. *A* will prevail under §9-307(1) because *A* is a buyer in ordinary course. It does not matter that *A* knows of the security interest. Just as you and I know that most retailers have granted a security interest in their inventory to a bank or finance company or to

a seller, we take free despite that knowledge, which does not prevent us from rising to the level of a buyer in ordinary course. *See* §1-201(9).

Although the cases are not entirely consistent, there is persuasive authority that *A* becomes a buyer for buyer-in-ordinary-course purposes at the point *A* has the right under Article 2 to receive delivery of the goods. A promise to pay is value. The fact that *A* has not paid does not prevent *A* from becoming a buyer in ordinary course. The law protects *A*'s expectation interest.

b. *B* has knowledge that infects him and prevents him from claiming buyer in ordinary course status. Under §1-201(9), *B*'s knowledge that the sale is in contravention of the bank's rights is fatal.

The bank's failure to enforce its prohibition of sale has convinced some courts that the bank has waived or is estopped from asserting its rights under the prohibition clause. The cases are not totally convincing.

c. A pawnbroker cannot be a buyer in ordinary course. *See* §1-201(9) (last clause, first sentence).

d. This horizontal sale is probably in ordinary course. Although it is customary to think of retailers as parties that sell only to vertical customers, in fact, dealers often sell to other dealers. Automobile dealers, for example, may need a model that is no longer available from the manufacturer. Such a dealer will seek to obtain the model from another dealer through a service that keeps track on a computer of every dealer's inventory. Courts accept such sales as sales in ordinary course.

e. *E* is a buyer in bulk and cannot qualify for buyer in ordinary course status. *See* §1-201(9).

f. *F* sounds like a lender that is taking security in a transaction disguised as a sale. The disguise should not work. Article 9 applies to all secured transactions, no matter the form. *See* §9-102(1)(a). If *F* is a secured party, it must comply with the attachment and perfection rules of the article and will be subject to the priority rule of §9-312(5)(a), which will render *F* subordinate to the bank.

g. *G* also runs the risk of being characterized as a lender. Prepaying buyers that lend sellers funds to acquire the parts and raw materials or other inventory that is the subject of the sale to the buyer may be able to take advantage of the purchase money priority rule of §9-312(3). They must, however, comply with the terms of that provision, which requires notice to the bank and filing of a financing statement.

122. a. *B* does take free, but note that *B* has created a new interest, which at the moment resides in *D*. If *B* takes free of the bank's security interest, *C* comes within the shelter of *B* and also takes free of it.

b. No. *B* has created a new security interest in favor of *D*.

c. No. The assignment makes the bank a secured party, succeeding to the rights of *D*. Because *B* is probably not a consumer, *D* must file to perfect. Because *D* is perfected, the bank need not file, as the assignee of a perfected security interest. *See* §9-302(2).

123.   a.   Under the Code, *B* will not defeat the PCA, because a buyer of farm products from a farmer does not defeat the secured party even if the buyer is a buyer in ordinary course. Failure of the state to enact one of the options under the Food Security Act of 1985, 7 U.S.C. §1631(d), however, reverses that result, and *B* will defeat the PCA unless the PCA notified the buyer. *See* 7 U.S.C. §1631(e).

b.   *K* cannot defeat the PCA under the Code, because *K*, even if it is a buyer in ordinary course, cannot take free and clear of a security interest created by someone other than its seller. *B* did not create the PCA's security interest; *F* did. Under the Food Security Act, however, because *B* defeats the PCA, *K* will come within the shelter of *B* and defeat the PCA.

c.   *T*'s rights are the same as those of *K* under the same reasoning set out in the preceding answer.

d.   All of them. You may relax, however, as you sit at the breakfast table eating some of production credit association's collateral. It is not economical to sue the consumer here. *B* and *K*, however, are tempting targets, liable as they are in conversion to the PCA.

124.   a.   *B* prevails either under §9-306(2) or under §9-307(1).

b.   *C* cannot avail itself of the protection under either provision. Clearly, the priority rule of §9-312(5)(a) applies here, and *C* will lose to the bank.

c.   This disposition is probably not authorized. *E* cannot use §9-306(2) and is not a buyer; he, therefore, cannot qualify for protection under §9-307(1).

d.   *F* is a bulk buyer, and the sale to *F* is probably not authorized or at least is not the type of sale that secured lenders authorize. *F*, moreover, being a bulk buyer, does not meet the buyer in ordinary course definition. *See* §1-201(9).

125.   a.   This is the same question that we saw in problem 122 above. The difference here is that this buyer is a consumer. *B*, in any event, defeats the bank's security interest but creates a new security interest in the dealer.

b.   Again, *B* does not take free of the security interest *B* created under the installment sales agreement.

c.   *C* will defeat the bank because *C* comes within the shelter of *B*, who defeats the bank. *C* will take free of *R*'s security interest under the rule of §9-307(2). This is a consumer-to-consumer sale, sometimes referred to as the garage sale exception. The dealer's security interest is automatically perfected because it is a purchase money security interest in consumer goods. *See* §9-302(1)(d).

d.   If *R* had filed, as it had the option to do under Article 9, *R* would have defeated *C*.

126.   a.   *Y* does not defeat the security interest because although *Y* is a buyer in ordinary course, *Y* only defeats security interests created by its seller, *X*. *See* §9-307(1). The security interest in this problem was created by *B*.

b.   No. *Y* would take subject to the bank's security interest.

127. The New York Court of Appeals thinks so, but some commentators disagree. Clearly, the crucial fact is that which states that *C* is a buyer in ordinary course. It is difficult to see how a party familiar with bill-and-hold practices could qualify as a buyer in ordinary course when it buys and pays without checking to see that *M* will honor its requests for delivery of the goods. If *B* is a buyer in ordinary course, perhaps the courts should fashion an exception for *M*, that is, an exception to the rule of §9-307(1) when a secured party is in possession of the goods. See the next two problems.

128. The same arguments advanced to protect *M* in the preceding problem should protect the bank here. The bank has done all it can do to protect itself, and there perhaps should be an understanding that §9-307(1) does not operate to defeat a secured party in possession of the goods. This is a very common practice. The bank has taken possession precisely to avoid sales by the debtor. One can also argue, of course, that there can be no sale in ordinary course because a buyer that prepays for a carload of goods it cannot see is barmy, and a barmy buyer is not a buyer in ordinary course.

129. This question describes the field warehouse, a once popular device to deprive the debtor of possession of his collateral to prevent him from selling it. The arguments in the preceding two questions apply with equal vigor here. *M*, in the judgment of most writers, should be protected either by holding that the sale is not in ordinary course or by engrafting an exception onto §9-307(1) to exclude secured parties that retain possession of the collateral from the reach of this buyer protection provision.

130.   a. Yes. That is the import of §9-306(2).
       b. Bank can maintain an action in replevin to recover the goods or an action in conversion to recover their value from *B*.
       c. No. An innocent donee will take subject to the bank's security interest, which is to say that the donee will be liable to the bank in replevin or conversion.
       d. Yes. Section 9-306 not only provides that the security interest follows the goods into the hands of the purchaser, it also gives the bank a security interest in the proceeds. The bank, of course, may have only one recovery.

Section 19.   *Chattel Paper and Account Problems*

131.   a. Yes to both. Retailer obtained a security interest in the snowblower by virtue of the installment sales agreement. When Retailer assigned the paper to First Bank on May 2, the bank became an assignee of the security interest in it.
       b. Yes as to the contract. By taking possession of the paper, the bank perfected. *See* §§9-304(1), 9-305.
       c. Yes. Retailer was perfected under the automatic perfection rule of §9-302(1)(d). When it assigned the paper to First Bank, the

bank did not need to file. *See* §9-302(2). The assignment is complete without transfer of possession of the paper. The bank would not have a perfected security interest in the contract, however, not having taken possession of it and not having filed. First Bank should file in the state where the retailer's chief executive office is located, and the retailer must sign the financing statement.

132.   a. First Bank has no interest in the computers, not having taken a security agreement in the reversionary interest in the computers or any security interest in the computer company's inventory.

b. First Bank has a security interest in the leases and in the stream of payments due under the leases. That interest is perfected by virtue of the bank's filing. Leases are chattel paper. *See* §9-105(1)(b).

c. Those leases that cover the credit sales are also chattel paper, and First Bank has a perfected security interest in them. The computer company took a security interest in the computers subject to those "leases." Section 2-401(1) stipulates that any attempt by a seller that has delivered goods under a sale to reserve title, as this seller did in the sale disguised as a lease, has a security interest. The computer company, then, had a security interest in the equipment on May 1. When it assigned that interest to First Bank, the bank became a secured party. Note, however, that neither the bank nor the computer company filed *as to the equipment*. First Bank's interest, therefore, is unperfected.

If, then, the leasing company becomes bankrupt, First Bank will defeat the trustee's claim to the leases, the chattel paper, because the bank is perfected. If a lessee becomes bankrupt, however, the bank will not defeat the lessee's trustee's claim to the equipment because the bank does not have a perfected security interest in the equipment. This answer applies only if the leases are not true leases, that is, if they are sales disguised as leases: sales with the computer company retaining a security interest in the equipment.

133. This lease is a true lease. *See* §1-201(37). First Bank has a security interest in the lease (chattel paper). Under a true lease, the lessor has a reversionary interest in the equipment. Leasing Co. granted a security interest to First Bank in the reversionary interest in the equipment.

a. Second Bank, by virtue of the security interest it takes from Construction Co., the lessee, obtains a security interest in the construction company's leasehold interest in the equipment. The claims of Second Bank and Leasing Co. are not in conflict. Leasing Co. has conveyed away the leasehold interest to the construction company and cannot interfere with the leasehold as long as the construction company or somebody else makes the lease payments. In the event the payments cease, presumably, the leasehold comes to an end; Second has no collateral; and the leasing company will assert its reversionary rights under the lease. Second Bank would perfect its security interest by filing a financing statement, signed by the construction company, in the state where the equipment is located.

b. First Bank can perfect its security interest in the lease by taking possession of it or by filing. *See* §9-304(1). If it files, it should take a financing statement from the leasing company, its debtor and the owner of the interest being conveyed (described in the statement as "lease" or "chattel paper"), and should file in the state where the leasing company maintains its chief executive office. *See* §9-103(4). First's interest in the equipment is limited, of course, by Leasing Co.'s interest. Leasing Co. only has a reversionary interest, but a reversionary interest in equipment with a useful life of eight years that is subject to a lease of only four years could be quite valuable. The debtor on First Bank's financing statement should be Leasing Co., and the collateral should be described as "inventory held for lease" or something similar. First should file in the state where the equipment is located.

c. The trustee of Construction Co. will be able to hold the equipment during the term of the lease, provided that the trustee makes lease payments. Nothing in the transaction permits First Bank to interfere in the trustee's rights. Second Bank, of course, does have rights against the trustee, but the question does not ask about those rights.

When Leasing Co. files in bankruptcy, First Bank will defeat the leasing company's trustee's claim to the lease and the payments under it because First Bank has a perfected security interest in the lease payments. The bank will also defeat the trustee's claim to Leasing Co.'s reversionary rights because the bank has filed as to the inventory in the state where the inventory is located. First should file in New Jersey as to the reversionary interest in the equipment. Possession of the chattel paper would be sufficient to perfect the bank as to the stream of lease payments.

134.   a. No. Unless the secured party notifies the account debtor (Buyer), the account debtor may make its payment directly to the assignor of the account. *See* §9-318(3).

b. Yes, if the notice also directed Buyer to pay the bank. *See* §9-318(3).

c. i. Yes. *See* §9-318(1).
   ii. It depends on whether the setoff arose prior to or after the notice of assignment. In the former case, yes; in the latter, no. *See* §9-318(1) and comment 1.

d. Such a waiver of defense clause is enforceable if Buyer is a merchant. FTC rules limit the right of a consumer to waive its defenses, however. *See* Federal Trade Commission, Holder-in-Due-Course-Regulations, 16 C.F.R. Part 433 (1994).

135.   The fact that §9-318(1)(b) renders the assignee subject to "any other defense or claim of the account debtor" prompted at least one account debtor to argue that the bank took subject to his claim. The court held, however, and most of the writers agree, that the bank does not take subject to this claim.

Section 20.   More on Purchasers, This Time of Paper

136.   a.   Yes, even though the bank has a perfected security interest in the lease as proceeds of inventory, Finance Co. wins. The transaction appears to be regular in all respects. The filing of the bank's financing statement covering inventory does not give the finance company knowledge. *See* §9-308(a).

b.   Yes. First Bank is claiming the lease as proceeds from the disposition of its inventory collateral. Finance Co. wins. *See* §9-308(b).

c.   No. Taking on account of an antecedent loan is not "new" value, though it would be value. Section 9-308 protects the finance company that takes with knowledge only if it gives new value.

d.   If the bank's security agreement indicates that the bank has a security interest in the lease, which is chattel paper, the bank has a good argument that it is protected from the reach of §9-308(b). *See* PEB Commentary No. 8. If the bank can show that it relied, its argument is that much stronger. These arguments do not avail the bank, however, if Finance Co. takes without knowledge of the bank's interest.

e.   The promissory note would be proceeds, but it is an instrument, not chattel paper. *See* §9-105(i). If Finance Co. takes a negotiable instrument properly endorsed and if it gives value and acts without notice and in good faith, it is a holder in due course and will cut off all claims of the bank. *See* §§3-302, 3-306 (previously §3-305(1)). *See also* §9-309 (nothing in Article 9 limits the rights of a holder in due course). If the finance company does not qualify as a holder in due course, it may benefit from the protection of §9-308, which covers transfers of instruments.

f.   First Bank might have policed its collateral more sedulously by taking possession of the chattel paper as soon as Dealer leased or sold a golf cart. By taking possession, the bank would have preempted the operation of §9-308, which applies only if the finance company takes possession of the chattel paper. The bank might also have stamped the paper with a legend indicating that it was the collateral of the bank, in which case §9-308(a) cannot apply. Section 9-308(b) might also be inapplicable in that case because the stamping of the paper may indicate that it is not merely proceeds and because it may not be ordinary to take stamped paper.

137.   a.   Under §9-306(2) (if the sale is authorized) or §9-307(1), *B* defeats First Bank's security interest. Of course, because the paper is proceeds from the sale of the bank's collateral, the bank has a security interest in the paper; and the paper includes a security interest in the boat.

b.   Well, §9-306(5)(a) says it does, though it makes little sense to give the bank a security interest unless its security agreement extends to repossessed inventory. Anyway, subsection (a) seems to say that the bank gets a security interest automatically.

    c. Yes. The "sale" of the paper (chattel paper) to the finance company is an Article 9 secured transaction. *See* §9-102(1)(b). It operates to vest in Ace the dealer's rights under the sales agreement.

    d. Ace Finance Co. has priority. Section 9-306(5)(b) clearly favors the finance company over the bank as to the boat, just as §9-308 favors the finance company as to the chattel paper. Note the language in §9-306(5)(d), however, which suggests that the finance company cannot defeat "creditors of the transferor" unless the finance company is perfected. The finance company will not have a perfected security interest in the sailboat, however, because the dealer's assignment document, which functions as a security agreement, will only refer to an assignment of the chattel paper, and because the finance company has not filed any financing statement. Remember that it perfected as to the paper by taking possession of the paper, but it does not have possession of the boat and never filed as to inventory. The commentators are in agreement that subsection (5)(d) is not meant to alter or limit the effect of subsection (5)(b) and applies to creditors of the dealer other than the bank. There is at least one case, however, going the other way. *See* PEB Commentary No. 5

138.   a. Yes, under the cited sections.

    b. Yes. The repo is a secured transaction. *R* is perfected by possession. *See* §8-313(1)(a).

    c. Under §9-312(5)(a), the first to perfect would prevail. Bank perfected first and would prevail, but the section does not apply.

    d. Yes. Section 9-312 is something in Article 9. Section 9-309 says that nothing in Article 9 can limit the rights of a bona fide purchaser under Article 8. *R* is a bona fide purchaser. *See* §8-302(1)(a). Section 8-302(3) makes it clear that the bona fide purchaser cuts off prior claims such as the bank's security interest.

    e. Yes. Negotiable certificates travel without baggage. Section 8-302(3) cuts off the bank's adverse claim.

139.   a. Yes. *See* §9-304(4).

    b. Ace has a security interest under the same section, and it is perfected. Section 7-502(1)(a) indicates that Ace also has title to the document, but that would be an extraordinary result. Lenders do not speculate in commodities. They take security interests in them. Banks are forbidden by law from speculating in them. I think §7-502(1)(a) is a little hyperbolic and doubt that any lender would ever expect to realize more than the amount of its loan on the sale of the commodity or the receipt. Any excess surely belongs to the debtor or its trustee in bankruptcy. Buyers of soybeans would take title, but lenders against soybeans probably do not.

    c. Section 9-312(5)(a) would give the receipt to the bank, which perfected first, but the section does not apply.

    d. Yes.

      e. Yes. This is the proper analysis.

      f. Yes.

140.

      a. I would argue that First Bank has only a security interest in the receipt and the goods it covers, the language of §7-502(1)(a) notwithstanding. See answer b to the preceding problem.

      b. Whether First Bank's security interest is created by *B* may not always be clear. Under §§2-505, 2-506, and 4-210(a) (previously §4-208(1)), the bank that pays the beneficiary of a letter of credit has a security interest by operation of law. Most letter of credit issuers, furthermore, insist that the buyer execute a reimbursement agreement at the time *B* applies for the letter of credit. That agreement typically includes language granting the issuer a security interest in the documents and in the goods that are the subject of the sale between the foreign party and *B* to secure the advance the issuer makes when it pays the foreign party (the beneficiary).

      c. No, §9-307(1) cannot apply here because the bank issuer is a holder to whom a negotiable document of title has been duly negotiated. Section 9-309 protects the bank issuer by limiting the application of Article 9 to the bank.

Section 21. *Bailments*

141. There are three ways to take a security interest in goods that are not subject to a negotiable document of title. Note that this category includes goods in the hands of a bailee that has issued a nonnegotiable document as well as those in the hands of a bailee that has issued no document. In this problem, the pipeline company's acceptance of the delivery order operates as the issuance of a document of title. An accepted delivery order is the equivalent of a warehouse receipt. *See* §7-102, comment 3.

    The three ways of *perfecting* a security interest include (1) having a document issued in the name of the secured party, (2) notifying the bailee and thereby rendering it the agent of the secured party rather than of the original bailor, and (3) filing as to the goods. Note that the notice to the bailee option can be quite efficient. Once the secured party notifies the bailee, as a matter of bailment law, *see* §7-401(3), the bailee must deliver to the secured party. The same is true if the bailee issues a warehouse receipt directly to the bank, as they often do in these cases. In the event of notice to the bailee or bailee issuance of a nonnegotiable document to the bank, the secured party is then in possession of the goods through its agent, the bailee. That possession, of course, satisfies both the attachment provisions and the perfection provisions of Article 9. *See* §§9-203(1)(a), 9-305. In the third case, however, filing, the bank should also take a security agreement from the buyer. In all probability, the bank will take a security agreement in all three cases, because the security agreement covers matters that would otherwise not be covered.

    If the bank, then, follows one of these three arrangements, it will have a perfected security interest in the propane.

142.   a.   Yes, it probably is. Note the language in the second clause of the subsection. Prior to the Code, it was the prevailing view that goods subject to a negotiable document of title were "mere simulacra," that is, merely a shadow, their existence being wrapped up in the commodity paper, the warehouse receipt. The Code changes that view, however, when it indicates that the bank may take a security interest in the goods themselves and perfect by filing. Note, however, that the security interest so perfected will be subordinate to Second Bank's security interest.

           b.   Yes. This is the preferred method of taking and perfecting a security interest in goods that are in the hands of a bailee that has issued a negotiable document for them.

           c.   Second will prevail, as the language of the subsection suggests. This rule, being more specific than the rule of §9-312(5)(a), will govern and is an exception to the rule of §9-312(5)(a) to the effect that generally the first to perfect will prevail.

143.   a.   All four of them.

           b. T fails to rise to the level of a holder by due negotiation. The problem does not tell you that the receipt was negotiable. There is no indication that there has been an endorsement. T does not take in good faith, or for value, or in the ordinary course of business or finance.

144.   Any of facts a through g would prevent B from rising to the level of a holder by due negotiation. Facts h and i, however, would not prevent B from being a holder by due negotiation, because banks in the ordinary course of business and finance take and transfer negotiable warehouse receipts.

145. B would have greater rights than T and greater rights than the producer. It does not matter whether B is a lender or a broker, because both entities take negotiable receipts in the ordinary course of their affairs. Note that B will be a holder by due negotiation only if the producer left a receipt in bearer form where a thief could get it or endorsed the receipt in blank and left it where a thief could get it.

146. C takes the same rights that B enjoyed. C comes under B's umbrella. *See* §7-504(1).

147.   No. A person who does not take by due negotiation comes under the "nemo dat" rule of §7-504(1); she gets the rights of her transferor. T, the transferor, did not have rights superior to the producer.

148.   a. B qualifies for holder by due negotiation status, but B is subject to the paramount rights rule of §7-503(1). The producer's rights arise *before* the bailment. *See* comment 1 (second sentence).

           b. B will also lose to First Bank because the bank also enjoys paramount rights in the cotton. Id.

           c.   If T were a truck driver, his transfer of the receipt to B would not be in the ordinary course of business or finance. Truck drivers do not deal in warehouse receipts. Thus, B, not taking by due negotiation, has only those rights given it under §7-504(1) and loses to the true owner, the producer. The result is the same, but the analysis differs.

149. If the producer entrusts the cotton to *T*, and if *B* takes by due negotiation (that is, if *T* is someone whose business it is to deal in warehouse receipts covering cotton, another cotton producer, for example), *B* may be able to escape the effect of the paramount rights rule of §7-503(1). That section makes exception for the operation of the rule for situations in which the party with the paramount rights clothes the bailor, *T* in this case, with actual or apparent authority to bail the goods. The facts suggest that the producer has indeed clothed *T* with such authority, in which case *B* will prevail over the producer.

150. The bank should make an estoppel by deed type of argument under §7-502(1)(c). Under this theory, the late delivery of the ore by *W* to the carrier "feeds" the earlier issued negotiable bill. This provision codifies a pre-Code case, *Baldwin v. Childs*, 249 N.Y. 212, 163 N.E. 737 (1928), in which the court invoked the estoppel. The bank would lose, however, had the bill been nonnegotiable. A nonnegotiable bill is like a quitclaim deed; its taker receives only those rights that the transferor possessed. When *W* conveys a nonnegotiable bill to the bank, the bank is not a holder by due negotiation and does not benefit from estoppel rules of §7-502(1)(c), but comes under §7-504(1).

Section 22. *Fixture Priority Rules*

151.
    a. This question falls into the general rule of Article 9's fixture priorities. That rule appears, of all places, in §9-313(7). Heating Co. cannot fit itself into any of the "preceding subsections" and therefore is subordinate to S&L's mortgage. Under the given facts, Heating Co. cannot qualify for the priority of subsection (4)(a) because the facts do not indicate that Heating Co. has a purchase-money security interest.

    b. Mortgage Investment Co. would defeat Heating Co. under the first rule of conveyancing law. Mortgage would succeed to the rights of S&L. Because S&L defeats Heating, Mortgage would defeat Heating. That result is consistent with the rule of subsection (4)(b).

    c. Under the altered facts, which do give the heating company a purchase-money security interest, the heating company would defeat the S&L and Mortgage Investment. *See* §9-313(4)(a).

152.
    a. S&L will have priority. Generally, to defeat the real estate encumbrancer's interest in a fixture, the secured party must make a fixture filing before the encumbrancer records its mortgage. Here, Heating Co. failed to make a fixture filing and cannot qualify for the protection of subsection (4)(b). Thus, the general rule of subsection (7) applies, and the encumbrancer wins.

    b. The answer would be the same even if Heating Co. made a fixture filing within ten days of the installation of the furnace. Although subsection (4)(a) contains a grace period, the heating company has not satisfied the requirement that its fixture be affixed after the encumbrancer obtains its mortgage. Any other rule would mislead the mortgagee. It would be lending against real estate that it thought had a new furnace, when in fact it was going to lose the furnace to the heating company. Subsection (4)(a) requires the purchase-money secured party to show that the rights of the encumbrancer arose when the old furnace was in the building.

153.   a. Here the heating company can avail itself of the purchase money rule of subsection (4)(a), having complied with all of its requirements.

        b i. In the event the mortgage were a construction mortgage, the heating company loses. Under subsection (6), the construction mortgagee is not subject to the purchase money rule for reasons adequately set out in Comment 4(e).

            ii. Heating Co. loses if it fails to file within ten days of affixation. May 13 is the tenth day.

154.   a. First Bank wins.

        b. There is no dispute with a real estate encumbrancer here, so §9-313 does not apply. Section 9-312(5)(a) governs.

        c. No.

        d. The banks should be able to defeat a real estate encumbrancer under §9-313(4)(c). This machine fits the notion of a readily removable office machine. Central filing is sufficient to defeat the real estate encumbrancer who should not reasonably rely on such collateral, whether or not state fixture law deems it a fixture. Note, however, that this exception is available to the banks only if they perfect before the goods are affixed. *See* comment 4(d). The exception is not limited in any way by the time that the encumbrancer obtains its mortgage. This is an important rule for equipment lessors, many of whom are really secured parties but who are not in a position to bother with the trouble of making a fixture filing, such filings involving, as they do, a legal description of sorts and a determination whether the debtor has an interest of record in the premises. *See* §9-402(5).

155. If the collateral were a mobile home, the readily removable office machine exception would not apply. The bank, then, would have to look for another rule to protect it. If it made a fixture filing before the encumbrancer obtained its mortgage, the bank would win. If it did not file ahead of the mortgagee, the bank will have to show that it satisfies the purchase-money rule of subsection (4)(a).

156. Subsection (4)(d) protects the banks against the trustee if they file centrally. The trustee has the rights of a lien creditor against the real estate. Thus, even though a court finds that the machine is a fixture, if the secured parties have filed centrally, they will defeat the trustee. Note that the Bankruptcy Code anticipates this rule by denying good-faith purchase status for the trustee in fixtures, though otherwise does grant the trustee good-faith purchase status as to real estate. *See* Bankruptcy Code §544(a)(3).

157. The S&L will get the window. The exception for consumer goods in subsection (4)(c) only applies to replacements of domestic appliances. Dealer should have made a fixture filing within ten days of the installation to gain priority over the mortgagee. If, however, the collateral had been a new refrigerator to replace an old one and assuming that the court held it to be a fixture, Dealer would win, having qualified for the protection of subsection (4)(c).

If the dispute were between the dealer and the debtor's trustee in bankruptcy, the dealer would prevail as to the window because the trustee's rights are limited under subsection (4)(d). This security interest is automatically perfected. Dealer, then, would qualify for the protection of subsection (4)(d). That assumes, of course, as the question states, that the window is a fixture. The court might find that it is not a fixture but ordinary building materials incorporated into the real estate, in which case the dealer cannot obtain a security interest in it. *See* §9-313(2).

158. This is a review of the purchase-money rule of subsection (4)(a). The central filing is not good against the mortgagee. The subsection requires a fixture filing. Such a filing on June 9 would be sufficient to give the heating company priority. A filing on June 19 would not. If the mortgage is a construction mortgage, of course, subsection (4)(a) does not apply. *See* §9-313(6).

159.   a.   These facts invoke the general rule of subsection (7). They do not fit into any of the preceding sections. First Bank, the real estate encumbrancer, prevails.

b.   If First took its mortgage on May 3, the result would differ. This would then be a subsection (4)(b) case. The mortgagee would have a warning that Second Bank was in the picture. Second Bank's filing would be of record before First Bank, the mortgagee, recorded. Mortgagees traditionally do not disburse funds until they have filed their mortgages and run a search to make certain that there are no filings made between the date of the mortgagee's commitment to lend and the date of the recording. If they see a fixture filing, they do not disburse the loan proceeds until matters are ironed out.

160. St. Paul will defeat the trustee even if the court finds that the minicomputer is a fixture. *See* §9-313(4)(d). St. Paul will defeat the mortgagee under subsection (4)(c), the computers falling within the definition of readily removable office machines. Note that St. Paul's strategy makes sense. It avoids the expense of a fixture filing, and it avoids the risk that a court might find the computers to be non-fixtures. In that case, a fixture filing in the local real estate records office would not be sufficient to defeat other secured parties or the trustee in bankruptcy of the debtor. Subsections (4)(c) and (d) apply only if the court finds that the goods are fixtures. If the court finds that they are not fixtures but plain, ordinary equipment, the local filing will be defective, but a central filing is good as to equipment that is not a fixture. *See* §9-401, second alternative subsection (1)(c).

Section 23. *Further Scope Questions*

161. The garage's lien prevails. The rule is in the nature of a purchase-money rule. Note that the garage loses the lien if it loses possession. The rule is otherwise if the lien is statutory and if the statute provides that the secured party will have priority, but not if the lien arises at common law, even though the common law would render the lien subordinate to the security interest. For a statute rendering the lien subordinate, see §7-209(3)(a) and Comment 3.

162. a. This is a sale. *See* §1-201(37)(d). Lessor should file but may use a filing that designates the parties as "Lessor" and "Lessee." *See* §9-408.

b. This is a true lease. It is not clear that the lessee will exercise the option. That decision not having been made and not being a foregone conclusion, the transaction is still a lease. No filing is necessary. If the consideration for the option is nominal, the Code assumes that the lessee will exercise it and, therefore, that the lease is a disguised sale, as it clearly is during the option term. In that case, the lessor should file.

c. This is also a true lease. A buyer does not agree to return to the seller goods it has bought when the goods remain useful.

d. This is clearly a sale. *See* §1-201(37)(b).

e. This is a sale. *See* subsection (a). The estimate is as of the date the parties enter into the transaction.

f. i. This is a sale. *See* subsection (c).

ii. One hundred dollars is probably nominal. This is also a sale.

iii. While the authority is in conflict, a price that is considerably below fair market value is nominal in the view of many. In that case, this is also a sale, and a filing is necessary.

g. In these cases, it is important to know whether the lessee has the right to terminate the lease. If it has that right, there is no sale. A lessee that can terminate the lease has the right to avoid paying for the goods, can put the goods back on the lessor, and will undoubtedly do so if the market for the goods falls. These rights are not normal incidents of a buyer under a contract for sale. They are incidents of a true lease.

163. a. *M* might argue that the indication that the bicycles are *M*'s overcomes the presumption of subsection (3). The trouble is that overcoming that presumption does not, at least under the language of the statute, prevent the court from finding nonetheless that there is a sale or return, that is, a consignment. This arrangement sounds very much like a consignment. If it is, the creditors of *R* will be able to claim the bicycles.

b. This language may also have an impact on the application of the presumption under subsection (3), but it is difficult to see how it makes any sense to decide the competing claims to the inventory on the basis of this small sign and this rather insignificant fact. It appears that *M* is financing *R*'s inventory. In that case, *M* should notify the world through a public filing or some equivalent. Arguably, these signs do not do the job. Bear in mind that at the present time there are no states with sign laws.

c. This is not an attempt to show compliance with a sign law, there not being any, but one to show that *R* is known by the people with whom it does business to hold goods on consignment. One might ask whether that sign puts the utility companies or parts suppliers of *R* that sell on credit on notice. Such creditors often do not visit the establishments to which they sell on credit.

d. This filing is the safest procedure for *M* to follow and protects *M* from *R*'s creditors and its trustee in bankruptcy. Note that subsection (3)(c) says that a filing overcomes the rule of subsection (3). Courts have uniformly held that it overcomes the rule of subsection (2) as well.

164. *B* is either a consignor or a seller of inventory on credit that is trying to retain a security interest. In either case, the Code is willing to give *B* priority over First Bank but only if *B* complies with §9-114 (if *B* is a consignor) or §9-312(3) (if *B* is a secured party). Note that the provisions of the sections are similar. *B* must give notice and file before it delivers the goods to *W*. *Compare* §9-114 *with* §9-312(3).

165. a. Under strict security of property analysis, the trustee has no rights in the cotton because *G* has no rights in it. *G* is only a bailee. Courts might be concerned, however, that the practice evident here is not commercially harmless.

This transaction does not fit the facts in subsection (3) of §2-326 that creates a presumption that the bailment is a sale or return. The setting, nonetheless, is redolent of pre-Code consignment arrangements that misled creditors of the bailee. Under modern credit practices, the argument that the bailment creates ostensible ownership in *G* is weak. Few, if any, of *G*'s creditors will rely on its naked possession of inventory. Even *G*'s inventory lender will soon learn, if it is at all sophisticated, that the cotton belongs to the farmers and not to *G*.

That may not convince a court, however, to find that this is not a consignment (sale or return) that renders the goods subject to *G*'s creditors. If the reason for the anti-consignment rule in the Code is to protect the integrity of the filing system and to avoid fraud by inventory lenders, the court should find against the farmer here and rule for the trustee. It should make no difference, of course, that the trustee had knowledge. *Cf.* §9-301(1)(b) (lack of knowledge not necessary for trustee to defeat unperfected secured party).

b. Again, the nature of the arrangement suggests that this may deserve treatment as an inventory loan by the farmer. In that case, the bank wins regardless of knowledge. *See* §9-312(5)(a). If, on the other hand, the courts see the arrangement solely as a bailment, the farmers will prevail because under the *nemo dat* rule, the gin cannot give its creditors anything more than it has. As a naked bailee, it has no right to hold the goods against the claim for their return by the farmers.

166.   a.   No. It is not ordinary for a buyer to take goods in satisfaction of a debt. This transaction is out of the ordinary course.

b.   No. The facts do not indicate that Aussie had a security interest. Aussie is simply a transferee and a creditor of Wool Co.

c.   Section 2-402(2) refers to common law fraud rules (Twyne's Case, 76 Eng. Rep. 809 (Star Chamber 1601)) under which it was a fraudulent conveyance when a buyer paid for goods and left them with the seller. Both the common law rule and §2-402(2) make exception for such arrangements when there is an innocent explanation for them. The facts do not provide such an explanation, and this transaction between Wool and Mill may be a fraud on Aussie, in which case Aussie has a better claim to the wool than Mill.

167.   Generally, if the lease is a true lease, the creditors of the lessee take subject to the terms of the lease. *See* §2A-307(1). It does not matter whether the lease payments are nominal or reasonable. In the facts of this problem, the arrangement may well be a true lease. Note, however, that the lessee might use the equipment up. In other words, it may be that the lessor is selling the equipment or giving the equipment to the lessee. If the lease provides that the lessee must return the equipment if the lessee does not buy strapping from lessor, the arrangement sounds more like a true lease. This may be a case for a cautionary filing designating the parties as lessee and lessor. *See* §9-408.

Section 24.   *The Seller's Right to Reclaim*

168.   a.   *B* has a special property, which is to say that it has an interest, the contours of which depend on the rights and remedies of the parties. *See* §2-501(1).

b.   Yes, as the section indicates. In view of *B*'s breach, *S* may withhold delivery and may resell the goods free of *B*'s interest. *See* §2-703(a), (d), and (f).

c.   Almost certainly *B*'s inventory lender will have taken a security interest in *B*'s after-acquired inventory; and once *B* has a property interest in the goods, the inventory lender's security interest will have attached under §9-203(1). Under the first rule of conveyancing law, the lender's interest, however, will stand no higher than *B*'s. Because *S* defeats *B*, *S* will defeat *B*'s inventory lender.

169.   If it learns that *B* is insolvent, *S* may stop delivery while the goods are in transit. If *B* is in breach, *S* may stop delivery of goods in transit if the goods comprise a carload or container load. *See* §§2-702(1), 2-705(1).

170.   Absent fraud by *B*, once the goods are delivered, *S* has no rights in them. To retain rights, *S* must have *B* execute a security agreement granting *S* a security interest. *B*'s inventory lender and *B*'s trustee in bankruptcy will obtain interests in the goods when *B* obtains an interest. To the extent that *B*'s interest defeats *S* (and *B* will defeat *S* under the facts of this problem, even if *B* does not pay), the lender and the trustee will defeat *S*. All of this follows from the first rule of conveyancing.

171. If a buyer fraudulently (either as a matter of fact or a matter of law) induces a seller to deliver goods on credit, the buyer has voidable title, and the seller has the right to avoid that title, a right to reclaim. The demand required by §2-702(2) is described by some as a perfection feature of the right to reclaim, but it may be more accurate to view it as a limit in the nature of a statute of limitations. In any event, the seller must make it for the right to reclaim to survive. Bear in mind that this right to reclaim is an extraordinary claim against property delivered under the contract of sale. Normally, a seller loses all rights in goods once it delivers them. True, the seller can retain a security interest, but that retention must be pursuant to agreement. (The seller's Article 2 security interest, a security interest that arises not by the agreement of the buyer but by operation of law, *see* §2-505(1), expires on delivery to the buyer of the goods or the negotiable document of title covering them.) The right to reclaim arises by operation of law and is in the nature of a non-possessory lien — an extraordinary commercial concept. Courts have generally and rightly enforced the demand requirement strictly. Note that the section does away with the demand requirement if the buyer has made written representation of its solvency. Most courts do not consider the check a written representation of solvency, though at least one did. Common law fraud is good enough. Receiving goods on credit while insolvent, whether buyer knows it or not, is fraud at law. Paying for goods in a cash sale with a check drawn on insufficient funds is also fraud at law. It does not matter that the buyer is unaware that it is overdrawn. Note that §2-702 does not apply to cash sale fraud, because the cash sale is not, by definition, a credit sale.

172.   a. *S* has a right to reclaim.
        b. No.
        c. Comments to §2-507 originally provided that *S* was required to protect his interest by giving the demand required by the credit sale section (§2-702). The Permanent Editorial Board changed the comment, however, and the requirement for the demand is now omitted. (Check your state's version of §2-507.)
        d. It does not matter whether *B* knew that the check was an overdraft. If the check is post-dated, however, §2-507 does not apply. As §2-511, comment 6 indicates, a post-dated check renders the transaction a credit sale, and the governing section is §2-702, not §2-507.

173.   a. The reference in comment 3 to the effect that the right to reclaim conforms with the policy of the good-faith purchase sections of the Code supports the view that the seller's right to reclaim does not defeat a purchaser for value who takes the goods in good faith from the fraudulent buyer *B*. A buyer in ordinary course is a good-faith purchaser for value.
        b. A secured party is a good-faith purchaser for value whether or not it is perfected and, therefore, defeats the reclaiming seller. (Note that a lien creditor, not being a good faith purchaser, will not defeat the reclaiming seller under this analysis.)

174. Not under the current version of the comments. Under the former version, however, the demand was necessary. See your state's version of §2-507, comment 3.

175. Traditionalists might call it "the property" or "title."

176. Voidable title. *See* §2-403(1) (second sentence).

177.   a. Good title. *See* §2-403(1) (second sentence).
    b. Good title. *See id.*
    c. Good title. *See* id. (A buyer in bulk is not a buyer in ordinary course, but it clearly is a purchaser and it can be a good-faith purchaser for value.)

178. No. The lien creditor is not a purchaser and cannot defeat the right to reclaim. The words "subject to," as courts have construed them, mean that the seller's right to reclaim is subject to the rights of the lien creditor, whatever those rights happen to be. Those rights, moreover, arise not under the Code but under non-Code law. In most jurisdictions, Pennsylvania being an exception, the non-Code law provides (mostly in nineteenth century cases) that the lien creditor's rights are indeed *subordinate* to those of the reclaiming seller. The words "subject to" in §2-702(3) should be read not to mean "inferior to" but to mean subject to whatever rights the common law gives the lien creditor.

179.   a. It is not clear whether Bankruptcy Code §546(c)(1) is meant to be a provision that excludes the cash seller's right to reclaim fashioned by UCC §2-507 or by the right to reclaim at common law. The cash seller's right to reclaim, of course, arises in bankruptcy much less often than the credit seller's claim. It may be that the omission was unintentional. In that case, the cash seller may retain the right to reclaim against the trustee, a lien creditor, in bankruptcy. If the section is meant to codify the only circumstances in which a seller has a right to reclaim, the cash seller will lose to the trustee, and so will the seller relying on common law fraud for its right to reclaim the goods. Only the credit seller will be able to use the provision against the trustee.
    b. Yes, the seller must perfect by making a *written* demand. The UCC does not require the demand to be in writing. Note also that the timing language in the two sections is different. The UCC says "within ten days after receipt"; the Bankruptcy Code says "before ten days after receipt." Check the cases in your circuit.
    c. Clearly, everyone assumes that the words "subject to" in Bankruptcy Code §546(c)(1) mean "subordinate to." That conclusion may be incorrect, however, in light of the cases construing the same terms in UCC §2-702(3) differently. See Problem 178. In Pennsylvania, the lien creditor defeated the reclaiming seller at common law. In most other jurisdictions, the lien creditor lost to the reclaiming seller. If the words "subject to" do not mean "inferior to" but mean that the court must determine outside the UCC and the Bankruptcy Code what the rights of the lien creditor against the reclaiming seller are, the result may be in favor of the seller in most jurisdictions and against him in Pennsylvania and perhaps elsewhere. Note, however, that most writers and courts ignore the history of the meaning of "subject to" in these cases and read Bankruptcy Code §546(c) as giving the seller's right to reclaim priority over the trustee's lien.

        d.   Such statements protect the seller outside the bankruptcy context under UCC §2-702(2) but do not avail the seller in bankruptcy, Bankruptcy Code §546(c)(1) not having an analogous provision.

180. *S*'s right to reclaim is not a security interest. Historically, it stems from the seller's lien, the notion that a seller wrongfully deprived of the goods by the buyer could get them back. The idea that a seller's lien can exist when the goods are out of the seller's possession is an extraordinary one because it is a secret lien. To extend the secret lien to proceeds from the sale of the goods by the seller would be extraordinary treatment of an extraordinary right. One court has so ruled, however, and raised the question posed in this problem. It is probably best to avoid these questions by refusing to let the reclaiming seller have a claim to the proceeds; but if the reclaiming seller does have a right to the proceeds, that right should be subordinate to other parties claiming proceeds that would defeat the seller. The inventory and account lenders are good-faith purchasers for value and should have a better claim to the proceeds than the reclaiming seller. The trustee and the lien creditor, on the other hand, would lose the goods to the reclaiming seller and arguably should lose the proceeds to the reclaiming seller.

181. As the preceding answer suggests, the seller's right to reclaim is neither an Article 9 nor an Article 2 security interest. First, Article 9 applies to consensual secured transactions. The right of the seller to reclaim arises by operation of law. Second, the seller's right to reclaim extends to the full value of the goods. A secured party in Article 9 is entitled to realize on the collateral only to the extent of the debtor's debt. The reclaiming seller's interest is not so limited. The reclaiming seller can take the goods back, sell them for more than what the original buyer agreed to pay, and pocket the difference between the original purchase price and the resale purchase price. Finally, the reclaiming seller need not comply with any of the debtor protection rules of Part 5 of Article 9 and need not perfect its interest.

    The right to reclaim is similar to the Article 2 security interest defined in §2-505(1)(a), and it may be that that security interest, which arises by operation of the law of negotiable documents of title and is not subject to any of the strictures that apply to Article 9 security interests, is misnamed. The security interest defined in §2-505 looks much like the seller's right to reclaim. Note, however, that comment 1 to §2-505 states that the security interest of the seller "is restricted to securing payment or performance by the buyer." That language suggests that the seller cannot reclaim the goods, resell them, and pocket the difference between the original contract price and the resale price. There are no cases that I can find. The security interest defined in §2-711(3), though it arises by operation of law and not by consensual transfer, clearly sounds like a security interest. The buyer may resort to the goods only to the extent of the sum due from the defaulting seller. After the buyer satisfies that claim against the seller, the buyer must return the goods or any excess value in them to the seller.

Section 25. *Article 9 and the Powers of the Trustee in Bankruptcy*

(At this point, it would be worthwhile to review UCC §9-301. *See* Problems 105 through 107.)

182. Generally, a perfected secured party such as the bank will defeat the trustee's lien creditor rights, even in after-acquired equipment, though it may have problems with the trustee's power to avoid a preference. Here, however, the debtor acquired the equipment after the date of bankruptcy. In that event, the Bankruptcy Code interdicts application of the UCC. Bankruptcy Code §552 makes it clear that the bank has no rights in equipment acquired after the debtor files in bankruptcy.

183. No. The trustee's rights in the inventory were subordinate to those of the bank as of the commencement of the bankruptcy case, that is, the filing of the bankruptcy petition. The subsequent sale should not deprive the bank of its collateral. The section makes it clear that proceeds from the sale of collateral belongs to the secured party. *See* Bankruptcy Code §552(b).

184. Normally, the automatic stay section, Bankruptcy Code §362, prevents creditors from taking any action against the debtor's property after the commencement of the case. Here, however, the effect of the stay would be to impair the rights of an innocent purchase-money creditor. The cited sections make it clear that it is not a violation of the automatic stay to file the financing statement. That filing renders Manufacturing Co. perfected as of the time of filing. *See* UCC §9-301(2).

185. The automatic stay does not inhibit the giving of the seller's reclamation notice as required by UCC §2-702(2) and Bankruptcy Code §546(c).

186. All of the proposed actions violate the automatic stay. Note that the attempt to file a financing statement after the commencement of the case would be a useless act in any event because the trustee, having the rights of a lien creditor as of December 1, would defeat the secured party under the rule of Bankruptcy Code §544(a)(1) and UCC §9-301(1)(b). This is not a purchase-money security interest.

187.
    a. As we will see later in the study of the timing provision of the preference section (§547(e)(2)(A)), for preference purposes, this transaction occurred on August 30, outside the preference period; the trustee may not set the transaction aside as a preferential transfer voidable in bankruptcy.

    b. Yes, Electric Co. will defeat First Bank under UCC §9-301(1)(b), because Electric Co. became a lien creditor prior to the time that the bank perfected. For purposes of UCC §9-301(1)(b), perfection occurred on September 4, which is after the date on which the electric company obtained its lien.

    c. Yes, the trustee may set the electric company's lien aside as a preference. It is a transfer of the debtor's property on account of an antecedent debt while the debtor is presumed to be insolvent and during the preference period. The trustee will be able to set aside the electric company's lien.

d. Yes, that is the effect of Bankruptcy Code §551.

e. Yes, the answer is that the trustee is limited by the amount of the electric company's lien. The trustee may not upset the secured party's claim entirely. Under the rule of Moore v. Bay, 284 U.S. 4 (1931), a curious rule that almost never applies, the trustee may upset the whole claim, but *Moore* applies only to unsecured bankruptcy claims. *See* §544b.

Section 26.   Preferences

188.   All of these transactions, the payment of money, the creation of a security interest, and the obtaining of a judicial lien are transfers of the debtor's property on account of an antecedent debt during the 90-day period while the debtor is presumed to be insolvent. In virtually every case, such transfers permit the transferee creditor to obtain more from the debtor's estate than the creditor would have obtained in a Chapter 7 liquidation. In short, all three of the transfers are preferences that the trustee may avoid.

189.   a. This is probably a preference because the note is a demand note.

b. If, however, the payment were made on a debt that was completely secured, there is no preference because the bank would get no more by virtue of the payment than it would get in a Chapter 7 liquidation. Note, moreover, that when a creditor is completely secured, payment on the debt reduces the debt and frees up collateral. By virtue of the payment, the debtor's "equity" in the collateral increases by the amount of the payment. In such cases, it is difficult to see how the payment satisfies the preference definition. The payment does not deplete the estate. On the debtor's balance sheet the cash account is reduced, but the equity value in the equipment account increases by the same amount.

c. This is a preference. Transfers to insiders are avoidable if they occur within one year of the commencement of the case. The president would be an insider. *See* Bankruptcy Code §101(31)(B)(ii).

d. Unlike the payment under the demand note in Problem a above, this regularly scheduled installment payment on the note is protected by the exception in Bankruptcy Code §547(c)(2).

e. If the grant of the security interest and the making of the loan by the secured party are contemporaneous, the trustee will not be able to set the security interest aside. If the transaction is intended by the parties to be contemporaneous and if the transaction is substantially contemporaneous, the exception in Bankruptcy Code §547(c)(1) applies. It is critical, then, for the secured party to be able to show that the loan and the grant of the security interest occurred on the same day or thereabouts. The timing rule of Bankruptcy Code §547(e)(2)(A) indicates that if the secured party perfects its security interest within ten days of the time the interest attaches, the time of the transfer is the time of attachment. (In Bankruptcy Code parlance, "at the time such transfer takes effect between the transferor and the transferee" is the equivalent of the UCC concept of "attachment".) If the secured party does not file until after November 13, the timing rule indicates that the time of the transfer is the time of perfection — November 14, say. In that case, we have a transfer on November 14 of the debtor's collateral to a secured party that made a loan on November 3. That is not a substantially contemporaneous transfer. It is a transfer on account of an antecedent debt and would be a preference that the trustee could avoid.

f. Yes, it matters because a filing within the ten-day period allowed by the timing rule renders the transfer effective on August 31, a day which falls outside the preference period, while a filing more than ten days after attachment renders the transfer effective on the date of filing, which will fall within the preference period and will be a transfer that meets the other elements of the preference definition.

g. There are two ten-day periods here. The first is under the timing rule of subsection (e)(A). That period begins to run on the day of attachment. The second ten-day period arises under the purchase-money exception in subsection (c)(3). That ten-day period begins to run on the day the goods are delivered and may give the secured party more time within which to file than the timing rule allows.

h. This is really an attachment problem. The timing rule governs and says that as long as the secured party perfects within ten days of attachment, the transfer shall be deemed to have occurred at the time of attachment. If perfection is later, the time of the transfer shall be deemed to be the time of perfection. Attachment does not occur until the bank makes a loan on the 10th. Because the bank perfected within ten days of the 10th, the bank's transfer occurs on September 10, and the transfer is contemporaneous with the bank's loan. There is no preference. Note that if the bank had given value on August 15 by making a binding commitment, attachment would have occurred on that date, and the perfection on September 17 would constitute a transfer outside of the ten-day grace period. This result may seem harsh, but it is consistent with the Bankruptcy Code's (and the UCC's) policy of encouraging prompt perfection of security interests. Remember that the secured party that does not file is holding a secret lien.

i. These facts illustrate the operation of the netting exception in subsection (c)(4). The transfer of the security interest on September 15 is a preference, but the subsequent unsecured loan on October 15 prompts the netting of the two transactions, so that the trustee's avoidance of the September 15 transfer is limited to $30,000, the difference between the $50,000 preferential transfer on September 15 and the unsecured advance on October 15.

j. The two monthly payments to the trade creditor are precisely the kind of payments that subsection (c)(2) excepts. Otherwise, these payments are clearly transfers that would be voidable under the definition in subsection (2).

190.   a. The bank cannot obtain an interest in an account until it arises. When an account arises within the preference period, the bank obtains an interest on that date. Bear in mind, the bank's claim here is not to proceeds from the sale of inventory. This bank is an account lender, not an inventory lender.

b. Yes, this is a transfer that fits the definition of a preference. No, courts cannot invoke UCC §9-108, which is an attempt by state legislatures to override bankruptcy law. Bankruptcy Code §547(e)(3) neuters UCC §9-108.

c. Yes, it would be a problem if the Bankruptcy Code did not make allowances. Account lenders typically rely on after-acquired property, and that perfectly legitimate business practice runs afoul of the preference section unless there is an exception for it.

d. The Bankruptcy Code does make allowance for account lenders that rely on after-acquired accounts and inventory lenders that rely on after-acquired inventory. The rule is set forth in subsection (c)(5).

e. Secured equipment lenders tend to rely on discrete items of collateral and not on after-acquired equipment. They will not be offended by a preference rule that says security interests in after-acquired equipment that the debtor obtains during the preference period will be voidable. It is true that some working capital lenders rely on after-acquired equipment. The preference section tells them not to rely too heavily.

191.   a. Under the first set of facts, there is no preference. Subsection (c)(5) is an improvement-in-position test. The secured party that is oversecured on the 90th day cannot improve its position. That secured party, therefore, will not receive a preference by virtue of the debtor's acquisition of additional inventory during the preference period.

b. If the secured party is undersecured on the 90th day, there may be an improvement in position. Under the modified facts, the secured party was undersecured in the amount of $14,000 on the 90th day and was fully secured on the date of bankruptcy. The secured party has improved its position to the extent of $14,000 and will have to return all but $5,000 worth of the inventory to the trustee.

c. This is simple math. Under the first example, there is a preference of $2,000; under the second and third there is no preference, there being no improvement in position; the secured party is still $2,000 undersecured.

Section 27. *The Trustee as Lien Creditor*

192. Yes. The transfer occurs immediately before the commencement of the case and, therefore, falls within the preference period. Note also that this secured party is unperfected at the time of filing and, therefore, will lose to the trustee under Bankruptcy Code §544(a)(1).

193.   a. The analysis differs, but the trustee still wins. Because the filing occurs after the commencement of the case, the trustee will defeat the secured party under Bankruptcy Code §544(a)(1). In this case the trustee will not be able to attack the transaction as a preference. The grace period in the preference section, in this example, Bankruptcy Code §547(e)(2)(C), gives the secured party ten days to perfect. That grace period only protects the secured party from a preference attack, however. The timing rule of subsection (e) applies only "[f]or the purposes of this section," id., that is, the preference section. The secured party may not avail itself of the timing rule when the trustee makes a strong-arm challenge under Bankruptcy Code §544(a)(1).

b. It would matter that the secured party had a purchase-money security interest. A purchase-money secured party is not subject to attack under Bankruptcy Code §544(a)(1) if the purchase-money secured party perfects within ten days of the time the debtor receives the collateral. *See* UCC §9-301(2).

194. As long as the parties intended from the time of the loan that it would be a secured loan, the transaction is not a preference. It fits the exception in subsection (c)(1) for substantially contemporaneous transactions. If, however, the bank made the loan and then thought better of it and asked for collateral, there is a preference.

Section 28. Proceeds in Bankruptcy

195.   a. These proceeds go to AC under §9-306(4)(a).

b. These proceeds go to AC under §9-306(4)(b).

c. These proceeds go to AC under §9-306(4)(c).

Beware. The facts are never as simple as this problem makes them. AC will often have a difficult time demonstrating, as it has the burden to do, that the items mentioned came from the sale of AC appliances. Also, in the event of insolvency, there often are few proceeds left, especially cash proceeds, which tend to be spent quickly by a debtor approaching insolvency.

196.   a. AC can claim $25,000 less any payments made to it from cash proceeds received by the debtor during the ten days and less anything it receives under subsections (a), (b), and (c) of subsection (4). It does not matter that the $10 is deposited outside the ten-day period. It is necessary only to show that AC's proceeds have been commingled with other funds in the account. The $10,000 would have to be subtracted from the $25,000. Proceeds received by the debtor from the sale of inventory other than AC products are not included in any of these calculations.

b. $0. AC must satisfy the burden of showing that proceeds from the sale of its collateral (AC products) were deposited in the account.

c. $0. AC has not satisfied the requirements of subsection (4)(d). It has not shown that the debtor received any proceeds from the sale of AC products during the ten days. The maximum that AC can receive under subsection (4)(d) is that amount. If AC cannot show what that amount is, the court cannot use the formula.

This result may seem harsh. It is clear that under the lowest intermediate balance rule, $20,000 of AC's proceeds remain in the account. The rule of this subsection is a compromise between the rights of secured creditors and the rights of the trustee. The drafters assumed that it was unfair to burden the parties with tracing from the day of bankruptcy back to the deluge. They tried to fashion a compromise similar to that fashioned by the drafters of the Bankruptcy Code in the preference section, which contains a cutoff date (90 days) analogous to the ten-day cutoff in subsection (4) and contains presumptions similar to the presumptions in subsection (4). In the cruel, hard world of insolvency law, compromises fashioned by drafters of federal legislation work; compromises fashioned by drafters of state legislation sometimes do not.

d. Under the subsection, the secured party may recover proceeds, in fact may recover the whole account, even though under tracing rules the secured party would obtain nothing. This result may well offend the Bankruptcy Code, a federal statute that cannot be amended by the states. At least one court, in a confusing opinion, has found the subsection to violate the preference section. Arguably, the subsection also runs afoul the Bankruptcy Code's prohibition against statutory liens. *See* Bankruptcy Code §545(1)(A).

Section 29. Part 5: Default

197.   a. Yes, Debtor is in violation of the note and the security agreement. The secured party may enforce its rights. *See* §9-503.
b. No. The secured party defeats the rights of the lien creditor under §9-201 and 9-301(1)(b).
c. It does not matter that Debtor is current on the note. If she has breached a provision in the security agreement by permitting a lien creditor to assert an interest in the collateral, the secured party may proceed against the collateral. To let a creditor attach one's property is normally the prelude to bad things, and the bank's conduct is quite reasonable.

198.   a. This conduct is probably not improper. The issue is whether Bank has breached the peace. The cases are generally tough on the bank in this setting, but this conduct is probably not a breach of the peace.
b. This is probably not a breach of the peace. If the employee told Banker not to come into the premises, there might well be a breach.
c. This conduct is not permissible. It is a breach of the peace even if the security agreement gave Bank the right to go on the premises. The agreement did not give Bank the right to break the lock.

    d. Some courts object to this kind of repossession, but a majority seem to indicate that it is alright absent some additional fact, such as the debtor's brandishing a shotgun. (You were not aware that banking was such an exciting profession.)

    e. The consensus seems to have emerged that the bank should not act in the presence of the debtor if the debtor in any way objects to the repossession. The bank that does not train its repo agents to avoid foul language is asking for trouble.

199.   a. The fact that in retrospect we know the price was below the market price does not mean that the bank misbehaved. If the bank can show that it sought purchasers through advertisements and that it made inquiries of used equipment dealers as to the going price for the collateral, the bank has probably satisfied the requirements of §9-504(3). A few courts take the approach that a lower-than-market price indicates that the bank is liable for losses under §9-507(1).

    b. It is proper to use a dealer if that conduct will fetch (or arguably will fetch) the best price. The deduction for the commission is expressly envisioned by the language of §9-504(1)(a).

    c. The timing of the sale is relevant in determining whether the bank acted in a commercially reasonable fashion. The fact that an earlier sale would have yielded a better price is not evidence per se that the bank failed to act properly, but it is an indication that it did so. In all of these settings, the bank must guard against appearances of commercial unreasonableness and must be able to prove the actions that it took. Experienced bankers, then, log all telephone calls in connection with the preparation for the sale, keep copies of advertisements and correspondence in connection with the sale, and make a record of face-to-face conversations. These practices are tedious, but in subsequent litigation such records are valuable.

    d. The secured party may purchase the collateral at a public or a private sale; but if it purchases at a private sale, it must show that it paid a recognized market price. *See* §9-504(3) (last sentence).

200. Yes. *See* §9-504(4).

201.   a. The cases are split. Some say that the secured party's failure to comply with §9-504(3) bars it from a deficiency judgment. Others say that the failure merely shifts to the secured party the burden of proving that the secured party got the best price.

    b. The debtor's pre-default waiver is ineffective. *See* §§9-501(3)(b), 9-504(3).

202.   a. Yes. The debtor is in default, and the secured party may proceed. Default in an interest payment can be quite innocent, but it can also indicate that the debtor is in trouble. The acceleration clause will probably be enforced, though there was some indication during the heyday of lender liability that courts would examine the secured party's conduct for evidence of bad faith. Generally, however, the secured party can proceed against the collateral. Note that a bank cannot accelerate on the grounds that it deems itself insecure unless it acts in the good-faith belief that it is insecure. *See* §1-208. The right to accelerate the full debt in the event of default on an installment such as an interest payment, however, is generally not subject to good-faith inquiry.

b. Yes. The debtor is seeking, in effect, to redeem the collateral, a right that the Code and debtor-creditor law always gives to a debtor. *See* §9-506. Note that the debtor must also pay the secured party's reasonable expenses of repossessing the collateral and its expenses in connection with preparing for the sale.

PART TWO

PAYMENT SYSTEMS

Payment Systems: Problems

1. NEGOTIABLE INSTRUMENTS

Section 30. *The Effect of a Signature on a Negotiable Instrument: The "Contract" Liability Concept*

There are three categories of liability in negotiable instruments law: (1) contract, (2) warranty, and (3) tort (usually conversion). "Contract" liability is not a concept of contract law (offer, acceptance, consideration, mutual manifestation of assent, etc.) but of the law merchant. In the law merchant, a merchant's signature on a "specialty," which is an obligation enforceable by itself by mere production of the paper bearing the signature, was a signal event. The merchant's signature entailed liability without any other evidence of a promise or consideration. That concept — liability by virtue of a signature alone — survives in negotiable instruments law under the confusing rubric of "contract" liability.

The following problems deal with that kind of contract liability. The Code fashions these rules presupposing that a person's signature on an instrument signals a legal obligation to pay money. There is a converse rule at work here — the rule that no person has such "contract" liability unless that person signs the instrument.

In the problems that follow, the UCC sections cited without brackets are those of revised Articles 3 and 4. The sections appearing within brackets are from the old versions of the same articles.

Problems

203. Thief stole a blank check from Drawer's checkbook. Thief then forged Drawer's signature on a check that Thief drew for the amount of $1,000.

Thief made the check payable to Seller, who took it from Thief, thinking Thief was Drawer, in payment for goods sold to Thief. When Seller presented the check at the counters of First Bank, the drawee bank, First dishonored it.

    a. Does Drawer have contract liability on the check? §3-401(a) [§3-401].

    b. Did Drawer "sign" the check? Does his "signature" appear on it? Why is the imprinted name at the top of the check (Dave Drawer, 123 Main Street, Chicago, Illinois) not a signature? §§1-201(39), 3-401(b).

    c. Is Thief liable on the instrument? What is his engagement? §3-403(a) [§3-404(1)].

    d. Fashion a set of facts that occurs after Thief forges the instrument that would render Drawer liable. §3-403(a) [§3-404(2)].

204. Assume that Drawer prepared the check in Problem 203, that is, that the drawer's signature on the check is genuine and that First Bank, the drawee bank, dishonored when Seller presented the check for payment.

    a. Does Seller have a cause of action against the drawee bank on the instrument? §§3-401(a), 3-408 [§§3-401(1), 3-409].

    b. Can Seller use principles of law outside the Code to fashion an argument to hold the drawee? Would third-party beneficiary theory help Seller? Some tort theory? Has the drawee bank certified this check? §3-409(d) [§3-411].

    c. In answering Question b, does it matter to you whether, in fact, Drawer had sufficient funds in his account at First Bank to cover the check?

Section 31.   *The Concepts of Transfer and Negotiation*

In negotiable instruments law, there is a measure of literalness that modern lawyers find a bit tedious. Negotiable instruments, as we know them, were fashioned by merchants and lawyers in the seventeenth and eighteenth centuries. To them, the literal rules, some of which survive today, were evidence of regularity. If a party failed to observe the rules, they concluded that something was wrong; and if something was irregular or wrong, the negotiable instruments regime did not work. The sections cited in the following problems exemplify some of the literal rules that arose out of those old practices and that still have application in negotiable instruments law.

The more important rules these problems illustrate are the rules of contract liability: the contract liability of the maker of a note, that of the drawer (of a check or a draft), that of the acceptor (a certifying bank if the instrument accepted is a check), and that of the indorser whose signature can appear on any negotiable instrument.

Problems

205. *§§3-413, 3-414, 3-415 [§§3-413, 3-414]*. Assume that Drawer drew the check and that Seller indorsed the reverse side of it by signing her name and that she then handed it to *X*.
    a. Is the indorsement special or in blank? §3-205 [§3-204].
    b. Does the nature of the indorsement as special or in blank matter in determining whether *X* is a holder? §3-205(a) and (b) [§3-202(1)].
    c. Before Seller indorsed, was the check order paper or bearer paper? What kind of paper is it after the indorsement? §3-109 [§§3-110, 3-111].
    d. Assume that *X* is a holder. What parties are liable to him as a holder? If the drawee bank dishonors, may *X* enforce the instrument against Seller? Against Drawer?
    e. If Thief forged Drawer's signature, would *X* have a claim against Seller in the event the bank dishonored? Against Drawer? Against Thief?

206. Assume in the preceding problem that Crook stole the check from Seller after Seller indorsed and that Crook then indorsed and delivered to *X*. *X* then delivered the check for value to *Y*, who presented to the drawee bank, which dishonored.
    a. Is *Y* a holder?
    b. Does *Y* have a cause of action against *X*? (If *X* indorsed specially?) Against Seller? Against Crook? Against Drawer?
    c. If *Y* recovers from *X*, can *X* enforce the instrument against anyone? Would *X* be an indorser who paid the instrument under §3-415? [A subsequent indorser who took the instrument up under §3-414(1)?]

207. *§§1-201(20), 3-403(a) [§3-404(1)]*. Assume in Problem 205 that Seller indorsed the check by signing the reverse side under the following words: "Pay *X*," and that Thief stole the check, forged *X*'s indorsement, and delivered to *Y*. With these modified facts, answer question 206.

208. Thief stole Drawer's checkbook, forged Drawer's name as drawer, and made the check payable to Seller. Seller indorsed the check and deposited it at Second Bank, which sent it on to First Bank, the drawee bank. First Bank dishonored and returned the check to Second.
    a. Does Second have a cause of action against Drawer on the check? Against Thief? Against First? Against Seller?
    b. Who should bear the loss under these facts? Would §1-103 prevent use of supplemental principles of law to hold Thief liable to Seller?

209. Ace Corp. has a check-writing machine that imprints Ace's signature on checks payable to Ace's employees and suppliers. *C*, a clerk, used the machine without authorization to write a check to herself for $1,000. *C* indorsed the check to Second Bank, which gave value to *C* and sent the check through to First Bank, the drawee bank, which dishonored.

    a.   Does Second have a cause of action against *C*? Against Ace?

    b.   Would it matter to you that *C* found the check-writing machine in the storeroom next to the company's supply of coffee cups? §3-406.

    c.   How do you suppose corporations protect themselves from unauthorized use of a check-writing machine?

    d.   If the law imposes on the drawee bank any losses Ace incurs when First honors a check over a signature of the drawer that is unauthorized, how would the drawee bank protect itself?

210.   *§3-402 [§3-403(2)].*   Assume that Ace Corp.'s president, Joe Ace, signs four company checks in the following fashion: (1) Joe Ace; (2) Joe Ace, agent; (3) Ace Corp., Joe Ace; and (4) Ace Corp., by Joe Ace, President. If the drawee bank dishonors one of the checks, will a holder in due course have a cause of action against Joe? Would your answer be different if the instrument were a promissory note and the claimant were the holder of the note?

Section 32.   *Conditions of Contract Liability*

The following problems deal with the conditions of contract liability. Those conditions arise rather infrequently, and, in the case of a drawer, it does not make much difference whether the holder trying to enforce the instrument has satisfied them. If you work through the problems, you will be familiar with the few conditions that matter much. Note that Problem 211B for the old version of Article 3 has two scenarios, one with the dates not in brackets, one with the dates in brackets. You will see that the delays under the second set of dates can make a difference for indorser liability and, in the rarest of cases, for drawer liability. New Article 3 has simplified things a bit by making 30 days the time for both drawers and indorsers.

Problems

211A.   *§§3-414(f), 3-415(e), 3-503(c); this problem is for new Article 3.*   On May 1, Drawer drew a check in favor of *S*, who took it and indorsed it on that day to *X*, who indorsed it and deposited it for collection on June 15. The drawee bank dishonored on June 20 and gave notice to *X* on that day. *X* gave notice to Drawer on July 30. *X* also did not give notice to *S* until July 30. (Each of the following questions is asking (1) whether the initiation of the collection of the check through the banking system is timely, (2) whether the notice of dishonor is timely, and (3) whether if one or the other, or both, are late, it makes any difference. In the case of the drawer, it does not in this problem because the drawer's bank is not insolvent.)

    a.   Can *X* recover from any of the parties?

    b.   Can *S* recover from any of the parties?

211B. *[§§3-503(2), 3-508(2)]; this problem is for the old version of Article 3.* On May 1, Drawer drew a check payable to Seller, who indorsed to X on May 2 [May 10], who indorsed to Y on May 3 [May 15], who indorsed to Z on May 4 [May 20]. On May 5 [May 25], Z presented the check to the drawee bank, which dishonored.

    a.   Under the early set of dates, can Z collect from Y? From X? From Seller? From Drawer? [§3-502(1).]

    b.   Would your answers be any different if the dates in brackets were the dates on which the transactions occurred? (Assume that Z received notice of dishonor on May 31 and gave notice of dishonor to indorsers on June 2 and notice to Drawer on June 30.)

    c.   Assume that Z collected in Problem a above from Y. Against whom does Y have a claim, if anyone? [Review §§3-413(2), 3-414(1).]

    d.   If in Problem a above Z collected from Seller, against whom does Seller have a claim, if anyone?

Section 33. *Negotiable Instruments and the Underlying Transaction*

The law of payments systems balances two commercial interests when it concerns itself with the underlying transaction. First is the idea that a negotiable instrument travels without baggage, that is, the idea that third parties may deal with the instrument and not worry about the equities of the underlying transaction. The value reflected in this feature of negotiable instruments law is peculiarly commercial. The second concern is one of seeing to it that there not be unjust enrichment in the application of rules fashioned to achieve the first objective.

These problems also continue the investigation of the "contract" liability concept.

Problems

212. *§3-310(b)(1) [§3-802].* Drawer gave a check to Seller, Seller indorsed to X, who indorsed to Y. Y deposited the check at Second Bank, and Second then presented the check through the check collection system to First. If First pays the check,

    a.   Was there ever a party liable on it unconditionally, that is, liable without dishonor by First?

    b.   What happens to the conditional liability of Drawer on the check? Of Seller? Of X?

    c.   What happens to the liability of Drawer in the contract under which Seller sold goods to Drawer? Can Seller maintain a cause of action against Drawer for payment on the sales contract?

    d.   What do we call a check that bears the signature of the drawee? §3-409(d) [§3-411]. What is the contract of the certifying bank? §3-413(b) [§3-413(1)].

213. *§3-309 [§3-804].* Drawer, a buyer, gave a check to Seller, and Seller lost it.

    a. May Seller sue Drawer on the underlying sales contract if Drawer refuses to give Seller a replacement check? §3-310(b)(1) [§3-802]. Why might Drawer be reluctant to give Seller a replacement check?

    b. Can Seller sue Drawer on the lost check? §3-309 [§3-804]. Is Drawer liable on the check absent dishonor? Has there been dishonor? Does §3-309 [§3-804] do away with the necessity for presentment and dishonor?

Section 34.   *Holders in Due Course and Their Rights*

There is a grand bonus in store for the party that takes a negotiable instrument in entirely regular fashion: the bonus of having the right to seek payment on the instrument without regard to the equities of the underlying transaction. But that bonus generally benefits only the party that takes a negotiable instrument in "due course." Note that there are two stages to all of this. First is the benefit that accrues to a person holding a negotiable instrument to prove the debt by mere introduction of the instrument into evidence. The second stage becomes important when the obligor on the instrument claims that there are defenses in the underlying transaction. At that point the "due course" issue becomes paramount.

    Finally, holders in due course cut off claims, that is, they hold free of any prior owner's claim in conversion, replevin, or the like. Problem 218(d) and the problems under Section 37, Conversion, deal with that feature of holder in due course protection.

Problems

214. Maker gave a promissory note dated September 1, 1992, in the face amount of $100,000 "payable one year from date to Seller" to cover sums due for the sale by Seller to Maker of earth moving equipment. Maker claims that the equipment is defective and has attempted to revoke his acceptance of the equipment under the Code.

    a. If Seller proves that Maker executed the note, has he established a prima facie case under §3-308 [§3-307]?

    b. Why cannot Seller negotiate this note? [§3-104(a)(1).]

215. *§§3-302(a), 3-305(b) [§§3-302(1), 3-305].* Maker gave National Sales Corp. a negotiable promissory note dated September 1, 1992, in the face amount of $100,000, payable to the order of National Sales Corp. 120 days after date in connection with the sale of goods by National to Maker. National is financing its receivables with First Bank. National's president signed the back of the note with the company's signature. She then delivered the note to First. First is now attempting to collect the note from Maker, who claims that National sold shabby goods and that he has a defense to National's claim.

Will First take subject to the defense if First
  a. credited National's account for $99,500 when it took the note? §§3-302(a)(2)(i), 3-303 (a) [§§3-302(1)(a), 3-303(a)].
  b. took the note as security for an antecedent debt that National owed First or in payment of a debt due from National to First? §§3-302(e), 3-303(a)(3), 4-210, 4-211 [§§3-303(b), 4-208, 4-209].
  c. credited National's account in the amount of $99,500 with the understanding that National could withdraw the funds (if in fact National did not withdraw them)? §§4-210(a)(1), 4-211 [§§4-208(1)(b), 4-209].
  d. credited National's account without any right of National to withdraw but permitted National to withdraw $500 of the funds? §4-210(a)(2) [§4-208(1)(b)].

216. Assume in the preceding problem that the buyer of the goods gave National a check for $100,000. National deposited the check in its account at Second Bank. Answer Questions a through d of Problem 215 under these modified facts. Does the fact that the instrument is a check alter your answers?

217. Would your answers to the foregoing questions be different if Maker (whose name should now be "Drawer" because we are dealing not with a note but a check), at National's request, made the check payable to the order of First Bank? Did First Bank "deal" with Maker? [§3-305(2).]

218. *§3-306 (last sentence) [§3-305(1)].* Buyer gave Seller a check payable to the order of Seller in the amount of $1,000. Seller indorsed the check by signing it on the reverse side "Sally Seller." Thief then stole the check from Seller and delivered it to X, who took for value and without any notice that the check was stolen. X deposited the check at Second Bank, which also gave value. Second put the check through the collection chain, and First paid it.
  a. May Seller recover from Buyer on the underlying contract? §§3-309, 3-310 [§§3-802, 3-804].
  b. May Seller recover from Buyer under the stolen instrument section? §3-309 [§3-804].
  c. May Seller recover in conversion against Thief if she can find him? [§1-103].
  d. May Seller recover from Second in conversion? §3-306 (last sentence) [§3-305(1)]. In replevin? On some other common law claim? §1-103.

219. *[§3-302(1) (eighth word)].* Assume in the preceding question that Seller indorsed the check "Pay to the order of Y, Sally Seller," that Thief stole the check, forged Y's indorsement, and delivered the check to X. Now answer Questions a through d in the preceding question.

220. Buyer gave Seller a check in the amount of $1,000 as payment for the sale of a used automobile. Seller indorsed the check and deposited it at Second Bank, which sent it through the check collection system to First Bank. Before the check arrived at First, Buyer, angry that the car he bought did not function properly, stopped payment on the check. First dishonored and returned the check to Second.

a. May Second recover on the check from Buyer under these facts? §3-414(b) [§3-413(2)].

b. May Second recover from Buyer if Second demonstrates that Second credited Seller's account and that Seller withdrew all of the check's proceeds? Half of the proceeds? §3-308 [§3-307].

c. Would your answer to b differ if
    i.   Buyer claimed that Seller fraudulently induced Buyer to pay for the car?
    ii. Seller withdrew none of the check's proceeds, but Second Bank had a security interest in Seller's inventory of used cars? §4-210 [§4-209].

d. Would your answer to b differ
    i.   if Buyer raised as his defense against Second the allegation that Buyer, being frail and of poor eyesight, thought he was signing a birthday card and not a check when he in fact executed the check? §3-305(a)(1) [§3-305(2)(c)].
    ii. if Buyer raised as his defense the argument that he was only 16 at the time of the transaction with Seller? §3-305(a)(1) [§3-305(2)(a)].

221. Seller, a pipe and pipe fittings distributor, sold pipe to Buyer and asked Buyer to make his check payable to Manufacturer, who had supplied fittings to Seller and remains unpaid.

a. If the pipe that Seller sold to Buyer is defective and therefore worthless, may Buyer successfully defend against Manufacturer's claim against Buyer when First dishonors the check? §§3-302, comment 4, 3-305(b) [§§3-302(2), 3-305(2)].

b. Would your answer be any different if Manufacturer had taken the check not in payment for fittings delivered but as a down payment for fittings that are to be delivered next month? §3-303(a)(1) [§3-303(a)].

222. Seller defrauded Buyer by delivering drums loaded with water instead of the linseed oil that he had agreed to sell Buyer. Before learning of the fraud, Buyer had given Seller a $100,000 check as a down payment on the oil. Buyer has stopped payment on the check and has gone to the newspapers with the story of the swindle. Seller indorsed the check for value to X before X heard the news. Thereafter, X indorsed and delivered the check to Y, who knew the story. Y then indorsed the check back to Seller. Could Buyer raise the fraud defense if he had been sued on the instrument by

a. X? §3-305(b) [§3-305(2)].

b. Y? Is Y a holder in due course? §3-302(a)(2) [§3-302(1)(c)]. Does Y have the rights of a holder in due course? §3-203(b) [§3-201(1)].

c. Seller? Does Seller come within X's or Y's umbrella? §3-203(b) (second clause) [§3-201(1) (second clause)].

223. *§3-407 [§3-407].*   Assume in the preceding question that the goods conform, that Buyer gave Seller a negotiable promissory note in the face amount of $10,000, but that Seller fraudulently raised the note to $100,000.

      a.   May *X* enforce the instrument? If so, for what amount? §3-407(c)
          [§3-407(3)].
      b.   May *Y* enforce the instrument? If so, for what amount?
      c.   May Seller enforce the instrument? §3-407(b) [§3-407(2)(a)].

Section 35.   *The Bank-Customer Relationship*

The following eleven problems deal with the questions that arise between the bank and its customer. This bank is the drawee-payor bank, and the customer is the drawer of the check. The question is one of allocating liability when the bank honors a check that it should not honor and when it dishonors a check that it should honor. The bank-customer deposit agreement entails some of the rules covering this relationship, but some of them come from cases decided long ago and are only alluded to in the Code sections.

Banks have lobbied hard in this area and have garnered a few victories. One of them is in the subrogation rules. Subrogation, you should bear in mind, is equity's response to unjust enrichment. The banks' arguments for subrogation under §4-407 are moderately complicated; but if you keep the unjust enrichment feature of subrogation in mind, you should be able to figure everything out.

Problems

224.   *§4-401(1).*   Indicate, giving your reasons, which of the following circumstances would render a check not properly payable:
      a.   Drawer's signature is forged.
      b.   Payee's indorsement is forged.
      c.   Holder of bearer instrument forges indorsement.
      d.   Payee alters sum payable from $100 to $1,000. §§3-407(c), 4-401(d)(1) [§§3-407(3), 4-401(2)(a)].
      e.   On May 2, Payor Bank receives a check the drawer issued on May 1 but post-dated to May 10. §4-401(c).
      f.   Payor Bank negligently fails to dishonor a check drawn on insufficient funds by its midnight deadline, §4-104(10) [§4-104(h)], thereby becomes liable for the amount of the item under §4-302(a)(1) [§4-203(a)] and debits Drawer's account.
      g.   Unbeknownst to drawee-payor bank, thief presents stolen check bearing payee's authorized indorsement in blank.
      h.   Payor bank pays check on which payee's endorsement is missing. Should the payor bank be liable to the drawer if it pays this item?

225.   If a drawee-payor bank pays a check and thereby creates an overdraft, does it matter for purposes of charging the drawer's account that

a. the payor failed to observe reasonable banking practices?
b. the payor violated its overdraft agreement with the drawer customer by, for example, creating an overdraft greater in amount than the overdraft agreement allowed? §4-401(a) and (b) [§4-401(1)].

226. *§4-402.*   May a customer whose check is wrongfully dishonored recover damages for
a. mental anguish?
b. ulcers?
c. the equity customer enjoyed in an automobile repossessed by the creditor to whom the customer wrote the overdraft?
d. lost business (that is, lost profits)?
e. loss of bargain on real estate transaction that fell through when down payment check bounced?
f. punitive damages?

227. [The first three parts of this question deal with issues that arose under the old version of §4-402.] In cases of dishonor, what damages are recoverable by the customer in the event of
a. payor bank bad faith?
b. dishonor as a consequence of a mistake of law?
c. dishonor as a consequence of a mistake of fact?
d. in a suit by a corporation's president and sole shareholder, dishonor of corporate check?

228. *§4-103.*   Can the terms of the customer-bank deposit agreement alter the results in the preceding question?

229. Is there any inconsistency in the fact that §4-103 does not permit a bank to disclaim liability for its want of due care while §4-401 appears to apply without regard to due care?

230. *§4-403.*   In which of the following cases may a depositor recover damages from the payor bank?
a. The customer proves only that the bank paid the customer's check after receiving timely notice to stop payment.
b. The customer proves only that the bank paid the check over a stop order when the payee had delivered defective merchandise to the customer.

231. *§4-407(3) [§4-407(c)].*   In case b of the preceding question, what should the bank do after it recredits its customer's account?

232. *§4-407(1) [§4-407(a)].*   Would your answer to Problem 230b differ if the evidence showed that the payee had deposited the check at Second Bank and had withdrawn the funds?

233. *§4-407(2) [§4-407(b)].*   In which of the cases described in the three preceding questions might the payor bank subrogate itself to the rights of the payee?

234. *§1-103.*   If the payor bank pays over its customer's stop payment order, may the bank recover from the payee in
a. restitution?
b. subrogation?

Section 36.   *Warranties*

In addition to "contract" liability, which makers, drawers, acceptors, and indorsers undertake when they sign a negotiable instrument, indorsers and transferors of a negotiable instrument also make warranties to certain parties that take or pay the instrument. It is the theory of warranties in negotiable instruments law that the party taking or paying an instrument (1) relies on certain unspoken representations of the person delivering the instrument or (2) relies on the signatures of prior parties. Most scholars are pretty much of the view that there is little, if any, reliance these days. Checks, the instruments that give rise to warranty disputes, usually find their way quite quickly into the banking system, where there is little reliance (though the banks argue to the contrary).

There are two sets of warranty sections, one in Article 3 and one in Article 4. See §§3-416, 3-417 [§3-417], 4-207, 4-208 [§4-207]. For our purposes and for most warranty issues that arise, the warranties are the same in both articles. The answers to the following problems cite the Article 4 sections. In the new version of Articles 3 and 4, the relevant comments are in Article 3. There will be references, then, in the answers and sometimes in the problems to comments in the Article 3 sections. As in all problems and answers, the citations to the old version of Articles 3 and 4 appear in brackets.

Problems

In the following problems, assume, unless otherwise indicated, that Buyer (B) wrote a check to Seller (S), that S indorsed and deposited it at Second Bank, and that Second presented it through the bank collection system to First Bank, the payor bank.

235. If *T*, a thief, stole the check from *S*, forged *S*'s indorsement and deposited the check at Second, and if First Bank, the payor bank, honored the check, can there be any successful claim for breach of a transfer warranty? §4-207 [§4-207(2)]. If First dishonored, can there ever be any successful claim for breach of a presentment warranty? §4-208 [§4-207(1)].

236. A thief, *F*, stole *B*'s checkbook, forged *B*'s signature, and used the check to pay *S* for goods that *S* delivered under a contract of sale.
    a.   If First honors, does First have a cause of action against *S* for breach of section §4-207(a)(2) or §4-208(a)(1)? [§4-207(2)(b) or §4-207(1)(a)?] May First debit *B*'s account? §4-401.
    b.   Do "transfer" warranties run to the payor bank?
    c.   If First dishonors the check, may Second make a successful breach of warranty claim against *S*? Does Second benefit from "transfer" warranties? If *S* is liable to Second for breach of warranty, how may *S* recoup her loss? May she recover from *B*? [§4-104]. May she recover from *F*? On what theory? [§§3-404, 3-413(2)].

237. *B* wrote a check payable to the order of *S*, *T-2* stole it, and forged *S*'s indorsement.

a. If First honors the check, has Second breached any transfer warranty? Does Second make transfer warranties? Does it make them to First? §4-207(a) [§4-207(2)].

b. If First honors the check, has Second breached any presentment warranty? Has Second breached §4-208(a)(1) [§4-207(1)(a)]? Is Second authorized to obtain payment? [Does Second have good title?]

c. Would your answer to Problem b above be any different if before the theft, S had indorsed the check by signing her name to it? Would Second breach a warranty of authority [good title] in these circumstances? Would Second be a holder? Would your answer be any different if T-1 had stolen the check from the mails after B mailed it? In that case, would T-1 be able to negotiate the check without forging S's indorsement? Why not? §§1-201(20), 3-201(a) [§3-202(1)].

238. B drew a check payable to S for $100 and delivered it to S. S raised the check to $1,000, deposited it at Second, and departed with the proceeds.

a. If First pays the check according to its altered tenor, may First debit B's account? By how much? §4-401(d) [§4-401(2)]. May First maintain a breach of warranty action against Second? §4-208(a)(2) [§4-207(1)(c)]. If so, what would First's damages be? §4-208(b).

b. If First discovers the alteration and dishonors the check, may Second recover from B under §3-414(b) [§3-413(2)] or §3-407(c) [§3-407(3)]? If so, what would Second's recovery be? May Second make a successful claim against S? On what theory? Breach of warranty? §4-207(a)(3) [§4-207(2)(c)].

c. If S pays Second under §4-207(2)(c) in the preceding Question b, may S enforce the instrument against B for the original amount of the check? §3-407(b) [§3-407(2)(a)].

Section 37.   Conversion

The third category of liability in negotiable instruments law is tort. When a thief steals a check, the rightful owner has a cause of action lying in tort against the thief. Conversion, the tort most commonly used in commercial transactions, gives the rightful owner a cause of action even against parties acting innocently. It is conversion at common law to intermeddle with the property of another.

Problems

239. §§1-103, 3-206(c), 3-420 [§3-419(1)].   Which of the following acts constitutes conversion?

a. T-2 steals the check from S, the payee.

b. T-1 steals the check from B, the drawer.

c. X maliciously grabs the check from S and tears it to shreds.

d. X negligently shreds S's check in the shredding machine.

e. First honors the check after *T-2* steals it from *S* and forges *S*'s indorsement. §3-420(a) [§3-419(1)(c)].

f. Second cashes the check for *T-2* after *T-2* steals it from *S* and forges *S*'s indorsement. §3-420(a) [§3-419(3)].

g. Second cashes the check for *T-2* after *T-2* steals it from *S*, who has indorsed the check in blank. Would the answer differ if Second's teller required *T-2* to indorse?

240. *B*, the drawer, delivered a check for $1,000 to *S* in payment of services rendered. *T-2* stole the check, forged *S*'s indorsement, and deposited the check at Second Bank. Later the same day, *T-2* withdrew the $1,000 from the account.

a. If First, the payor bank, honors the check, may it debit *B*'s account? [§4-401].

b. If First honors the check, may *S* maintain an action against First in conversion? §3-420(a)(second sentence) [§3-419(1)(c)].

241. By way of further review of conversion, in each of the following cases, indicate whether the check has been converted, name the converter, and identify the person that has the cause of action and the person that is liable in conversion.

a. *T-2* stole the check from *S*, the payee.

b. *T-1* stole the check from *B*, the drawer.

c. Second "cashed" the check for *T-2* after *T-2* forged *S*'s signature. [Does it matter in most jurisdictions under the old version of Article 3 whether Second has any proceeds remaining? Whether Second observed reasonable banking practices? Whether Second "cashed" the check instead of taking it for deposit and then giving *T-2* credit? §3-419(3) (old version).]

d. First paid the check after *T-2* stole it from *S* and forged *S*'s indorsement.

242. *F* stole *B*'s checkbook and wrote a check payable to *S* for services *S* rendered to *F*. *F* forged *B*'s signature on the check and mailed it to *S*. *T-2*, a dishonest employee of *S*, stole the check, forged *S*'s indorsement, and deposited it at Second. Second sent the check through the check collection system, and First paid it. *T-2* then withdrew the funds from Second. Thereafter, *B* learned of the forgery.

a. From whom may *B* recover?

b. From whom may *S* recover?

c. If First suffers a loss by being forced to recredit *B*'s account, may First recover in breach of warranty from Second? Did Second breach a presentment warranty? Is the policy of Price v. Neal strong enough to overcome the presentment warranty of §4-208(a)(1) [§4-207(1)(a)]? Note that Second does not warrant to First that the signature of the drawer is authorized. *Compare* §4-207(a)(2) [§4-207(2)(b)] *with* §4-208(a)(3) [§4-207(1)(b)].

243. *B* issued a check to *S* payable to the order of *S*, and *S* indorsed it by signing her name on the back of the instrument. *T*, a thief, stole the check and gave it to *X* as payment for goods *X* sold to *T*. Assume that *X* took the check in good faith and without notice that anything was wrong.

   a.   Does *S* have a cause of action against *T*? §3-420.
   b.   Does *S* have a cause of action against *X*? §3-306 [§3-305(1)].
   c.   If *X* transfers the instrument to *Y* after *Y* learns of the theft by *T*, does *S* have a cause of action against *Y*? §§3-203(b), 3-302(c) [§§3-201(1), 3-304, comment 1.]
   d.   Would your answers to any of the preceding questions differ if (1) *S* had indorsed the check "pay *Z*," and (2) *T* had forged *Z*'s signature when *T* delivered the check to *X*?

Section 38.   *Estoppel*

After positing three categories of liability ("contract," warranty, and tort) negotiable instruments law finishes the job by denying or limiting the remedies of those three categories to parties whose conduct is commercially blameworthy. Estoppel, or "preclusion" as the Code calls it, is the instrument of this last adjustment to negotiable instrument law liability. As a matter of general law, estoppel, which is a creature of equity, is available to a party only if the party relied to its detriment. The Code and other areas of commercial law sometimes ignore the reliance and detriment features of estoppel. In those cases, the law often speaks of "preclusion" rather than estoppel. In some instances, *see* §§3-404(b), 3-405(b), the Code merely says that an unauthorized indorsement is effective, which is another way of saying that a party is estopped or precluded to say that the indorsement is unauthorized.

New Article 3 has attempted to rationalize the estoppel rules by dividing them among four sections. The first, §3-406, deals with the general rule that negligence that substantially contributes to a forgery or alteration will preclude the negligent party from asserting the forgery or alteration.

The second provision, §3-405, deals with an historic character, the faithless employee, who is charged with responsibility for handling checks and who fraudulently forges an indorsement, either of a check that is payable to the employer or a check drawn by the employer payable to another employee or a creditor.

The third provision, §3-404, deals with the imposter rule and with other faithless employees who write checks to fictitious parties (typically by padding the payroll or the payables) or who write a check for the employer to a real payee with the intent from the beginning to intercept the check before it is mailed and to forge the indorsement.

Finally, in a fourth provision, §4-406, the Code deals with the customer who is negligent in examining its checking account statement.

[Old Article 3 deals with most of the same questions but does so in three provisions, grouping rules for fictitious payees, faithless employees, and imposters in one provision, §3-405. Old Article 3 puts the general rule in §3-406 and the negligent bank customer rules in §4-406, as do new Article 3 and new Article 4.]

In new Article 3, the drafters have fashioned comparative negligence rules for the estoppel sections. [In old Article 3, the effect of contributory negligence varies from an absolute bar to use of the estoppel rule to no consequence at all.]

Problems

244. *§3-406(a) [§3-406].*   This problem deals with the general negligence provision.

B left his checkbook and a check writing machine in the supply room next to the styrofoam coffee cups. F, a truck driver delivering stationery supplies to B's office who was in need of a cup of java, found the checks and the machine and wrote a check payable to himself. F then indorsed the check and deposited it at Second Bank. Second sent the check through to First Bank, which paid it. F has withdrawn the funds.

    a. May First charge B's account?

    b. Would your answer differ if First was negligent in paying the check?

245. *§3-406 [§3-406].*   This is another general negligence problem.

B wrote a check to S in payment for goods that S delivered under a contract. B forgot the price of the goods, though he knew it was in the neighborhood of $100. He sent the check, which he had signed and dated, without any amount and told S to fill in the amount. B added to the check a legend at the bottom as follows: "Not good for more than $125." S, needing cash to pay his withholding taxes, inserted $1,000 as the amount on the check and deposited it at Second. Second's operations clerk did not notice the legend at the bottom of the check and encoded it for $1,000. Second sent the check through the system, and First paid it.

    a. May First debit B's account?

    b. Has Second breached a presentment warranty?

246. *§§3-405, 3-406 [§3-406].*

    a. B wrote a check to S, whose secretary, T-2, an employee with no "responsibility" or authority to deal with B's checks or financial affairs, forged S's indorsement and cashed the check at Second, telling Second that S needed petty cash at the office. T-2 had been engaging in this fraud for over two years and had cashed more than $3,000 in checks in this fashion. Does S have a cause of action in conversion against Second? Against First? Does it matter whether Second or First failed to observe reasonable banking practices? Would your answer to any of these questions differ if this were the first time T-2 had fraudulently indorsed one of S's checks?

    b. Would the answer differ if T-2 did have responsibility to handle checks? §3-405(a)(3) and (b).

247. *§§3-404, 3-405 [§3-405].*   F, the human resources manager of ABC Co., padded the payroll, that is, he gave the payroll clerk names and addresses of fictitious parties and instructed the clerk to draw checks for the fictitious employees. The clerk, unaware of the manager's fraud, drew the checks and put them in envelopes addressed to the fictitious parties at addresses supplied by F. Before the mail messenger took the checks out of the clerk's tray, F surreptitiously removed the checks, indorsed them in the names of the fictitious parties and deposited them at his account at Second. Second sent the checks through to First, which paid them. F has withdrawn the proceeds of the checks.

a. May First debit ABC's account? In the alternative, may it recover from Second for breach of the presentment warranty of authority [good title], §4-208(a)(1) [§4-207(1)(a)]? Is there any way for Second to avoid these warranty claims? §4-208(c).

b. If First had dishonored the checks and returned them to Second, could Second recover from ABC? Under these facts would Second be a person entitled to enforce the check [a holder]? Would it do ABC any good in this setting to stop payment on the checks? §3-405 [§3-405].

c. Has Second done anything negligent in crediting F's account with payroll checks made payable to third parties? §3-405, comment 4 (illustration of depositary bank conduct that would probably constitute lack of due care). If so, would Second's negligence result in a comparative negligence rule? [Under the old version of Article 3, would that negligence bar Second from enforcing the checks against ABC? §3-405.]

d. Would your answers to any of the foregoing questions differ if, rather than an innocent clerk, F himself had signed the checks on behalf of ABC?

e. Would your answers differ in Questions a through c if the checks has been made payable to real employees of ABC but as overtime paychecks, which had in fact been earned?

f. Would your answers to Questions a through c differ if the checks had been made payable to fictitious suppliers of ABC? To real suppliers, but for materials that had in fact not been supplied?

248. *§4-406 [§4-406].*   On May 1, A wrote a check in the amount of $1,000 to L, its landlord, who altered the check by raising it to $10,000. L deposited the check at Second, which gave L value ($5,000 in cash and $5,000 credit on a loan balance) and forwarded the check to First, which paid it in the normal course on May 5. On May 10, A received a bank statement, including the altered item, from First. Because A's bookkeeper was away on business, A did not reconcile the statement until June 15, when the bookkeeper discovered the alteration.

a. Did A satisfy the duty required under §4-406(c) [§4-406(1)]? If not, may First properly refuse to recredit A's account in the amount of $9,000?

b. §4-406(d)(2) [§4-406(2)(b)]. If on June 5, A wrote a second rent check to L in the face amount of $1,000 and if L again altered the item, deposited the check at Second, and obtained payment through the banking system on June 14, may First properly refuse to recredit A's account for the second $9,000? May First, instead of debiting A's account, recover from Second for breach of the presentment warranty under §4-208(a)(2) [§4-207(1)(c)]? §4-406(f) (last sentence) [§4-406(5)].

c. Would your answer to Question a or b differ if, instead of an altered item, the problem involved L's forgery of A's signature? Or if the problem involved the forgery of the payee's indorsement of a check A had written to the payee? §4-406(d) [§4-406(2)].

d. Would your answer to Question a differ if L maintained his account at First and did not withdraw the $9,000 until June 14?

e. Would your answers to any of the foregoing questions differ if you decided that First had not observed reasonable care in paying the check?

f. How long does a customer have to assert against the payor bank a claim for

i. paying a check with a forged drawer's signature or a material alteration? §4-406(f) [§4-406(4)].

ii. paying a check bearing a forged indorsement? §4-111 [§4-406(4)].

249. *§3-404(a) [§3-405(1)].* B, sitting on the terrace of a seaside resort, met I, an imposter, who passed himself off as Baron de Richi and claimed to own the yacht that was anchored just offshore. After ample drinks and insufficient investigation, B gave I a check payable to de Richi in the amount of $100,000, to be used as a down payment on the yacht. The next morning, when B arrived at the appointed place to close the deal with I, B learned of the fraud. In the meantime, I, whose name was Smith, indorsed the check by signing "Baron de Richi" to the reverse side and cashed it at First Bank, the drawee-payor.

a. Can First charge B's account? §3-404(a) [§3-405(1)(a)].

b. Would your answer to the prior question differ if First failed to observe reasonable banking practices? §3-404(d) [§3-405(1)(a)].

250. *§3-404(b) [§3-405].*

a. O, a dishonest officer of ABC Corp. who had no authority to write checks, drew checks in the amount of $1,000 payable as indicated below and signed them with fraudulent intent. After drawing the checks, O indorsed them in the name of the payee and deposited them in various accounts to his own name. Thereafter, First Bank, the payor bank, paid the checks. May First charge ABC's account?

i. A check payable to a fictitious payee. §3-404(b) [§3-405(1)(b)].

ii. A check payable to a real company to which ABC owed money but with the intent that the real payee never receive the check. §3-404(b) [§3-405(1)(b)]. Does it matter that O is not an employee of ABC? §3-404, comment 2, Case #4.

iii. A check payable to a real company to which ABC was not indebted.

b. In any of the foregoing examples, would the depositary bank breach a warranty to the payor bank if the payor paid the check?

Section 39. Final Payment

The doctrine of final payment is designed to determine at what point a drawee-payor bank loses the right to invoke restitutionary concepts or the law of mistake in order to recover a payment it has made to a payee or other person enforcing the instrument.

The problems in this section deal with checks because it is in the check setting, once again, that the issue has arisen. Generally, the rule is simple enough: The payor bank may recover the payment if the party holding the proceeds is unjustly enriched or if the payment was by mistake. If the potential defendant gave value in good faith for the check or changed its position in reliance on the payor's payment, the Code invokes the final payment doctrine and forbids restitution and the law of mistake.

Bear in mind, however, that the final payment doctrine does not displace Article 4 claims for breach of warranty or subrogation. If a depositary bank, for example, gives value for a check bearing a forged indorsement, it will be able, under the final payment doctrine, to resist the payor's claim for restitution; but it will not be able to resist the payor's claim that the depositary bank has breached the presentment warranty of authority [good title].

Problems

251. *§3-418 [§3-418].*   Seller entered into a contract to sell grain to Buyer for $100,000, payment against Seller's delivery of a negotiable bill of lading to Buyer. On May 1, Seller gave Buyer a negotiable bill covering the grain, and Buyer gave Seller a check for the contract amount. Later that same day, Buyer learned that the grain was moldy and insect-infested. Buyer stopped payment on the check. The next day, Seller took the check to Second Bank, which, acting in good faith, gave Seller value. Second presented the check to First, the drawee-payor bank, which inadvertently paid it over the stop payment order.
    a.   May First recover the payment from Second?
    b.   Would the answer be the same if Second had given Seller provisional credit for the check but had not permitted Seller to withdraw the funds?
    c.   Would your answer in Question a differ if *T*, a thief, stole the check from Seller, forged Seller's indorsement, and deposited the check at Second?
    d.   Would the answer to Question a differ if, instead of paying over a stop payment order, First had paid the check out of an account that had insufficient funds?
    e.   If the final payment doctrine prevents First from recovering from Second, may First pursue Seller under §4-407 [§4-407]?
    f.   What effect, if any, does the care or lack of care of First have on the analysis of the preceding questions?

252. Seller entered into a contract to sell grain to Buyer for $100,000, delivery against Buyer's payment. On May 1, Buyer gave Seller a check for the contract amount, and Seller took it directly to First Bank and asked for payment. First paid Seller the $100,000 that same day, and Seller released the grain to Buyer. Subsequently, First learned that Buyer's account was overdrawn, and First is now seeking to recover the funds from Seller on the grounds that First paid the check by mistake.
    a.   May First recover from Seller?
    b.   Would your answer differ if Buyer claimed that the grain was partly moldy and insect-infested?

     c. Would your answer to Question a differ if *T*, a thief, stole the check from Seller, forged Seller's signature, and obtained payment from First?

     d. Would your answers to the preceding questions differ if First's mistake had been one of paying over Buyer's unauthorized signature, that is, would the results differ if *T-2* obtained Buyer's checkbook and wrote the check to Seller signing with Buyer's name?

2. DOCUMENTS OF TITLE

Section 40. *The Documentary Draft Transaction*

The documentary draft transaction was a staple of domestic sales until the advent of reliable credit reporting and the open account sale that largely displaced the documentary sale in domestic commerce. The transaction survives in international trade, usually with a letter of credit as an adjunct.

    We study the documentary draft transaction in part because it remains an important component of international trade but more importantly because it is instructive. The draft, bill of lading, and letter of credit, all of which are still part of the payments system, developed out of the documentary draft transaction. That transaction illustrates their features.

Problems

253. In which of the following contracts does the buyer have the right to examine the merchandise prior to payment?

     a. In general. §§2-512, 2-513.

     b. FOB vessel or FAS. §§2-319(4), 2-513(3)(b).

     c. CIF or C&F. §2-320(4).

     d. COD. §2-513(3)(a).

254. Seller and Buyer agreed to a contract for the sale of diamonds. Seller drew on Buyer, that is, Seller drew an order payable to itself for the amount of the purchase price designating the buyer as the drawee. (Assume that the draft is payable at sight.) When Second Bank takes the draft for collection from Seller, does Second become a holder in due course if

     a. Second Bank takes the draft as collateral for a pre-existing debt incurred by Seller? In payment of a pre-existing note? Would it matter whether the bank makes bookkeeping entries, that is, would the bank become a holder as soon as the draft, properly indorsed, comes into the bank's possession, or does the bank need to take some additional action? §3-303(a)(3) [§3-303(b)].

     b. Second Bank issues a cashier's check to Seller that Seller has yet to cash or deposit? §3-303(4) [§3-303(c)].

255. *§3-305(b) [§3-305(2)].*   In the preceding question, assume that Buyer bargained with Seller for credit terms and that the parties used a time draft, that is, a draft drawn by Seller on Buyer that called for Buyer to accept it by signing its face and to pay it 60 days after the date of that acceptance. If Buyer accepted the time draft and if Second Bank is a holder in due course of that draft, may Buyer assert underlying contract defenses against Second Bank when Second presents the draft (now called an acceptance) for payment?

256. *§3-502(b)(2) [§3-507(1)(a)].*   If Buyer refused to accept the time draft, has Buyer dishonored the draft? §3-502(b)(3) [§3-507(1)(a)]. Does Buyer dishonor an accepted time draft by refusing to pay it when it comes due? How does a Buyer dishonor a *sight* or *demand* draft?

257. *§3-305(a) [§3-306].*   If Buyer accepts a time draft, and if Second Bank is *not* a holder in due course because it gave value after it learned of Buyer's underlying contract defenses or after it learned that Buyer dishonored by refusing to pay the draft when it came due, may Buyer assert against Second Bank

    a.   recoupment, that is, one-half of the contract price of the diamonds on the grounds that the diamonds are defective and worth only one-half of the contract price or the value as warranted? §3-305(a)(3) [§3-306(b)].

    b.   setoff, that is, sums due Buyer from Seller for returns in connection with this contract? §3-305(a)(3), comment 3 (fifth paragraph) [§3-306(b)]. With other contracts? §2-717.

    c.   payment, that is, Buyer's cash payment of the contract purchase price? §3-305(a)(2) [§3-306(b)].

    d.   the defense that Seller never delivered the merchandise or that Seller delivered nonconforming merchandise and the Buyer rejected it? §3-305(a)(2) [§3-306(c)].

Section 41.   *The Bill of Lading*

Traditionally, the bill of lading was the merchants' device for incorporating goods, while they were being transported, into a piece of paper that merchants could transfer from one to another and use as collateral with their bankers. Traditionally, the bill was always negotiable, and the negotiable bill (sometimes "order bill") stood for the goods. The rules that developed for the negotiable bill reflect the merchants' need to use possession of paper as a substitute for possession of the goods.

In U.S. domestic commerce and recently in international trade, the nonnegotiable bill (sometimes "way bill" or "straight bill") made its appearance. The rules for the nonnegotiable bill differ from those for the negotiable bill in that the nonnegotiable bill does not stand for the goods but is largely a contract of carriage.

Problems

258. *§7-403.* If a seller shipped goods under an order bill of lading, is the carrier liable to the seller if the carrier
    a. delivers the goods to the holder of the bill but fails to require the holder to surrender it?
    b. delivers to a non-holder, that is,
        i. a thief's transferee of a bill bearing a forged indorsement?
        ii. a party in possession to whom the indorsements do not run?

259. *§7-403.* If the seller ships under an order bill and the carrier delivers to X, a stranger and not the holder, does the holder of the bill have a cause of action against the carrier? Against the seller?

260. *§§4-103(e), 4-202(a)(1) [§§4-103(5), 4-202(1)(a)].* Seller delivered to its own bank, Second Bank, a negotiable bill of lading and a negotiable draft drawn on the buyer in the sum of $25,000 payable at sight. Second forwarded the documents to Third Bank, which delivered the documents to the buyer before the buyer paid Third. In such a case, could the seller recover damages from Third? What damages could the seller recover?

261. A seller desiring to protect against losses is considering the following courses of action. What are the advantages and disadvantages to the seller in each case?
    a. Using a nonnegotiable bill of lading and consigning the goods to seller itself.
    b. Using a nonnegotiable bill, consigning the goods to the buyer, and changing shipping instructions after shipment but before delivery to the buyer-consignee, if the buyer becomes insolvent or otherwise loses its credit standing.
    c. Causing a negotiable bill to issue to seller's order and refusing to indorse the bill.

Section 42. *The Warehouse Receipt*

The negotiable warehouse receipt, much like its negotiable bill of lading counterpart, stands for the goods. By virtue of that feature, the negotiable receipt can play the traditional document-of-title role in the documentary draft transaction, and sometimes does.

The chief value of the negotiable receipt is the ability of merchants to transfer interests (usually title and security interests) in the goods without disturbing their storage. The merchants simply deliver the negotiable receipt much as they delivered the negotiable bill.

The nonnegotiable receipt does not stand for the goods and is largely a contract for the storage of the goods.

Problems

262. If a warehouse receives goods and redelivers them to a stranger by mistake,
   a.   does §7-204 apply? (If not, when does it apply?)
   b.   does §7-404 apply?
   c.   does §7-403 apply?

263. *[§7-403].*   To whom should a grain elevator deliver grain if
   a.   the elevator issued a nonnegotiable receipt to X, the bailor?
   b.   the elevator took the grain from X but issued him no receipt?
   c.   in Questions a and b, X instructs the elevator to deliver the grain to Y?
   d.   in Questions a through c, if the elevator had issued a negotiable receipt to X?
   e.   the elevator issued a negotiable receipt to X, which X negotiated to Y, but X told the elevator not to deliver to Y?

264. Thief stole grain from O and bailed the grain with the elevator, which issued Thief a negotiable receipt. Later, Thief presented the receipt to the elevator, and the elevator redelivered the grain to Thief.
   a.   At common law, has the elevator converted O's grain?
   b.   Is the elevator liable to O in conversion under the Code? §7-404.

Section 43.   *More on the Documentary Draft Transaction*

Problems

265. In a documentary draft transaction, the seller shipped goods under a negotiable bill of lading and drew a time draft on the buyer for the purchase price of the goods. Seller then discounted the draft at Second Bank, which sent the draft and the bill through the banking system for presentation to Buyer in Buyer's city. If the buyer dishonored the draft (either by refusing to accept it when it was first presented or refusing to pay it when it came due), the seller must reimburse any advance it received from Second Bank in which of the following cases?
   a.   The seller drew the draft with Second as payee. §3-414(b) [§3-413(2)].
   b.   The seller drew the draft payable to itself and indorsed it without recourse to Second. §3-415(b) [§3-414(1)].
   c.   The seller drew the draft without recourse payable to itself and indorsed to Second. §3-414(e) [§3-413(2)].
   d.   The seller drew and indorsed the draft "without recourse." §§3-414(e), 3-315(b) [§§3-413(2), 3-414(1)].

266. Seller brought two drafts to Second Bank. The first was accompanied by a negotiable bill of lading; the second by a nonnegotiable bill of lading.

Why might Second take the first draft but not the second? Why might the drawee, the buyer, honor the first draft but not the second?

267. *§§7-403(4), 7-502(1)(b), 9-304(2).* Assume that in the preceding problem Second took both drafts for value, the buyer dishonored both of them, and the seller is insolvent. Will Second be able to get the goods covered by the bills?

268. *§2-705.* If the seller consigns a shipment of goods to a buyer and if the seller has grounds that would otherwise permit stoppage of goods in transit, may the seller cause the carrier to stop delivery after
    a. the buyer receives the nonnegotiable bill?
    b. the buyer indorses the nonnegotiable bill to a sub-buyer?
    c. the buyer pays the seller for the goods?
    d. the carrier acknowledges that it holds the goods for the buyer?

269. *§5-113.* If the seller consigns goods to the buyer under a nonnegotiable bill of lading and if the buyer loses the bill, what happens? Would your answer differ if the shipment were under a negotiable bill?

270. *§7-301, cf. §7-203 (similar rule for nonreceipt or misdescription in the case of a warehouse receipt).* Assuming that the document contains no disclaimer such as "shipper's load and count," if a bill of lading includes a misdescription of the goods shipped or if the cartons are empty so that the carrier never received any goods, which of the following parties may recover from the carrier?
    a. Second Bank that gives value to the seller and that takes a straight (nonnegotiable) bill designating the buyer as consignee.
    b. A buyer that takes a straight bill designating the buyer as consignee after the buyer gives value to the seller.
    c. A bank that takes an order (negotiable) bill for value.
    d. A buyer that takes an order bill for value.

Section 44. *Negotiation and Transfer of Documents of Title*

The distinction between negotiation and transfer in document of title law is sharp. Note that commercial parties might transfer a negotiable document. If the conveyance does not meet all of the requirements for due negotiation, it is a transfer even though the document may be in negotiable form.

The effect of transfer is pretty hollow: the transferee gets what the transferor had (the first rule of conveyancing law, *nemo dat*). The benefits of negotiation are considerable, however.

Problems

271. *§7-501(4).* Which of the following parties is a good-faith purchaser of a negotiable document of title?

a.   A bank that takes the bill from Seller if the bill is to the order of the seller and is indorsed by Seller, or if the bill is to the order of the bank.

b.   *B*, a chemical company, that purchases from a grain broker negotiable warehouse receipts indorsed in blank covering corn.

c.   A bank that lends to a grain broker and takes possession of negotiable warehouse receipts that the broker has indorsed. Would it matter that the broker failed to indorse the receipts? Would it matter that the bank knew that the broker held the grain subject to the security interest of another bank? Would it matter that the bank took the receipts in satisfaction of the broker's debt?

d.   A cereal manufacturer that takes negotiable warehouse receipts, indorsed in blank,
   i.   from a homeless person.
   ii. from a law teacher.

272.   *§7-102, comment 3.*   Chicago Buyer entered into a contract with St. Louis Seller for 100,000 bushels of soybeans. Seller has advised Buyer that the beans are in an elevator in Ainsworth, Iowa. Buyer would like to pay for the beans but wants assurance of delivery. Seller is unwilling to ship until Buyer pays. Devise a method whereby the parties can conclude their transaction using a document of title, not a bill of lading and not a warehouse receipt.

273.   Brown is a tenant farmer on the old Wilson farm that is now owned by Doc Wilson, who practices medicine in Cleveland. The farm is in Tennessee. Each year Brown harvests the crop and markets it. This year, as in the past, Brown stored the crop, hoping that the price would rise. The elevator with which he stored it gave him a negotiable receipt, which he later used to sell the crop to National Chemical Corp. Every year, except this one, Brown would send half of the sales proceeds to Wilson under their oral lease arrangement. This year, however, Brown found himself in a cash bind and used all of the proceeds for his own purposes. Tennessee law gives farm landlords a lien for crop rent on the crop and on the proceeds from the sale of the crop, and Wilson now sues National for conversion.

a.   What result? *See* Cleveland v. McNabb, 312 F. Supp. 155 (W.D. Tenn. 1970) (similar fact setting in which court ruled for farm landlord). Is the holding consistent with the policy or letter of §7-503(1)(a) and (b)?

b.   Would the result differ if this were the first year that Brown farmed Wilson's land? *Id.*

c.   What would the result be if Brown sold the crop in the ordinary course of business without using a receipt? See §9-307(1); Food Security Act of 1985, 7 U.S.C. §1631 (1985). Should the result differ depending on whether Brown uses a negotiable document of title? In Hext v. United States, 444 F.2d 804 (5th Cir. 1971), the court held that it does.

274.   Foreign Seller and domestic Buyer agreed that Seller would ship goods under a negotiable bill of lading, payment under a commercial letter of

credit. Seller shipped the goods and presented the bill of lading along with a draft drawn on the bank that issued the credit. The bank paid the draft at sight and took the bill. When the goods arrived, the bank took possession of them and stored them under negotiable warehouse receipts. In the meantime, Buyer had entered into a contract to resell the goods to a sub-buyer. The sub-buyer paid Buyer, which is now insolvent and which never reimbursed the bank for the advance the bank made when it paid the foreign seller under the letter of credit.

    a.   When the bank honored Seller's draft, what interest did the bank have in the goods? §§2-506, 7-502(1), 9-304(2), 9-504(2).

    b.   Are the bank's rights determined by Article 9? §9-309.

    c.   Can the sub-buyer argue that it is a buyer in ordinary course that defeats the bank's security interest under §9-307(1)?

3.   LETTERS OF CREDIT

Section 45.   *Letter of Credit Transactions*

Article 5 is skeletal. It provides a basic legal framework for letters of credit but leaves much to the courts and to banking practice and custom. No commonly used commercial device is as sensitive to merchant innovation as the letter of credit. When the Code drafters prepared Article 5, the standby credit was sufficiently undeveloped that they ignored it. They may have been unaware of it, this despite the fact that bankers and bank lawyers were intimately involved as advisers to the reporter for Article 5, Professor Soia Mentschikoff. Yet, the standby has grown to prominence as a commercial device, and Article 5 has provided the legal framework for it.

Familiarity with transactions involving letters of credit is rather helpful in understanding the rules. It is beyond the scope of this book to explain those transactions fully, but it might help a bit here to note that the commercial letter of credit is the type used in international trade. When a foreign seller, for example, agrees to ship goods to a domestic buyer, the seller will want a letter of credit to secure payment. Once the goods begin their way across the ocean, it is costly for the seller to control them. He would at that point like to have his money or at least a bank obligation in place of the obligation of a U.S. buyer that he does not know. The buyer, at the same time, is reluctant to pay unless she has the right to the goods.

The commercial letter of credit protects both parties. It permits the seller to ship and secure the bank obligation he desires. It also permits the buyer to allow her bank to undertake that obligation, secure in the knowledge that the ocean carrier will deliver the goods to the bank or the buyer herself.

The standby letter of credit, the credit you are bound to meet in practice, is largely domestic. It operates to substitute the bank's credit standing for that of a weaker commercial party. A borrower, for example, may enhance the acceptability of his obligations (notes or bonds) by securing them with a standby. Under the terms of the standby, if the obligor does not pay, the holder may draw on the bank for payment.

From a pedagogical standpoint, the letter of credit is a lovely subject. It often involves an underlying contract of sale (Article 2); it frequently calls for a draft (Article 3) and a bill of lading (Article 7); the draft and bill usually wend their way through the bank collection system (Article 4); and the parties usually avail themselves of one or more security interests (Article 9). It is therefore a fitting capstone for Code study, providing an opportunity for review of much that we learn in the courses on Payment Systems and Secured Transactions.

Problems

275. U.S. Seller entered into a contract for the sale of goods with Dutch Buyer. The terms of the agreement call for payment by letter of credit. Buyer caused the Amsterdam office of Dutch Bank to issue a letter of credit directly to Seller.

   a. Under the Code, has Buyer complied with the sales contract? §2-325(3).

   b. Should the seller want an advice (from a bank local to seller) to the effect that the credit has been issued? How does the seller in these circumstances know that in fact Dutch Bank issued the credit? Do you suppose that sellers normally have signature books for foreign bank officers? A code book for foreign bank communications sent by telex equipment? Access to SWIFT (Society for Worldwide Interbank Financial Telecommunications)? How should the lawyer for the seller draft the letter-of-credit term in the sales contract to provide more protection for the seller? Why, moreover, would seller want a confirmed credit? §5-107(2)? Would you advise your client to ship against a credit issued by the First National Bank of Ho Chi Minh City?

276. Assume in the foregoing problem that the seller insisted on and got a credit confirmed by First Bank. In that case, identify

   a. the credit issuer.
   b. the adviser (advising bank).
   c. the confirming bank.
   d. the applicant (account party) (customer).
   e. the beneficiary.
   f. the bank and place at which the beneficiary seller must present his documents to have payment under the credit.
   g. The typical documents that a commercial letter of credit such as the one in this transaction might call for.

277. Your client, a small savings and loan association, is arranging to lend money to a borrower on the borrower's note secured by a mortgage. The S&L is asking the borrower to arrange to have its commercial bank issue a letter of credit in favor of the S&L for 10 percent of the face amount of the

note. This arrangement is in lieu of a down payment by the borrower. The S&L officer wants to be able to draw in the event of a default on the note. The commercial bank has proposed a letter of credit containing language indicating that the S&L may draw on the bank issuer and that the draw must be accompanied by "all documents causing this credit to be called upon." Your client would prefer the language "documentation of the borrower's default." One of your client's colleagues wants the language to read "upon borrower's default." What do you tell your client?

278. There is authority in contract law to the effect that courts should construe a contract so that it will have effect and will not be rendered a nullity. In an ambiguous credit, should courts construe the credit to promote payment to the beneficiary as an instance of this contract rule of construction?

279. In contract law, it is a general rule of construction that an ambiguous contract should be construed against its drafter. Who do you suppose drafts most of the terms of the letter of credit? In government contract cases, the government usually provides the bank with the language that must be incorporated into the letter of credit issued in favor of the government agency. Should these credits be construed against the government, if they are ambiguous? Do you agree with the view announced by the U.S. Court of Appeals for the First Circuit that letters of credit should be construed strongly against the issuer? *See* Banco Espagnol de Credito v. State Street Bank & Trust Co., 385 F.2d 230 (1st Cir. 1967), *cert. denied*, 390 U.S. 1013 (1968).

280. The International Chamber of Commerce (ICC), a trade group of enterprises engaged in international trade that has its headquarters in Paris, through its Commission on Banking Technique and Practice has fashioned a set of rules that apply to letters of credit, primarily to documents that are traditionally submitted under commercial letters of credit. The ICC revises these rules, the Uniform Customs and Practice for Documentary Credits (UCP), every ten years or so. When four U.S. jurisdictions adopted Article 5 (Alabama, Arizona, Missouri, and New York) they engrafted a nonconforming provision onto it to the effect that if the credit incorporated the UCP, Article 5 would not apply. In a case governed by New York law, should the courts invoke §5-111, a warranty rule, to an issuer's claim that the beneficiary received payment under the credit by presenting fraudulent documents? Does it matter that the Uniform Customs do not contain a presentment warranty? Make an argument that New York courts may invoke Code rules even when the credit incorporates the UCP.

281.   a. First Bank's letter of credit in favor of Seller Corp. stipulates that Seller must present, among other documents, an invoice in duplicate evidencing shipment of "approximately 100 Tons ¼-inch specialty steel rods at $142 per Ton (length not less than 6 feet, nor more than 8 feet)." If First Bank's document examiner receives an invoice referring to "steel rods," should the bank honor the seller's draft? If the issuer dishonors, will it be liable to the

> beneficiary for wrongful dishonor of its credit obligation? *See* UCP 500 art. 37(c).[1]
>
> b. Would your answer differ if the credit had not been subject to the UCP?
>
> c. If you were the lawyer for the seller, how would you draft the description of the goods in the invoice?

Section 46.   *Duties of the Credit Issuer*

The key to the success of the letter of credit is the integrity of the credit issuer's obligation to pay the beneficiary quickly and without regard to the equities of the underlying transaction. The independence principle teaches that the issuer must pay against facially conforming documents. While bank bad faith can subvert that principle, banks generally pay promptly, even when they have lost their right of reimbursement against the applicant for the credit.

Sections 5-109 and 5-114 define the independence principle first as to the applicant and then as to the beneficiary. Note that the latter section contains an exception for fraud. At times, the Iranian/U.S. diplomatic crisis being one of them, that exception has occupied much of letter-of-credit law.

Problems

282. *§5-109.*   If the documents conform on their face, but the letter-of-credit issuer pays the wrong beneficiary, that is, the draft is forged and a fraudulent party is presenting the documents for payment, may the issuer obtain reimbursement from the applicant? How might an issuer protect itself from losses of this kind?

283. *§§5-109, 5-114(3).*   A letter of credit calls for a bill of lading with an "on-board" stamp, that is, a certification by the carrier that the goods are not only received for shipment but have been loaded on board the vessel. The stamp is important to many buyers and banks because marine insurance does not cover the goods until they pass the ship's rail. The on-board stamp on the bill and the insurance certificate certifying that the seller obtained marine insurance will give the buyer and the banks comfort when they pay the seller's draft that the goods, if destroyed, will be covered by the insurance. Assume that the beneficiary presents to the issuer a bill of lading that does not bear the stamp.

a. Should the issuer pay the beneficiary's draft?

b. Would your answer differ if the credit called for an ocean bill of lading, and the beneficiary presented an air bill?

---

1. "The description of the goods in the commercial invoice must correspond with the description in the credit." International Chamber of Commerce, ICC Uniform Customs and Practice for Documentary Credits (ICC Pub. No. 500) (1993).

c. Would your answer differ if the credit called for a bill of lading with a clause requiring the carrier to notify "Mohammed Sofan" of the shipment if the bill presented directed the carrier to notify "Mohammed So*r*an"?

284. *§5-109(1).*   Assume in Part a of the preceding question that the document checker missed the fact that the on-board stamp was missing from the face of the bill but that the goods were in fact on board. Based on its error, the bank paid the beneficiary. Now the bank seeks reimbursement from its customer, the applicant, who is claiming that the bank erred by paying the beneficiary and should not obtain reimbursement.

a. May the issuer have reimbursement from the applicant?

b. Would your answer differ if the goods were not on board but on the dock, and were then destroyed by fire and not covered by insurance?

285. *§5-112.*   First Bank issued a letter of credit in favor of Mortgage Co. to secure 10 percent of the mortgage loan that Mortgage Co. made to First's customer, the applicant for the credit. Under its terms, the credit expired on May 1, a Thursday. Mortgage Co. mailed its draft and conforming documents under the credit on April 22, but because of a delay in the mails, the documents did not arrive at First Bank until May 2.

a. Must First pay Mortgage Co.'s draft?

b. Would your answer differ if the draft arrived with the documents on Wednesday, April 30, and the credit expired while the bank was examining the documents under the three-banking-day rule provided by §5-112?

c. Suppose the draft and documents arrived on April 23, and one of the documents, a certificate of default, was unsigned. If the bank waits until May 2 to give notice of the defect, is the bank liable to the beneficiary?

d. Would your answer to c differ if the bank could show that its delay did not cause detriment to the beneficiary, that is, that the beneficiary could not have cured the defect if the bank had given notice on April 26?

286. *§5-114(1) and (2).*   An issuer received documents that conformed on their face with the terms of the credit but learned from an independent source that the goods were, in fact, not up to industry standards.

a. May the issuer refuse to honor the beneficiary's draft?

b. Would your answer differ if the bank was relying on the goods as security for the advance it made when it paid the beneficiary's draft?

c. Would your answer differ if the documents included a certificate reciting that the goods satisfied industry standards and if the bank learned from another source that the goods were defective?

Section 47. *The Exception for Fraud*

Because fraud is a serious problem for commerce, courts have felt that they cannot ignore it, even though an exception to the independence principle for fraud creates serious problems for the letter of credit. Litigation over the fraud exception has yielded a judicial balancing of the equities of the defrauded party against the integrity of the letter of credit as a commercial product. Once the courts established the fraud exception (§5-114(2) being a codification of those cases), they strained to cabin it. They did so primarily in two rather ingenious ways. First, they defined fraud narrowly, so that only egregious fraud would satisfy the exception. Second, they vigorously invoked equity prerequisites for injunctive relief, requiring the applicant to show that it had no adequate remedy at law and that it had a strong likelihood of success on the merits. The net effect of these two judicially confected limits on the judicially confected fraud exception has been to guard the credit's integrity but to allow injunctions against payment in the most compelling cases, but not as a matter of course. The solution is not always successful but is largely a happy one.

Problems

287. *§5-114(2)(b).* Seller and Buyer entered into a contract for the sale of diodes with payment to be made under a letter of credit. Seller presented facially conforming documents to the letter of credit issuer, but Buyer alleged that the bill of lading was fraudulent in that Seller had shipped rubbish in the cartons instead of diodes.

   a. Is this an example of the kind of fraud that will justify court interference with the independence principle?

   b. If it is such a case, should the court issue an injunction against payment of the credit? What further demonstration would you as trial judge want before you would issue the injunction?

288. First Bank (FB) issued a credit in favor of Saudi Bank (SB), which had issued an international bank guarantee in favor of a Saudi buyer of goods manufactured by a U.S. seller. If SB certifies to FB that SB has paid under the guarantee and if that certification is all that FB's letter of credit calls for, is there any way that the U.S. seller can prevent payment under the credit? If it cannot stop payment, is all lost?

289. In which of the following cases do you think that a court might issue a preliminary injunction?

   a. The letter of credit calls for a certificate from the beneficiary, a landlord, to the effect that the tenant has not paid its rent. The landlord presents the certificate with a demand for payment under the credit. The tenant claims that because the landlord has breached a covenant in the lease, the rent is not due; that the certification is, therefore, false; and that an injunction forbidding payment under the credit should not issue.

   b. The credit calls for beneficiary-seller's certificate that its invoices to the applicant-buyer have not been paid. Buyer alleges that the goods were defective, that it does not owe the money covered by the invoices, that the seller's certification is therefore fraudulent, and that an injunction should issue.

290.   a. Applicant for a credit issued in favor of a large corporation has learned that the documents that the corporation is submitting under the credit contain false assertions. If Applicant pleads these facts, should a court issue a temporary restraining order against payment under the credit?.

b. Would your answer to the preceding question differ if payment under the credit and the issuer's subsequent charge against Applicant's account would render Applicant insolvent? Would it matter that the payment would not render Applicant insolvent but, according to Applicant, would embarrass Applicant in the trade by having industry members learn that its standby had been drawn against?

c. Applicant for a credit issued by First Bank, a large money center bank, has learned that the beneficiary of the credit has supplied the bank with documents that are facially nonconforming. Applicant fears, however, that the bank is about to honor the beneficiary's draft. If applicant pleads these facts, should the court enter a temporary restraining order?

291. Applicant is a limited partner in a venture that was to construct a gambling casino. Under the terms of the partnership agreement, Applicant gave the partnership $100,000 and a promissory note for $400,000. Applicant secured the note by a letter of credit payable to Lending Bank. Lending Bank took the note from the partnership as security for a loan to the partnership. The partnership has defaulted on the loan, the bank has called Applicant's note, and Applicant has refused to pay the bank. Applicant has learned that the general partner of the partnership who sold the limited partnership interest to Applicant made false and seriously misleading statements to Applicant. These fraudulent statements are in violation of state and federal securities laws. If Applicant pleads these facts, should a court issue a temporary restraining order against Lending Bank preventing it from drawing on the letter of credit?

Section 48.   *Transferring Interests in Letters of Credit*

It is an oversimplification but nonetheless helpful to think of letters of credit as obligations that are generally not transferable. There are exceptions. First, the parties can agree to the contrary by stipulating in the credit that the credit is transferable. Second, the fact that a credit is not transferable does not prevent the beneficiary from assigning the credit's proceeds. The Code treats that assignment as the creation of a security interest subject to the rules of Article 9. See §5-116. Note, moreover, that transfer, a concept different from the assignment of proceeds, entails the right to substitute beneficiaries, that is, the right to let a third party draw on the credit. Assignment does not entail that substitution. The third method of transferring the benefit of the credit is to have the issuer issue a negotiation credit. Under the negotiation credit, which the following problems describe, the beneficiary takes its documents to a bank that negotiates them. That bank thereby wins rather extensive rights against the credit issuer under the credit. Credits come in two varieties: negotiation credits and straight credits; and a bank cannot become a "negotiating bank" under a straight credit, even though it negotiates the beneficiary's draft.

Problems

292. *§§3-308, 5-114(2)(a), [§3-307].*   FNB issued a negotiation letter of credit in favor of Seller calling for a draft payable 60 days after sight. Seller discounted its draft at Second Bank, which now seeks acceptance under the credit.

    a.   Is it necessary for Second to prove that it is a holder in due course to enforce the credit?

    b.   If the buyer-applicant alleges that the seller defrauded the buyer and delivered fraudulent documents to Second, may the buyer obtain an injunction against acceptance or payment of the draft when Second presents them to FNB? In this setting, does Second's status as a holder in due course become relevant? If so, who has the burden of proof regarding that status?

    c.   If the buyer seeks an injunction in this case on the grounds that the bill of lading is fraudulent, should buyer's petition allege that Second is not a holder in due course? Absent that allegation, is the complaint deficient? May a court issue an injunction if the petitioner fails to demonstrate the likelihood of success on the merits? Would the buyer have a likelihood of success on the merits in this case if Second is a holder in due course?

    d.   Would your answers to the foregoing questions differ if the credit was a straight credit?

    e.   Under either a straight or a negotiation credit that calls for time drafts, may the applicant buyer obtain an injunction after the time drafts have been accepted by the issuer?

293. *§5-116.*   If corporate planners decide to merge a subsidiary into its parent, why might they be interested to know whether the subsidiary is a beneficiary of a letter of credit?

294. May the trustee in bankruptcy of the beneficiary draw on a credit issued to the beneficiary before bankruptcy? May the personal representative of a decedent draw on a credit issued to the decedent? What might issuers do to avoid problems in these cases?

295. FNB issued a letter of credit in favor of Second Bank, which is now insolvent. FDIC is the receiver of Second and by operation of law succeeds to all of Second's assets. May it draw on the credit? If FDIC as receiver transfers the credit voluntarily to itself as insurer of Second's deposits, may FDIC (now in its corporate capacity, that is, for itself and not for the estate of Second) draw on the credit?

296. *§9-305.*

    a.   Exporter Co. has entered into a contract with a Ukrainian buyer for 100,000 bushels of hops. The buyer caused a German bank to issue a nontransferable letter of credit in favor of the exporter, and a New York bank has confirmed the credit. Exporter is now seeking to purchase the hops from a Seattle broker and needs credit to induce Exporter's bank to (1) issue a back-to-back credit in favor of the Seattle broker, or (2) lend Exporter the funds to pay the Seattle broker. How should the parties proceed?

    b.   If Exporter effectively assigns the proceeds of his credit to his bank, who will draw the draft under the credit, Exporter or his bank?

Section 49.   Issuer Insolvency

When the issuer becomes insolvent, the beneficiary's expectations are surely frustrated. Whether the law should protect a beneficiary that takes a letter of credit from a bank that soon thereafter becomes insolvent is an interesting policy question, the kind of question that this book does not address. To some extent the Code, however, does address the problem, and there has been some litigation. The following problem attempts to clarify some of the moderately confusing issues that arose during the bank insolvency crisis of the 1980s.

Problems

297. *§5-117.*   First Bank issued a credit for $90,000 to Seller Co. When Seller Co. was about to present its documents and draft under the credit, Seller learned that First was insolvent.

    a.   Is Seller an insured depositor under the Federal Deposit Insurance Act?

    b.   Would it be a preference in violation of the policy of that Act for the receiver (the FDIC) to pay seller 100 percent of his claim and to pay other creditors less than 100 percent?

    c.   If Buyer, the applicant for the credit, had deposited funds with the specific purpose of providing for the payment of the credit, can the receiver keep the funds and dishonor the credit?

4. WIRE TRANSFERS

Section 50.   Wire Transfers

It would leave a law teacher with a guilty conscience to teach a course in payments systems and not cover wire transfers. After all, the electronic payments system transfers more funds, more quickly, with more reliability than all of the other systems put together.

Yet, one cannot fault tepid interest in the law of wire transfers. It is simply not very exciting at the moment. Primarily the domain of large business corporations, government agencies, and financial institutions, electronic transfers outside of the debit and credit card system have yielded little litigation, well-established principles, a few fireworks in the legislative process, and a disgruntled law professor here and there.

The net effect of the situation is something of a disappointment to lawyers and law teachers — the system works well, and there is little controversy and less litigation. For the student, the challenge here may be more one of understanding the transactions than understanding the law. These problems illustrate the few questions that have arisen and that might be the subject of class study.

The diagram illustrates a simple wire transfer over, in this case, Fedwire. Note the terminology developed by the industry and recognized by Article 4A. Note also that a bank will usually play two roles. It is a receiving bank when it receives a payment order (hereafter "p/o"); and it is a sender when it retransmits the order to the next receiving bank.

> Buyer (Originator) — p/o → (Receiving Bank) Buyer's Bank (Sender) — p/o → (Receiving Bank) Federal Reserve Bank of San Francisco (Sender) — p/o → (Receiving Bank) Federal Reserve Bank of Atlanta (Sender) — p/o → (Receiving Bank) Seller's Bank — funds → Seller (Beneficiary)

Problems

298. In the foregoing illustration, an Atlanta insurance company and its San Francisco customer agreed that on May 1, the customer would pay its monthly premium by wiring $1 million to the insurance company's account at Second Bank of Atlanta. The customer's financial officer authorized the payment and caused the payment order to be sent by wire from a computer terminal at the customer's offices to a wire transfer terminal at First Bank in San Francisco. Thus the customer became an originator.

  a. When First Bank sends the order (p/o) to the Federal Reserve Bank of San Francisco, the Federal Reserve Bank will forward the funds to Atlanta's Federal Reserve Bank. How does the San Francisco Federal Reserve Bank reimburse itself? Reg. J, 12 C.F.R. §210.28(a) (1994).

  b. If the payment order misnames the beneficiary's bank but contains the correct number for that bank, what might the Federal Reserve Bank of Atlanta do? *Id.* §210.27(a). *See also* Problem 300 below.

  c. When does acceptance of the p/o occur between First Bank and the San Francisco Fed?

  d. When does the payment of the insurance premium occur? UCC §4A-209(b).

e. Under the Code, must Second Bank of Atlanta take action to accept the p/o? UCC §4A-209, comment 8. Reg. J, 12 C.F.R. §210.31(a) (1994).

299. *§§4A-201, 4A-202(b), 4A-203, 4A-205.*   If a dishonest employee of the buyer manages to initiate a funds transfer through a funds transfer system, who will bear the loss? §4A-202. Will the result depend on the fact that the buyer's bank has made available to its customers a commercially reasonable security procedure?

300. *§4A-207.*   Crook obtained Widow's investment identification number with Mutual Fund, Inc. Crook used that information to request Mutual Fund to sell Widow's $750,000 interest in the fund and to wire the proceeds to Widow's account at Third Bank in Dallas, account No. 12345. In fact, that account is not in Widow's name but in the name of Coin Store, Inc., a legitimate coin dealer. Crook has selected $750,000 in rare coins with the dealer and will pick them up when Third Bank informs the innocent dealer that $750,000 has been wired to the dealer's account.

What should Third Bank do when it receives a wire transfer payment order designating payment to an account that does not bear the name of the beneficiary listed on the payment order? (This problem illustrates a fraudulent scheme that worked more than once.)

301. On May 1, Buyer originated a funds transfer to Insurance Co. in Atlanta. At 1:00 P.M. Third Bank, the beneficiary's bank in Atlanta, received a payment order from the Federal Reserve Bank of Atlanta.
   a. May the customer cancel the payment order before Third Bank accepts it? §§4A-209, 4A-211.
   b. May the customer cancel the order after Third Bank has notified the insurance company of the payment? §4A-209(b)(1).

302. *§4A-303.*   Buyer originated an order for payment to Insurance Co. of $1 million. Through a data entry clerk's error on the premises of Buyer's bank, the bank issued a payment order to the Federal Reserve Bank of San Francisco in the amount of $10 million instead of $1 million. How are the losses allocated?

303. *§4A-305.*   Buyer issued a payment order to Insurance Co. on May 1, the day the premium was due. Through the negligence of Buyer's bank, the payment was not received until May 2, the insurance company canceled the policy, and Buyer sustained a $25 million uninsured loss. Is the bank liable for Buyer's consequential damages?

Payment Systems: Answers

1. NEGOTIABLE INSTRUMENTS

Section 30. The Effect of a Signature on a Negotiable Instrument: The "Contract" Liability Concept

203.

a. No. As a general rule, no party is liable on an instrument unless he signs it. *See* §3-401(a) [§3-401(1)]. If the signature were authorized, of course, Drawer would be liable because the drawer of a check or other draft engages to pay the instrument if it is dishonored. *See* §3-414(b) [§3-413(2)].

b. Because the drawer did not intend the imprinted name to operate as a signature, that is, as an authentication of the check, the imprint does not operate as a signature. *See* §§1-201(39), 3-401(b).

c. Under the fiction of §3-403(a) [§3-404(1)], Thief has signed the instrument and engaged to pay a subsequent party that takes it for value if the instrument is not paid by the drawee bank, First Bank. If First pays the instrument to Seller or some other holder to whom Seller negotiates it, Thief is liable to the bank.

d. If Thief is a relative of Drawer or perhaps an employee, Drawer may be inclined to ratify the signature. If, for example, First Bank is suspicious of the signature and calls Drawer, Drawer might tell First to pay. In that case, Drawer would not be able to say subsequently that the signature is not his. Drawer would have ratified it. *See* §3-403(a) (last sentence) [§3-404(1) (first clause) and (2)].

204.

a. No. A draft is not an assignment under the Code. Seller may not argue, therefore, that the bank is obliged to honor the drawer's order. This rule is consistent with the general rule that no person is liable on an instrument unless he signs it. The bank has not signed. *See* §§3-401(a), 3-408 [§§3-401(1), 3-409].

b. The cases go against Seller. Section 1-103 incorporates extra-Code law only to the extent that the Code does not displace that law. The sections cited in Answer a probably displace any extra-Code theories. Note also that the Code does provide a procedure for imposing instrument liability on the drawee bank. *See* §§3-409(a) and (d), 3-413(a) [§§3-411(1), 3-413(1)]. Bear in mind that this discussion relates only to the holder's (Seller's) claim against the drawee bank. A drawee bank that dishonors a properly payable item may be liable to its customer, the drawer. There have been cases holding the dishonoring drawee bank liable to Seller, but only if Seller can show that she exacted an explicit promise from the bank to pay the instrument.

c. No, though it may make a difference in Drawer's claim against the bank for not paying Seller.

Section 31. The Concepts of Transfer and Negotiation

205.

a. This is a blank indorsement that renders the check bearer paper and permits subsequent negotiation of it by delivery alone. *See* §§3-109(a), 3-201(a), 3-205(b) [§§3-111, 3-202(1), 3-204(2)].

b. No. Once Seller indorses the check, X will become a holder. Whether a subsequent party is a holder depends on the way Seller indorses. If Seller indorses in blank, as she did in the problem, subsequent parties can become holders by mere delivery of the check. *See* §3-205(a) [§3-204(2)]. If Seller indorses specially, subsequent parties cannot be holders unless X indorses. *See* §3-205(a) [§3-204(1)]. The nature of X's indorsement will determine the status of parties subsequent to him as holders, as the analysis starts all over again. Note that once a holder indorses in blank, all subsequent negotiations may be effected by delivery without indorsement. If a holder indorses specially, however, there can be no negotiation without the indorsement of the party to whom the instrument is specially indorsed.

c. It was order paper before Seller indorsed and bearer paper after the blank indorsement. *See* §3-205(b) [§3-204(2)].

d. X is an indorsee-holder and, therefore, is entitled to enforce the instrument. *See* §3-301. X may enforce the instrument against Seller under §3-415 [§3-414(1)]. Assuming that Drawer's signature is genuine, X may enforce the instrument against Drawer under §3-414 [§3-413(2)]. Thus X will often have a choice and will select the party most amenable to service or most creditworthy as the target defendant or may sue both parties in the same suit if that is possible. X, of course, must satisfy conditions to recover from these parties and will have only one recovery. Note that if Seller satisfies her indorser obligation to X, Seller will be an indorser who "paid the draft under Section 3-415" (an indorser who has "taken the instrument up" under §3-414(1)). In case Seller pays X, then, Seller will be able to enforce the check against Drawer under §3-414(b) [§3-413(2)].

e. X may recover from Seller under §3-415(a) [§3-414(1)] and, because he is liable as a drawer, from Thief under §3-414(b) [§3-413(2)] but not against Drawer, whose authorized signature does not appear on the instrument.

206. The following is a diagram of the transaction:

Drawer → Seller → [Crook] → X → Y → First Bank

a. Y is a holder because the indorsement is not unauthorized; it is a good indorsement by Seller. *See* §1-201(20).

b. As a holder, Y may enforce the contract liability of X, an indorser; of Seller, also an indorser; of Crook, also an indorser; and of Drawer, as a drawer. It does not matter whether X indorsed specially or in blank. X's indorsement gives rise to indorser liability. *See* §3-415(a) [§3-414(1)].

c. In these circumstances, X is an indorser that "paid the draft under Section 3-415." §3-414(a) (last sentence). [Under the parlance of old Article 3, X is an indorser that "takes [the instrument] up," §3-413(2). Such an indorser can enforce the instrument against Crook and Drawer. *See* §§3-413(2), 3-414(1).]

207. Under the modified facts, Y is not a holder. Because Crook's signing of X's name does not operate as X's signature, *see* §3-403(a) [§3-404(1)], X's indorsement is missing. Unless Y obtains X's indorsement, Y is not a holder, *see* §1-201(20), and cannot enforce the instrument.

208. The following diagram illustrates the transaction:

[Thief] → Seller → Second Bank → First Bank

a. Second may not recover from Drawer who, in this case, is not a drawer, not having signed the instrument. Thief's forgery operates as Thief's signature and renders Thief a drawer, *see* §3-403(a) [§3-404(1)]; Second may enforce Thief's liability as drawer. First is not liable on the instrument to anyone, not having signed it. *See* §3-401(a) [§3-401(1)]. Second, despite the forged drawer's signature, is a holder; Seller is liable as an indorser to Second. *See* §3-415(a) [§3-414(1)].

b. Thief should bear the loss but is usually insolvent or missing. Generally Seller, having dealt with Thief, was in the best position to avoid the fraud and will bear the loss. There is no reason to prevent Seller's use of supplemental rules of tort [fraud] or equity [unjust enrichment] to permit Seller to recover from Thief. But remember that Thief is liable to Seller on the instrument because Thief's forgery of Drawer's signature acts as Thief's own signature and makes him liable, being a drawer, to Seller, as an indorser who pays the instrument [a holder who takes the instrument up].

209. a. As an indorser and as a drawer, C is liable to Second, the holder. *See* §§3-414(b), 3-415(a) [§§3-413(2), 3-414(1)]. Unless one of the

estoppel rules applies (and one of them may, namely §3-406), Ace is not liable because its signature is not on the instrument. *See* §3-401(a) [§3-401(1)].

b. Yes. These facts establish an estoppel under §3-406. Ace's negligence has substantially contributed to *C*'s forgery.

c. They keep it under lock and key.

d. Under the doctrine of Price v. Neal, 3 Burr. 1354 (K.B. 1762), the law does impose on the drawee bank losses for payment over a forged drawer's signature. The drawee bank may be able to avoid that liability by invoking the estoppel of §3-406, but most banks avoid it in this setting by telling Ace that they will not accept a facsimile signature machine signature unless Ace agrees to hold the bank harmless from Price v. Neal liability when an unauthorized person uses the machine. The courts have been willing to enforce those agreements, and the Code anticipates them. *See* §3-404, comment 2, case #4.

210. Preprinted checks will bear the name of the Company and should show unambiguously to any holder that Joe is signing only for the company. New Article 3 makes that result explicit. *See* §3-402(c). It is probably best in other cases for officers of corporations always to sign "Ace Corp., by Joe Ace, President." The results are more serious to Joe in the case of a promissory note. Many lenders to closely held companies rely on the credit of the individual officers and stockholders of the company; the name of the company will not appear on the note as a matter of course, as it does on a preprinted check; and Joe will have to argue that the signatures unambiguously show that he signed in a representative capacity. In the fourth case, he will surely prevail.

Section 32. *Conditions of Contract Liability*

211A. (This is the answer to the problem for new Article 3.)

a. *X* has "contract" rights against *S* as an indorser and against Drawer as drawer. *See* §§3-414, 3-415. To hold the indorser, however, *X* must get the check into the banking system within 30 days of the date of the indorsement and must give notice of dishonor within 30 days of the day *X* receives notice of dishonor. *X* can hold the drawer even if the initiation of collection is late and even if the notice of dishonor is late. As long as the delays do not cause the drawer to lose its deposit, the drawer is not discharged. *See* §3-414(f). *X*, then, can hold Drawer as drawer but loses *S* because *X* did not deposit the check within 30 days of *S*'s indorsement and did not notify *S* within 30 days of the time the bank notified *X* of the dishonor. *See* §3-415(e). *X* is late as against the drawer in depositing the check and in giving the notice, but the delays do not discharge the drawer. *See* §§3-414(f), 3-503(c).

b. *S* does not need to hold anyone, because she is not liable on the instrument. The party that can enforce contract liability against *S* is *X*, *see* §3-415(a); but *X* has lost his rights by virtue of the delays. *S*, then, does not need to enforce the instrument against anyone.

211B. (This is the answer to the problem for old Article 3.) The following diagram illustrates the transaction:

Drawer [5/1] → Seller [5/2 or 5/10] → X [5/3 or 5/15] → Y [5/4 or 5/20] → Z [5/5 or 5/25] → First Bank

- a. Under the early set of dates, Z may recover from all parties because he has acted promptly enough and within the time limits necessary to hold the drawer and to hold the indorsers. [*See* §3-503(2)(a) and (b).] This answer assumes that Z gives timely notice of dishonor to the indorsers. [*See* §3-508(2).] These are the important conditions of indorser liability that may prevent Z from recovering under old §3-502(1)(a). They are also conditions of drawer liability but are not so important in light of old §3-502(1)(b), under which drawer discharge virtually never arises.
- b. The answers are different. On May 25, Z can hold the drawer and the last indorser. The first two indorsers, Seller and X, are discharged under the seven-day rule of old §3-503(2)(b). [*See* §3-502(1)(a).]
- c. Under the early set of dates, it is not too late for Y to hold Seller or X. Y, however, can also still hold the drawer.
- d. Seller's only claim is against the drawer because the other indorsers came after Seller and are not liable to her. [*See* §3-414(2).]

Section 33. *Negotiable Instruments and the Underlying Transaction*

212.
- a. No. First, not having accepted the check by certifying it, *see* §§3-408, 3-409 [§§3-411, 3-412], was never liable on the instrument; and the other parties that signed, the drawer and the two indorsers, were liable only in the event of dishonor.
- b. When the check is paid, the parties are discharged. *See* §3-310(b)(1) [§3-802(1)(b)].
- c. Drawer is discharged. *See* §3-310(b)(1) [§3-802(1)(b)].
- d. A certified check. *See* §3-409(d) [§3-410]. The certifying bank undertakes to honor the check as presented. *See* §3-413(a) and (b) [§3-413(1)].

213.
- a. The rule of §3-310(b)(1) [§3-802(1)(a)] that issuance of the check to the seller suspends the drawer's liability on the underlying contract must admit of an exception in these circumstances, as §3-309 [§3-804] suggests. Yes, Seller may sue on the underlying contract. Drawer is reluctant to draw a replacement check because if the first check finds its way into the hands of a holder in due course, that person will be able to enforce it against Drawer even though Drawer is discharged on the underlying transaction. A holder in due course takes the instrument free from that kind of defense.
- b. Seller has a choice of suing on the check under §3-309 [§3-804] or suing on the underlying contract. In either case, Seller will have to post a bond or other security to protect Drawer against the eventuality that the check turns up in the hands of a holder in

due course who can enforce it. Section 3-309 [§3-804] in a sense does away with the conditions of the drawer's liability, that is, presentment of the check to the drawee bank and dishonor by that bank. Seller cannot present the lost or stolen check.

Section 34.   *Holders in Due Course and Their Rights*

214.   a. No. Note how much easier it would be for Seller to prove a prima facie case on a negotiable instrument under §3-308 [§3-307].
         b. This note is not negotiable because, in order to be negotiable, a note must be payable either to order or to bearer. *See* §§3-104(a)(1), 3-109 [§§3-104(1)(d), 3-110, 3-111]. Only negotiable instruments may be negotiated.

215. The issues here turn on the value requirement of the holder in due course definition. A holder in due course will cut off the defense, but the bank is a holder only if and to the extent it gave value. It gave value in all four problems, but in Problem d only to the extent of $500. *See* §4-210(a) [§4-208(1)].

216. The answers are largely the same, though the bank is now a collecting bank, not an owner of the instrument. It is more likely in this scenario that the bank has not advanced funds to National, in which case, of course, the bank is not protected. It would not need protection in that case, not having parted with value in fact or in theory. Note, however, that the collecting bank may also assert rights as a secured party, say, for instance, where it has made loans to National and taken a security interest in National's negotiable instruments or the proceeds from the sale of its equipment or inventory. In that case, §4-211 [§4-209] would come into play.

217. The answers are still the same. Even though First Bank is now a payee, it can be a holder in due course and would be in this setting if it meets the definition in §3-302 of one taking for value, in good faith, and without notice. First Bank "has not dealt" with Maker as those terms are used in old §3-305(2). That language in old Article 3 is intended to make it clear that National cannot assert the rights of a holder in due course against Maker.

218.   a. Seller may not recover. When the drawee bank, First, paid Second, it paid a holder in due course and thereby discharged the contract liability of the drawer and the indorsers. Buyer is discharged on the underlying contract and on the instrument. *See* §3-310(b)(1) [§3-802(1)(b)]. Note that this rule puts the loss on Seller, who should not have indorsed the check in blank thereby permitting the thief to make subsequent parties holders.
         b. No. Buyer is discharged under §3-310(b)(1) [§3-802(1)(b)].
         c. It makes sense.
         d. No. Second has the protection of §3-306 [§3-305(1)], which shields it from all claims. Replevin and conversion are claims.

219. Under the revised facts, we have a forged indorsement by Thief. Seller, by using a special indorsement, has protected herself. Now, the subsequent parties are not holders; the indorsements do not run to them. *See* §1-201(20).

    a.   Buyer, therefore, is not discharged. Payment must be to a "party entitled to enforce the instrument," §3-602(a) ["to a holder," §3-604(1)]. Payment to a stranger does not discharge anybody. Discharge not having occurred, the primary and secondary parties are still liable for their "contract" liability. They are not discharged, and Seller may sue on the underlying contract.

    b.   Seller may also recover on the stolen instrument.

    c.   Again, yes.

    d.   Generally, yes. There are some limitations, which the problems in Section 37 discuss.

220.   a.   Yes, for the instrument has been dishonored, and Buyer is liable as drawer. *See* §3-414(b) [§3-413(2)]. (This part of the question is strictly review.)

    b.   Whether Second gave value is not an issue until Buyer establishes a defense. Assuming Buyer does have a defense, we would want to know the extent of the value that the collecting bank has given. *See* §§4-210, 4-211 [§4-208, 4-209].

    c.   Now the question of value becomes critical. If Second has a security interest in the check (as it would under ii), *see* sections cited above, the bank will cut off the defense under §3-305(b) [§3-305(2)].

    d.   Under new Article 3, the first defense is a defense that the holder in due course does not cut off. Whether the holder in due course takes free of the infancy defense is a question that depends on the extent of the infancy defense in contract law. *See* §3-305(a)(1). [Under old Article 3, the first of these is a real defense under §3-305(2)(c). The second is a real defense only if non-Code law renders it so. *See* §3-305(2)(b). The holder in due course does not take free of real defenses.] Note that the defenses the holder in due course does not cut off are commercially unimportant. Failure of consideration and fraud in the inducement are the two frequent commercial defenses; and the holder in due course takes free of them.

221.   a.   No. Manufacturer is a holder in due course, even though it is a payee. *See* §3-302, comment 4 [§3-302(2)]. Manufacturer is not subject to Buyer's recoupment defense in Buyer's transaction with Seller. *See* §3-305(a)(3). [Note that under old Article 3, Manufacturer did not "deal with" Buyer. *See* §3-305(2).]

    b.   Now Manufacturer fails the value test of Article 3. An unexecuted promise is not value in negotiable instruments law under §3-303(a)(1) [§3-303(a)], though it would be consideration in contract law and in other articles of the Code. *See* §1-201(44). In contract law we are dealing with only two parties, and it is generally fair to hold Seller to his promise if Manufacturer has made a return promise. In negotiable instruments law we are dealing with three parties. The Code is not trying to hold Seller but Buyer and is trying to hold him when he has a defense. If, therefore, Manufacturer has not performed, the Code will deprive him of his expectation; but if he has performed, it will not deprive him of his reliance damages measured by the contract price.

222.   a.   No. *X* is a holder in due course who takes free of the defense. *See* §3-305(b) [§3-305(2)].

b.   No. Even though *Y* is not a holder in due course, having taken with notice, *see* §3-302(a)(2) [§3-302(1)(c)], he has the rights of a holder in due course. *See* §3-203(b) [§3-201(1)]. The law gives him those rights to protect *X*'s market for the check.

c.   The law does not protect *X*, however, to the extent of letting the fraudulent seller come within the umbrella of *X*'s holder in due course status. *See* §3-203(b) (second clause) [§3-201(1) (second clause)].

223.   a.   *X* may enforce the note but for the amount originally drawn only. The law assumes that *X* is in a better position to prevent Seller's fraud than Buyer is. *See* §3-407(c)(i) [§3-407(3)]. (This answer assumes, of course, that Buyer's conduct does not contribute to Seller's fraud. If Buyer is negligent and somehow makes it easy for Seller to raise the note, Buyer may run afoul of an estoppel rule. *See* §3-406.)

b.   *Y* comes within the shelter of *X*'s holder in due course status and thus can recover, but only according to the original tenor of the item. *See* §3-203(b) [§3-201(1)].

c.   Under §3-407(b) [§3-407(2)(a)], Seller may not enforce the instrument at all. This is a rare instance of moral outrage in the normally amoral Code. Here, Buyer enjoys a windfall, and the Code punishes Seller for her fraud.

Section 35.   *The Bank-Customer Relationship*

224.   a.   Not properly payable. If the payor bank pays this item, it will not be obeying the order of its depositor. The depositor never gave an order, so the payment is improper.

b.   Not properly payable. The drawer ordered the bank to pay to the order of Payee. Bank paid to the order of forger.

c.   This forged indorsement is dispensable. §3-201(b) [§3-202(1)]. A party taking the instrument would be a holder with or without the indorsement, and the payor may pay the holder because that payment would be consistent with the drawer's instructions.

d.   The check is properly payable only according to its original tenor: $100. *See* §§3-407(c), 4-401(d)(1) [§§3-407(3), 4-401(2)(a)]. Note that this rule puts the risk of alterations on the payor bank, not on the customer. This is a general rule subject to an estoppel exception. *See* §3-406. The general rule is based on the assumption that the party taking after the alteration is better able to prevent the fraud than the party issuing the check before the alteration.

e. Under the old version of Article 4, most courts considered a post-dated check not properly payable. In the check collection industry it is currently the fact, however, that bank reader-sorter equipment is incapable of reading the date. On all but the largest checks, which banks intercept and handle manually, the bank's equipment pays the check without regard to its date. The rule that the check is not properly payable permits the drawer to use the banking system in a way that most people do not use it. For the banks to look at every date on the checks, most of which are handled by machine, would increase check collection costs prohibitively, though evolving imaging processing technology may give bank equipment that capacity in the future. The banking practices are efficient, and the rule is inconsistent with them, but the losses from payment of post-dated checks have been minimal. The revised Article 4 permits customers to use the post-dated check and hold the bank to the date, but only if the customer notifies the bank and, presumably, if the customer pays the bank's reasonable charges. *See* §4-401, comment 3. In view of customary bank practices of not examining all but checks in the largest denominations, new Article 3 and revised Article 4 define "ordinary care" in a way to relieve a bank from the responsibility of examining checks unless the bank's internal practices require it. *See* §3-103(a)(7); *cf.* §4-104(c) (incorporating Article 3 definition of "ordinary care").

f. A check drawn on insufficient funds is not for that reason alone improperly payable. *See* §4-401(a) [§4-401(1)]. The bank-customer deposit agreement disposes of the question. *See* §4-401, comment 1. *See also* Problem 225(b) (dealing with the same question).

g. This check is properly payable. If the thief is gone with the funds, the Code puts the loss for this fraud on the payee, who should not have left a check with a blank indorsement lying around. Careful payees do not indorse checks until they are about to deposit them. If they choose to indorse them earlier, they can indorse them restrictively, *see* §3-206(c) [§3-206(3)], and protect themselves; or they can indorse in blank and take the risk of loss.

h. This check is not properly payable, but if the payor pays the payee, the drawer cannot complain. The drawer has sustained no damages; the correct party will have received the funds. *Cf.* §4-401(b) (excusing customer from liability when customer did not sign check *and did not benefit from proceeds of check*). Under §4-401(b) and cases decided under the old version of Article 4, the customer cannot complain when the bank pays a check that is improperly payable if the funds go to satisfy the customer's debt.

225. a. No. As a general rule, the Code does not impose a duty of care on banks. In fact, it does not always impose a duty of good faith. The basis for these apparently loose rules is the assumption that banks will normally act honestly and that fact finders (usually a jury) should not be charged with the duty to review bank operations. In short, these rules reflect a measure of mistrust in the jury

system on the part of the Code drafters. The drafters did not want to reward dishonesty or lack of due care; they simply did not want to open the questions. (Some of your teachers will quarrel with this answer.)

b. Under the revised version of Article 4, the bank may not create an overdraft in excess of that permitted by the customer's agreement with the bank. *See* §4-401(a) (second sentence). Under the old version of Article 4, arguably, the bank may agree with its customer to surrender rights the Code gives it. In this problem, the payor has agreed that it will not pay overdrafts exceeding a certain amount. That agreement alters the rule of old Article 4's §4-401(1), which gives the bank the unlimited right to pay overdrafts. Under either version of Article 4, however, in all probability the customer will have a difficult time showing any loss by virtue of the bank's breach of the overdraft agreement. If the bank paid the customer's creditor, the customer has benefitted from the payment and probably will not be able to recover in a breach of contract action. *Cf.* §4-401(b) (relieving customer of liability to bank if bank pays an instrument the customer did not sign *provided customer does not benefit from payment*).

226.
a. Yes.

b. Yes, if he can prove that the payment caused them.

c. It is difficult to see any damages here. The question assumes that the automobile's fair market value exceeds the debt. In that case, a sale in accord with the rules of Article 9 would yield a surplus that the creditor would have to pay to the customer. *See* §9-504(2). The costs of the sale might be recoverable, however.

d. Yes, but lost profits are notoriously difficult to prove, as are mental anguish damages and the fact that a bounced check caused ulcers. Of course, there are witnesses that will testify to anything, and judges and jurors that will believe anything.

e. Sometimes checks bounce for quite honest reasons. When they do, drawers replace them. Often the process of replacing them is inconvenient to both the payee and the drawer; but it is difficult to imagine that the fact alone that a down payment check bounced will cause a customer to lose the benefit of his bargain under a contract. Of course, there are witnesses that will testify. . . .

f. No. *See* §1-106(1). This answer assumes that the payor has acted mistakenly and in good faith, as that term is defined in §1-201(19). In the event of bad faith (that is, intentional, wrongful dishonor), the old version of §4-402 suggests in the view of some that damages in the nature of punitive damages or presumptive damages under the "trader rule" are available. *See* §4-402, comment 1 (revised version).

227. [The first three parts of this question rehearse some of the issues under the old version of Article 4 that may not have survived revision of the article.]

a. All of the damages permitted in Problem 226 plus presumptive damages for "traders." [§4-402 (second sentence)].

b. Some case authority would lump this kind of mistake in with bad faith and allow the presumptive damages for the trader.

c. Mistake of fact probably is included in the mistake rule of §4-402 that limits recovery to actual damages proved.

d. No recovery under §4-402, but possible recovery under supplemental principles. *See* §4-402, comment 5. [The authority under old Article 4 is split with at least one case allowing recovery and other authority denying recovery on the grounds that the corporation, not the individual, is the customer.]

228. Such an attempt probably violates §4-103(a) [§4-103(1)] and is unenforceable.

229. No. Section 4-103(a) [§4-103(1)] denies freedom of contract to modify a duty of due care or good faith imposed by the Code. Arguably, by not imposing a duty of due care in §4-401 (see Answer 225A), the Code drafters intentionally left that issue out of the inquiry. Bear in mind that there is a difference between saying that we do not care that banks are negligent and saying that we do not want banks to have to defend their collection and payment practices to juries every time they pay a check. Only in fairy tales do juries always reach the fair and just result. In some counties and circuits of the real world, banks have a hard time obtaining a fair and just verdict from a jury deciding a due care question. The Code drafters evidently were aware of the problem and of the fact that verdicts against banks that are not justified are wasteful. (Some of your teachers will disagree with this answer too.)

230.

a. Arguably there should be no recovery because the customer has not proved any damages. *See* §4-403(c) [§4-403(3)].

b. Here, the customer has shown the damages. He cannot simply return the merchandise to the seller but is out the funds and holds defective goods. Customer should recover the difference between the goods as warranted and the goods as delivered. *See* §2-714(2). Note that the bank is not liable for consequential damages suffered by reason of the seller's breach of the sales agreement. Buyer, the bank's customer, is going to suffer those damages whether the bank stops payment or not. They are a consequence of the seller's breach, not of the bank's wrongful payment over the stop payment order.

231. As subrogee of the buyer-customer's rights in the sales contract between the seller and the buyer, it should proceed against the seller and assert the damage claim that Article 2 affords the disappointed buyer under §2-714. *See* §4-407(3) [§4-407(c)].

232. Yes. Under these facts, Second Bank is a holder in due course. The payor bank is subrogated to the rights of Second, which would be able to enforce the check against Buyer if the payor had dishonored. Thus the payor bank's failure to honor the stop payment order has not damaged Buyer. To recredit Buyer's account would be to enrich Buyer unjustly. Under these facts, the payor bank is under no duty to recredit Buyer's account. *See* §4-407(1) [§4-407(a)].

233. In Problem 230a, the payee has a right to be paid, and the bank might defend the customer's action for recovery under §4-403(c) [§4-403(3)] (no showing of damages) or §4-407(b) [§4-407(b)] (bank subrogated to rights of seller against buyer in underlying sales contract).

234. a. The answer depends on whether the courts read §4-407 as displacing non-Code law. Comment 5 to that section indicates that an action in restitution would lie.

 b. The payor bank may use subrogation against the seller in the setting outlined in Problem 230b. In that case, the payor is subrogated to the rights of the buyer against the seller in the underlying transaction. *See* §4-407(3) [§4-407(c)].

Section 36. Warranties

235. If First honors after *T* forged *S*'s indorsement, First may assert a breach of presentment warranty under §4-208(a)(1) [§4-207(1)(a)] against Second, which in turn may assert a breach of transfer warranty under §4-207(a)(1) [§4-207(2)(a)] against a prior party that has made such a warranty. Thus, if Thief steals the check from *S* and forges *S*'s indorsement, Second will breach its presentment warranty to the effect that it is authorized to obtain payment [warranty of good title under old Article 4]. A party holding an instrument through a forged indorsement is not entitled to enforce it and does not have good title. Thief will have breached its transfer warranty of authority [good title] to Second. If First dishonors, there can be no breach of a presentment warranty because the beneficiary of the presentment warranty, First, has not parted with funds. Second, however, will have a breach of the transfer warranty claim against Thief.

236. a. If First honors, it will bear the loss under the doctrine of Price v. Neal, 3 Burr. 1354 (K.B. 1762), a Lord Mansfield decision that held payors liable for paying against the forged signature of the drawer — *B* in our model transaction. Price v. Neal is at the bottom of the warranty rules. If your interpretation of a warranty section conflicts with this simple rule of *Price*, your interpretation is wrong. *Price* is an anti-bank rule with which banks are quite comfortable. To read the warranty sections to conflict with *Price* is inconsistent with everyone's understanding of what they mean. The §4-207(a)(2) [§4-207(2)(b)] warranty that all signatures are good is a transfer warranty that does not run to First, the payor. First does benefit from the §4-208(a)(3) [§4-207(1)(b)] presentment warranty that *S* does not know of any forgery of the drawer's signature. Seldom, however, will *S*, the victim of Forger's fraud, know of the forgery. First may not debit *B*'s account because the item, bearing a forged drawer's signature, is not properly payable. It is not *B*'s order. These results may not be crystal clear from the language of the respective provisions, but they are clearly dictated by the Price v. Neal rule. *See* §3-417, comment 3 [§4-207, comment 4].

b.   No. An affirmative answer would give the payor bank a breach of warranty action when the drawer's signature is forged and thus overturn *Price*, a result we know from the comment that the drafters did not intend.

c.   *S* is liable to Second for breaching the transfer warranty that all signatures are genuine. *See* §4-207(a)(2) [§4-207(2)(b)]. *S* may not recover from *B* because *B* did not sign the check. *S* may recover from the forger, if she can find him. By signing *B*'s name to the check, the forger is liable as a drawer. *See* §§3-403(a), 3-414(b) [§§3-404(1), 3-413(2)].

237.   a.   Second makes transfer warranties to subsequent banks in the collection chain but not to First.

b.   Second has breached the presentment warranty of authority [good title], *see* §4-208(a)(1) [§4-207(1)(a)], which it does make to First. Second does not have authority [good title], because a necessary indorsement, that of *S*, is missing.

c.   If the thief steals the check after *S* indorses, Second has authority [good title] and does not breach the presentment warranty. *S* will probably end up bearing the loss here by virtue of having indorsed in blank. *B* is not liable to *S* on the check, which is paid, thereby discharging *B* on the check and on the underlying sales contract. *See* Problem 212. If the thief steals the check before *S* indorses it, the thief will have to forge the indorsement before any bank will take the instrument. Once there is a forgery, Second will probably bear the loss because the thief will be gone or insolvent; and Second will breach its presentment warranty of authority [good title] if the payor bank pays. Note that if the payor pays, it will not be able to charge *B*'s account because the check, bearing a forged indorsement, is not properly payable. *B* would not be discharged on the check or on the underlying obligation and would still be liable to *S* for the goods or services *S* has provided. *S*, then, will not bear any loss if the thief steals it before *S* indorses.

238.   a.   First may debit *B*'s account only according to the original tenor of the item. *See* §§3-407(c), 4-401(d)(1) [§§3-407(3), 4-401(2)(a)]. First may then recover $900 from Second for breach of the §4-208(a)(2) [§4-207(1)(c)] presentment warranty.

b.   In the event First dishonors the check entirely, Second, if it has given value to the thief, would be able to recover from *B* according to the original tenor of the item ($100). *See* §3-407(c) [§3-407(3)]. Second could recover from *S* for breach of the transfer warranty in §4-207(a)(3) [§4-207(2)(c)].

c.   No. This is the case in which the Code in effect imposes a penalty and permits *B* to enjoy a windfall. When First dishonors, Second can enforce the instrument according to its altered tenor against *S*. *See* §3-415(a) [§3-414(1)]. If *S* makes Second whole, *B* will get the goods or services from *S* without paying for them, for *S* cannot enforce the instrument, even according to its original tenor against *B*. *See* §3-407(b) [§3-407(2)(a)]. *S*, of course, is usually not present or is financially irresponsible and cannot answer to Second's breach of warranty claim. Query, furthermore, whether *S* might not argue successfully that in the event Second makes a claim for breach of the transfer warranty that the amount of Second's recovery should be $900, because Second has a good claim against *B* for that amount. In that case, would *B* have a claim against *S* for the $100? (I do not know.)

Section 37. *Conversion*

239.

a. This is common law conversion. Note that it is not one of the enumerated acts of conversion in §3-420(a) [§3-419(1)] but is an instance of conversion of personal property, which is by the language of the section applicable to instruments. [The lack of any such reference to personal property law and conversion in old Article 3 tells you something about the list of conversion acts in that section, namely, that it is an incomplete list. This implication is made explicit in new Article 3.]

b. This is not conversion under new Article 3. *See* §3-420(a) (last sentence). *B* is an "issuer" and cannot bring an action for conversion of the instrument. [Under old Article 3, a convincing line of authority took the position that this is not conversion. The check has no value in *B*'s hands. Not all courts or writers agreed, however. *But cf.* §3-420, comment 1 (second paragraph) (endorsing line of authority under old Article 3).]

c. This is also conversion as a matter of personal property law and, therefore, is conversion under §3-420. [It is also conversion at common law and is incorporated by inference in §3-419(1).]

d. This is also conversion. Bear in mind that in tort law, conversion is a matter of strict liability. It matters not whether the converter is careful or acting in good faith. Any interference with a person's property rights is conversion.

e. This is conversion under §3-420(a) (second sentence) [§3-419(1)(c)].

f. This is conversion at common law and is conversion for which Second will be liable under new Article 3. *See* §3-420, comment 3. [This is also conversion under old Article 3, though in the view of some courts and commentators old §3-419(3) did away with it. There is strong authority under old Article 3 to the contrary. New Article 3 notes the controversy and opts for the view that the depositary bank should be liable. *See* §3-420, comment 3 (1990).]

g. The addition of an unnecessary indorsement is not conversion, nor is the payment by the drawer of a check bearing such a forgery, nor is the handling of such a check by a bank in the collection chain.

240.

a. This is a classic case. First cannot charge the account of its customer because the check, bearing a forged indorsement, is not properly payable. *See* Answer 224b.

b. If the bank does debit the account of *B*, *S* may sue First in conversion. *See* §3-420(a) [§3-419(1)(c)]. Ultimately, *B* and *S*, unless she is negligent in such fashion to contribute to the forgery, *see* §3-406(a), or unless she has ratified it, will shift the loss to First. Note, however, that First is not without recourse — against Second, which breached its presentment warranty of authority [good title], *see* §4-208(a)(1) [§4-207(1)(a)]. Second, in turn, has a breach of transfer warranty claim against *T-2*, if Second can find him. *See* §4-207(a)(1) [§4-207(2)(a)]. Note also, to complete the picture and this little review, that *S* could have sued Second in conversion under new Article 3 and under a line of authority construing old Article 3. *See* Answer 239f.

241.
a. *T-2* has converted the property of *S*, and *S* may recover from *T-2*.
b. Under new Article 3, *B*, issuer of the check, may not sue in conversion. *See* §3-420(a) (last sentence). [Under old Article 3, some courts argued that there is no conversion here because *B* has been deprived of no property interest other than the pennies that it costs *B* to have the check printed. New Article 3 accepts that analysis. *See* §3-420, comment 1 (second paragraph). Not all courts have accepted it under old Article 3, however.]
c. Under new Article 3, the answer is clear. Second is liable and it does not matter whether it does not have proceeds of the check, observed reasonable banking practices, or "cashed" the check. [Those facts do bear on the issue in some jurisdictions under old Article 3. This question elicits a rehearsal of the controversy of the meaning of §3-419(3) (old version). Some courts read the provision as protecting the collecting bank if it has paid out funds to *T-2*. Other courts, using pre-Code logic that is rather compelling, contend that the provision protects the collecting bank in only the narrowest of settings. In all events, under old Article 3, Second will be protected by the provision only if Second observes reasonable banking practices.]
d. First has converted the check and is therefore liable to *S*. *See* §3-420(a) (second sentence) [§3-419(1)(c)].

242.
a. *B* may force First to recredit his account. The check was not properly payable. *See* Answer 224a. [Under old Article 3, some courts would let *B* recover from Second and *F* in conversion; others would not. The comments to new Article 3 make it clear that the drafters of new Article 3 disapprove of cases letting *B* sue in conversion. *See* §3-417, comment 2 (new version).]
b. Unless an estoppel rule applies, *S* may recover in conversion from First, which has paid over a forged indorsement. *See* §3-420(a) [§3-419(1)(c)]. *S* may also recover in conversion from *T-2* and from Second. *See* §3-420(c) [Under old Article 3, some courts construed §3-419(3) to mean that *S* could not recover in conversion from Second, the depositary bank, if the bank acted in good faith and in accordance with reasonable commercial standards of the banking industry.]

c. Here we have a double forgery. Under Price v. Neal, First should bear the loss. First paid over a forged drawer's signature. Under the presentment warranty section, First should be able to recover from Second because Second breached its presentment warranty of authority [good title]. The few cases that have confronted this conflict in the subsections consider this to be a case of a forged drawer's signature and ignore the breach of warranty cause of action. Thus Lord Mansfield's rule in Price v. Neal enjoys a strong measure of vitality.

243.

a. *S* has a cause of action against *T* at common law for conversion of the check and under §3-420(a).

b. *S*'s attempt to recover from *X* on a conversion theory will fail. *X* is a holder in due course. Conversion is a claim, and §3-306 [§3-305(1)] provides that the holder in due course takes free of all claims.

c. *S* will not recover from *Y* because *Y* comes within the shelter of *X*. *See* §3-203(b) [§3-201].

d. If the indorsement is forged, the answers to b and c are different. In the case of a forged indorsement, *X* is not a holder and, therefore, is not a holder in due course. *X*, then, takes subject to the claims of *S*; and *Y* has no shelter.

Section 38.   Estoppel

244.

a. Probably yes, even though First paid over a forged drawer's signature. The facts indicate that the negligence of the customer substantially contributed to the forgery, thereby estopping the customer under §3-406 from asserting that the signature is not genuine. There remains, however, the matter of First's conduct, which Part b of this answer addresses.

b. Note that under subsection (b) of new Article 3, the bank's contributory negligence renders the liability comparative. [Under old §3-406, the bank's contributory negligence is a complete bar to its use of the estoppel rule.] If First did not examine the drawer's signature on the check, some courts might take the position that the bank has not observed reasonable banking practices, even though everyone knows that banks cannot examine all signatures and even though we do not want them examining all of the signatures. There are roughly four billion checks that run through the banking system each month. If banks examine all of the drawers' signatures, they will solve the nation's unemployment problems, but they probably will not catch many forgeries. Under new Article 3, a bank that does not examine the signature is not negligent if it has observed its own practices, as long as those practices are not unusually at variance from general banking usage. See §§3-103(a)(7), 4-104(c). If it is the bank's practice to examine signatures on checks above a certain amount, failure to observe that practice would render the bank contributorily negligent with attendant consequences.

245.   a.   Arguably, First may debit the account because the negligence of B substantially contributed to the unauthorized completion. *See* §3-406(a) [§3-406]. Article 3 treats an unauthorized completion as if it were a material authorization. *See* §3-115(c) [§3-115(2)]. Some courts have held that it is a violation of reasonable standards of the bank collection industry for the payor to pay the check without looking at it, a look that in this case would have revealed the limitation in the legend. In fact, the bank collection industry rarely, if ever, looks at a check in this amount; and it would cost us all a lot more to have our checks collected if it did. If the court finds, however, that First did not exercise due care, the loss will be apportioned under a comparative negligence rule as new Article 3 provides. §3-406(b). [Under old Article 3, if the bank failed to exercise due care, it will not be able to assert the estoppel. *See* §3-406.]

b.   Because this unauthorized completion is the same as a material alteration, Second Bank has breached its presentment warranty. *See* §4-208(a)(2) [§4-207(1)(c)]. In that case, First Bank would be able to recover from Second. The loss, then, would fall on Second (as it probably should if a bank is to take the loss) because Second is much more likely to examine the instrument than First. Second's encoding clerk will handle the check. At First Bank, only machinery will handle it. Yet, allocation of the loss to Second should not be complete under new Article 3, which adopts in the general negligence section a comparative negligence regime. Section 3-406(a) permits Second to raise the estoppel against B. [Under old Article 3, Second's negligence or First's negligence is a complete bar to use of the estoppel rule; and B will prevail against both banks if the court finds them to be negligent. *See* §3-406.]

246.   a.   There is a good argument that S has been negligent and that his negligence will estop him under §3-406. Employers should keep track of their financial affairs, and their failure to do so is probably an instance of negligence. *T-2* had been engaging in this misconduct for a long-enough period that S should have discovered it. The length of time, moreover, would have lulled Second into thinking that the practice was surely authorized. It is also possible, though the facts of the question are incomplete, that S is negligent under §4-406 [§4-406]. *See generally* Problem 245. [In the view of most but not all courts construing old §3-406 and of most commentators, Second is a holder in due course if S is estopped. Does the language of the section fit that conclusion? (No.) Does the intent of the section? (Yes.)] Under both the old and new sections, First is a payor that benefits from the section's estoppel rule if the payor observes reasonable banking practices. Remember that the consequences of the banks' failure to exercise due care varies under old and new Article 3. *See* Answers 243 and

244. If this were the first time that *T-2* had misbehaved, *S* is probably not negligent; there is no estoppel; and both banks are liable in conversion to *S*.

b. Yes, under new Article 3 if *T-2* has "responsibility" for checks, *B* is bound by *T-2*'s indorsement, *B*'s care or lack of care notwithstanding. This rule, which is a new one, is subject to a comparative negligence-type allocation of damages in the event the banks are guilty of failure to exercise due care. *See* §3-405(b).

247.

a. Yes. *See* §3-404(b) [§3-405(1)(b)]. Second has breached the warranty, but §4-208(c) prevents First from favoring its negligent customer by putting the loss on Second. [Section 4-406(5) of the old version of Article 4 indicates in a different setting that the Code drafters did not want First to be able to shift the loss to Second.]

b. Second could recover. ABC is estopped under §3-404(b) [§3-405(1)(c)] from claiming that the indorsements are bad. Second would be a holder and a person entitled to enforce the check, *see* §§3-301, 3-414(b) [§3-413(2)]. It would not benefit ABC to stop payment because Second would be able to enforce the instrument against ABC, whose obligation to pay Second in the event of dishonor is codified in §3-414(b) [§3-413(2).]

c. There is authority that Second's conduct violates reasonable banking practices. Under new Article 3, that negligence will result in allocation of the loss in accordance with comparative negligence principles. [Under old Article 3, the bank's negligence may not deprive Second of the estoppel rule in §3-405. Old §3-405, in contrast to old §3-406, does not fashion a contributory negligence bar. While some courts have read a contributory negligence bar into old §3-405, the better view is that there is no contributory negligence bar. Other courts have held that the policy of putting the loss on the employer of the faithless employee overrides concern for due care in the bank collection system, a matter not easily amenable to jury determination.]

d. No. *See* §3-404(b), comment 2, Case #1 [§3-405(1)(b)].

e. As long as it is clear, as it is in this problem, that the faithless employee intended from the start that the payees would not have any interest in the checks, §3-404(b) governs, and the indorsements are good. [There is some authority under old Article 3 that the existence of actual payees prevents the payor and the holders from contending that the faithless employee formulated the intent to defraud his employer at the time he drew the checks (payroll clerk fraud) or submitted the names and hours to the payroll clerk (human resources manager fraud). That authority relies heavily on literal interpretation of the words "intends" and "intending" in the old provision, §3-405(1)(b) and (c), at the expense, it would seem, of the provision's underlying reason. The Code, recall, commands the courts to interpret the sections according to their reason, not their language. *See* §1-102 and comment 1 (last paragraph). If the faithless employee formulates his fraudulent intent after he draws the check, new §3-405 applies. Note that new §3-405(b) overturns the literalist view. *See* §3-405, comment 3, Cases #6 and #7.]

    f.   If the checks are written to fictitious suppliers, the faithless employee had the requisite fraudulent intent when he drew the checks; and under new Article 3, §3-404(b) governs, and ABC may not contest the indorsements. Similarly, if the checks are payable to real parties who have not supplied anything to ABC, the faithless employee had the requisite intent at the time he drew the checks, and §3-404(b) prevents ABC from contesting the indorsements. *See* §3-404, comment 2, Case #2. [Under old Article 3, the result should be the same. *See* §3-405(1)(b) and (c).]

248.   a.   *A* has probably failed to examine the bank statement and report the alteration promptly as §4-406(c) [§4-406(1)] requires, but the failure did not cause the bank any loss. *See* §4-406(d)(1) [§4-406(2)(a)]. First gave *L* the money on May 5 before the statement and the check were available to *A*. First must recredit the account because the check was properly payable only according to its original tenor. *See* §4-401(d) [§4-401(2)(a)]. Note that the time limit in §4-406(d)(2) [§4-406(2)(b)] applies to multiple alteration or multiple forgery cases and does not apply to single alteration or single forgery cases.

    b.   The clear language of §4-406(d)(2) [§4-406(2)(b)] supports the bank's position that *A* is estopped here and cannot claim that the second check was not properly payable. First may recover from Second only if First cannot recover from *A*. *See* §4-406(f) (last sentence) [§4-406(5)]. [Note that under old §4-406(2)(b), in multiple alteration or multiple forgery cases, a customer had 14 days to examine the statement. Under revised §4-406(d)(2), the customer has 30 days.]

    c.   Subsection (d) [subsection (2)(a)] only applies to forgeries of the drawer's signature and alterations. There is no preclusion under revised §4-406 when a customer fails to detect a forged indorsement. There is no duty under the section for the customer to look for forged indorsements. [Subsection (2)(b) of old §4-406 refers to "an unauthorized" signature and arguably applies to forged indorsements. *A* is not in a position to discover forged indorsements easily; and the better view is that Subsection (2) does not apply to forged indorsements and that the language of the subsection is infelicitous.]

    d.   If *L* maintained an account at First and did not withdraw the funds until a date after the time that *A* should have reported the alteration, First can satisfy the requirements of subsection (d)(1) [subsection (2)(a)]; it can show that the customer's failure to examine the statement and report the alteration caused the bank loss. Had *A* notified First in time, First could have charged *L*'s account and avoided the loss.

    e.   If First does not observe ordinary standards of care, §4-406(e) allocates the loss in accordance with standard comparative negligence principles. [Under the old section, the bank's negligence operates to bar the bank from using the estoppel. *See* §4-406(3).]

    f.   i.   one year; *see* §4-406(f) [§4-406(4)].

        ii. three years; *see* §4-111 [§4-406(4)].

           Note that these rules are statutes of limitations and apply irrespective of due care or absence thereof by the bank.

249.   a. First may charge *B*'s account because *B* is estopped from asserting that the indorsement is forged. *See* §3-404(a) [§3-405(1)(a)].

    b. The preceding answer assumes that the bank exercised ordinary care. If it did not, the comparative fault rules apply under new Article 3. *See* §3-404(d). [There is no contributory negligence rule in §3-405 of old Article 3, and most courts hold that the bank's lack of due care is not relevant. A minority ignores the negative implication in the absence of any reference to the bank's conduct in §3-405 and would bar the bank from using the estoppel if the bank does not exercise due care.]

250.   a.   i.   First may charge the company's account if §3-406 [§3-406] or §4-406 [§4-406] applies to the unauthorized drawer signature. The facts on that issue are incomplete. The indorsement, whether or not the drawer's signature is authorized, operates as an effective indorsement. [The result would be the same under old Article 3. *See* §3-405(1)(b).]

        ii. Again, §3-404 does not address the question of the unauthorized drawer's signature but does make the indorsement effective. [And again, the result under old Article 3 would be the same. *See* §3-405(1)(b).] If *O* is not an employee of the company, §3-404 would apply, as the comment indicates, but the bank will have to deal with the unauthorized drawer signature issue under other provisions. [Under old Article 3, the cases have reached a similar result, holding that the issue is one of whether the drawer's signature is effective. The courts ignore the forged indorsement and treat the double forgery as a forged drawer's signature or "forged check" case.]

        iii. Because this is an instance of an employee's drawing a check with fraudulent intent that the payee not have any interest in the check, §3-404 applies; and the bank may charge the employer's account. [The result would be the same under old §3-405(1)(b).]

    b. In all of the cases, as the sections and comments indicate, the depositary banks have not breached any warranty because §3-404(b) makes them persons entitled to enforce the checks. In other words, because the forged indorsements are effective, the depositary banks do not breach the warranty of authority in §4-208(a)(1). [There is no section in old Article 3 that directly corresponds with subsection (b) of §3-404. In some cases, §3-406 would apply. As the preceding discussion indicates, courts that have precluded the drawer on the drawer forgery issue have ignored the indorsement issue and effected the results that new section §3-404(b) prescribes.]

Section 39. Final Payment

251.   a. The final payment doctrine applies here, and First may not recover from Second. *See* §3-418(c) [§3-418].

b. The answer would be different. Under these facts, Second is unjustly enriched (and Seller will soon be if First does not recover the payment) because it has not parted with value. *Id.*

c. The final payment doctrine does not prevent First from enforcing Second's presentment warranty of authority [good title], a warranty that it has breached by virtue of the forged indorsement. *See* §§3-418(c) (second sentence), 4-208(a)(1) [§§3-418 (first phrase), 4-207(1)(a)].

d. No, the answer would be the same. The final payment doctrine applies when the payor's mistake consists of paying an overdraft. *See* §3-418(a).

e. Yes. The final payment doctrine protects Second, a party that has given value in good faith. It does not protect the seller in these circumstances. *See* §3-418(c) (last sentence) [§3-418 (first phrase)]. For a case in which a seller is protected, see Problem 252.

f. The final payment doctrine applies irrespective of the bank's care or lack of care. *See* §3-418(a) (last sentence).

252.   a. No, the final payment doctrine applies. Seller changed its position in reliance on the payment. *See* §3-418(c) [§3-418].

b. No. The final payment doctrine would still apply, but the bank might have a partial recovery by subrogating itself to the recoupment rights of the buyer against the seller in the underlying transaction. *See* §4-407(3) [§4-407(c)].

c. *T* is not one of the parties protected by the final payment doctrine, and First could recover the payment from *T*.

d. The answer would be the same. First has paid by mistake and will not be able to charge Buyer's account, but First will be able to recover from a payee that has not given value or changed its position in reliance on payment.

2. DOCUMENTS OF TITLE

Section 40. The Documentary Draft Transaction

253.   a. Generally the buyer has the right to examine the goods unless he agrees to pay "against documents" or otherwise expressly agrees that he will pay before inspecting the goods. *See* §§2-512, 2-513(1).

b. In these contracts, which traditionally appear in international trade, the buyer has agreed, in effect, that it will not have the right to examine the goods before payment. These contracts assume that the document of title covering the goods will arrive in the buyer's country before the goods do and that the buyer must honor the draft that accompanies the document of title at the time the documents arrive.

c. The CIF and C&F sale are still relatively common in international trade. These contracts are similar to the FOB contract in that they assume that the documents will arrive before the goods do and that the buyer will honor the draft when the buyer receives the document of title.

d. The cash on delivery sale also assumes, under Article 2, that the buyer will pay before examining the goods.

254. a. In both of these events, Second has given value. It is not necessary for the bank to make any bookkeeping entries. Delivery of a properly indorsed draft to the bank in satisfaction of a pre-existing debt or as security for a debt is sufficient to satisfy the value requirement of §3-302(a)(2) [§3-302(1)(a)]. *See* §3-303(a)(3) [§3-303(b)].

b. Under §3-303(a)(4) [§3-303(c)], the bank has given value.

255. No. Under this scenario, when Seller delivers the draft to Second for collection, Second forwards the draft to a bank (Third Bank) in Buyer's city. That bank presents the draft to Buyer for acceptance. In the normal course, Buyer will accept the draft by signing it on its face and returning it to Third. Third will hold for Second or will buy the draft from Second. In either case, the bank holding the item will be a holder in due course and will have the power under §3-305(b) [§3-305(2)] to cut off Buyer's underlying contract defenses.

256. Buyer dishonors the time draft either by refusing to accept the draft when it is presented by Third Bank for acceptance or by refusing to pay the draft when it comes due 60 days after acceptance. *See* §3-502(b)(3) [§3-507(1)(a)]. Buyer dishonors a sight draft by refusing to pay it when it is first presented. *See* §3-502(b)(2) [§3-507(1)(a)]. A sight draft need not be presented for acceptance but is presented for payment, unless presentment is excused.

257. a. Yes. *See* §3-305(a)(3) [§3-306(b)]. The failure of Second to be a holder in due course renders it subject to all defenses that are good in the underlying contract.

b. Yes as to the first setoff defense, but no as to the second. The first setoff is a valid defense under contract law. The second is not because it would not be valid against Seller. *See* §2-717, comment 1.

c. Payment is a defense in the underlying contract. It is folly, of course, for the obligor on a negotiable instrument to pay the underlying obligation without obtaining surrender of the instrument, for if the instrument finds its way into the hands of a holder in due course, the obligor will have to pay the holder. In this problem, the acceptor got lucky. The acceptance did not find its way into the hands of a holder in due course.

d. These facts constitute failure of consideration. *See* §3-305(a)(2) [§3-306(c)].

Section 41.   The Bill of Lading

258.   a. No. *See* §7-403(4). The carrier has erred, but the error has not caused the shipper any loss. The error may cause the carrier loss, however, if the bill finds its way into the hands of a holder by due negotiation. In that case, the holder will be able to recover losses from the carrier when the carrier cannot deliver the goods to the holder. Because the buyer received the goods, under the facts of this problem, the seller, the shipper of the goods, will be unable to show that the carrier caused the seller any damages.

            b. Yes. In these settings the carrier has violated its duty under §7-403(1) to deliver the goods to the person entitled as defined in §7-403(4). Seller must still show damages, however. Presumably it could do so because the misdelivery to a stranger will prevent the buyer from obtaining the goods and will render the seller-shipper in breach of the sales contract.

259.   The holder does indeed have a cause of action against the carrier under §7-403. The carrier has an obligation to deliver to the holder. Also, the holder, if he is the buyer, may have a cause of action against the seller for failing to deliver and thereby breaching the underlying contract.

260.   Here, Third has failed in its duty as a collecting bank. Although it is not clear from the section, in law and in fact, Third has not observed due care in the presentment of the item and is liable. *See* §4-202(a)(1) [§4-202(1)(a)]. A bank that presents an item (the draft) should not permit the drawee to have the document of title until the drawee honors. The issue here is one of determining the liability that attends that failure. Unless there are mitigating circumstances, Third is liable for the face amount of the item. *See* §4-103(e) [§4-103(5)]. Note, however, that there is no notion in Article 4 supporting recovery of consequential damages in the event the collecting bank is negligent. That is an important principle.

261.   a. The problem with this arrangement is that is forces the seller to have an agent at the point of delivery to take the goods from the carrier or to give the carrier instructions changing the name of the party entitled to receive the goods under §7-403(4).

            b. If the seller changes the designation of the consignee, the buyer would no longer be the person entitled under §7-403(4), and the carrier should not deliver to the buyer. The problem with the arrangement is obvious. The seller may not learn of the buyer's credit problems in time to change the consignee designation. Essentially, this is a sale on open account, and sellers should not use the arrangement unless they are confident of the buyer's credit worthiness or are willing to assume the risk.

            c. Until the seller indorses the bill, no one but the seller can take delivery because the holder of the bill is the person entitled under §7-403(4). Thus, the seller or her agent will have to be at the destination to take the goods from the carrier.

Section 42.   The Warehouse Receipt

262.   a.   No. Section 7-204 applies when a bailor delivers goods to a warehouse and the warehouse loses them or the goods are destroyed, in which cases, of course, the warehouse cannot redeliver when the bailor requests the goods. Section 7-204 is a lost goods section, not a misdelivery section.

b.   Section 7-404 is confusing and has quite limited application. It is a legislative attempt to protect warehouses from conversion liability when they take goods from one not entitled to them and return the goods to that person at the end of the bailment. If a thief, for example, bails stolen goods, the warehouse that returns the goods to the thief will be liable in conversion at common law to the true owner. This provision, §7-404, alters that common law rule. That is its sole purpose.

c.   Yes, this is the section that governs when the warehouse misdelivers the goods.

263.   a.   X.
b.   X.
c.   Y.
d.   The holder of the receipt.
e.   Y.

264.   a.   Yes.
b.   No. *See* §7-404.

Section 43.   More on the Documentary Draft Transaction

265.   a.   Seller must reimburse under its engagement as drawer to pay the person entitled to enforce the instrument (the holder) in the event of dishonor. *See* §3-414(b) [§3-413(2)]. Seller avoided indorser liability by making the draft payable to the bank and thereby avoiding the need to indorse, but Seller drew the draft and thereby engaged to pay the holder in the event of dishonor.

b.   By endorsing without recourse, Seller avoided indorser liability, *see* §3-415(b) [§3-414(1)], but it is still the drawer and must pay the holder of the dishonored draft.

c.   By drawing without recourse, Seller avoided drawer liability, *see* §3-414(e) [§3-413(2)], but by indorsing has incurred indorser liability. *See* §3-415(a) [§3-414(1)].

d.   Second has no right of recourse, Seller having avoided both drawer and indorser engagements. *See* §§3-414(e), 3-315(b) [§§3-413(2), 3-414(1)].

266.   The first draft, being accompanied by a negotiable bill of lading, is more valuable than the second draft, which is accompanied by a nonnegotiable bill. If Second Bank takes the first draft and gives value for it, Second will have an Article 4 security interest in the bill and the goods it represents.

See §4-210(a) [§4-208(1)]. If Buyer honors the first draft, it will have the right to insist on a properly indorsed bill and will then hold the bill by due negotiation. *See* §7-501. A holder by due negotiation takes title to the bill and to the goods it represents. *See* §7-502(1). Takers of the nonnegotiable document do not enjoy these rights. *See* §7-504(1). If Second discounts the second draft, it will hold a nonnegotiable bill and arguably will have a security interest in it, for whatever a security interest in a nonnegotiable bill is worth. It is worth very little because the nonnegotiable bill does not represent the goods. Similarly, if Buyer honors the second draft and takes the nonnegotiable bill, Buyer will not be a holder by due negotiation because only the holder of a negotiable bill can rise to that level. *See* §7-501(4). Buyer's rights under the bill, then, will be no greater than his transferor's rights. *See* §7-504(1). The bank, having only a worthless security interest, can only transfer that worthless interest to Buyer.

267.   Second will be able to get the goods covered by the negotiable bill because, as the holder of the negotiable bill, it is the person entitled. *See* §7-403(4). It will also be protected in Seller's bankruptcy by virtue of a perfected security interest under Article 9. *See* §9-304(2). All of this is verified by the rule of Article 7 to the effect that the taker by due negotiation of the bill holds "title" to the goods. *See* §7-502(1)(a). Whether Second has any rights under the goods covered by the nonnegotiable bill depends on the seller's instructions to the carrier and on the Bankruptcy Code. In all probability, Second will have an unsecured claim in Seller's bankruptcy.

268.   a.   Yes, none of the events listed in Article 2 that prevent the seller from exercising the right have occurred. *See* §2-705(2).
        b.   Yes. Indorsement of a nonnegotiable document of title is meaningless.
        c.   Yes. The buyer that does not trust the seller does not pay against a nonnegotiable bill.
        d.   Yes. Note that acknowledgment by the carrier, which would be quite unusual, does not cut off the seller's right to stop shipment. *See* §2-705(2)(b).

For further instances of Buyer jeopardy when it is purchasing goods under a nonnegotiable bill, see §7-504(2).

269.   The carrier will deliver the goods to the consignee under a nonnegotiable bill without surrender of the bill because the consignee is the person entitled under §7-403(4). The carrier will not deliver the goods to a party that has lost the negotiable bill unless someone indemnifies the carrier against liability for misdelivery under §7-403. Note that Article 5 contains a provision facilitating that practice, which sometimes occurs in international shipments of goods under letters of credit. *See* §5-113. When the seller is shipping on open account, that is, when there is no documentary draft transaction, it will not ship under a negotiable bill. Most truck and rail bills in the U.S. are nonnegotiable.

270.   This problem is a warning that not all parties may rely on the description of goods in a bill of lading. First, even if the carrier does not disclaim liability, as it may under §7-301(1), only certain takers are protected, as the

problem and the answer indicate. Most of the time, the carrier will disclaim. Carriers are not inspectors of the packages and containers they receive from the shipper. If the banks and the buyer want protection of this kind, they usually must pay for it by having an independent inspector open the packages. The rules under the Carriage of Goods by Sea Act differ, however, making it more difficult for the carrier to disclaim. *See* 46 U.S.C. App. §1303 (1988).

With the advent of containerization, many commercial parties began the practice of arranging for inspection of the container at the seller's facility as the seller "stuffs" the container. After inspection, the seller and the inspector seal the container. The buyer relies on this procedure rather than on the description of the goods in the bill of lading.

   a. No recovery because, with respect to nonnegotiable bills, only the consignee of the nonnegotiable bill that takes for value in good faith may rely on the description in the bill. The buyer, not the bank, is the consignee under this bill. *See* §7-301(1).

   b. This buyer, assuming it is named in the bill as the consignee and that it takes in good faith, will be able to recover. *Id.*

   c. The bank takes by due negotiation and will be able to recover under the section. *Id.*

   d. This buyer is also a holder by due negotiation and will be able to recover from the carrier for misdescription under §7-301(1).

Section 44.   *Negotiation and Transfer of Documents of Title*

271.   a. If the bank gives value and otherwise satisfies the requisites for due negotiation in §7-501(4), it is a good-faith purchaser of the bill, that is, it is "a holder to whom a negotiable document of title is duly negotiated." §7-502(1). The key point here is that this bank is taking in the ordinary course of financing — a requirement of due negotiation. *See* §7-501(4).

   b. Assuming that it acts in good faith, *B* is acquiring the receipt in the regular course of business and would take by due negotiation under the section.

   c. Under the first set of facts, and assuming that it acted in good faith, the bank is taking in the regular course of financing and would benefit from status as a holder by due negotiation. If the broker fails to indorse, however, the bank would not be a holder and would not qualify for good-faith purchase protection. The law is moderately tough here. Indorsements matter. Failure to obtain the indorsement may mean that something was fishy. It would also matter if the bank knew of a prior interest in the grain or if the bank took the receipts in satisfaction of a debt. In both of those cases, the bank would not take by due negotiation. *See* §7-501(4).

   d. The manufacturer does not satisfy the requirements for due negotiation. *See* §7-501, comment 1 (second paragraph).

272.   a. The documentary draft does not appear to work here because the seller is not willing to ship the product until he receives pay-

ment. If the buyer pays, of course, he loses some leverage and may even lose the goods if the seller is dishonest or files in bankruptcy. Note, however, that the banking system might still be able to serve the parties by using a check, probably certified, and a delivery order. Buyer can ask his bank to initiate the delivery of the check on the condition that the bank in Seller's community not deliver it until the seller obtains the elevator's acceptance of the delivery order. Should the delivery order be in negotiable form? Yes, so that the resulting accepted delivery order, the equivalent of a warehouse receipt (*see* §7-102, comment 3) will be negotiable.

273.   a.   Arguably, the *McNabb* case is contrary to the purpose of §7-503(1)(a) and (b). *See* §7-503, comment 1 (third and fourth sentences).

　　　　　　b.   Yes, because in this event, Wilson is less culpable. It is more difficult to consider this conduct as clothing Brown with actual or apparent authority to bail the goods or as acquiescing in the bailment. *Id.*

　　　　　　c.   If the landlord's lien is comparable to a security interest, under the Code, National Chemical will lose to Wilson if Brown sells without a receipt because the buyer in ordinary course rule of §9-307(1) does not defeat a security interest created by this farmer. The landlord's lien, however, is not created by the farmer but by operation of law, and Article 9 does not deal with such liens. If this state of affairs is not confusing enough, the Food Security Act confuses it royally. But that is a matter for Article 9 study.

274.   a.   The bank is loaded with rights. Under §2-506, it has the rights of the seller. Under §7-502(1), it appears to have "title" to the document and to the goods it represents. Under §9-304(2), it has a perfected security interest in the document and in the goods. The Code's protection of the bank is limited, however, by the reality that the bank is not a purchaser here but a lender. Banks do not buy and sell commodities; they take security interests in them. This is a secured transaction; and if the value of the goods exceeds the bank's loan, the bank must account to the seller or the buyer or their respective trustees in bankruptcy for the excess. *See* §9-504(2).

　　　　　　b.   Section 9-309 says that nothing in Article 9 diminishes the rights of a holder by due negotiation who has rights under Article 7. Literal application of that rule would prevent the court from requiring the bank to disgorge the excess referred to in Answer a. That literal reading is not tenable.

　　　　　　c.   Here, literal application of §9-309 makes sense. The bank has behaved in commercially reasonable fashion. It has taken steps to protect its security interest by depriving Buyer of possession of the goods. Sub-buyer has behaved quite irresponsibly by paying for goods it cannot see. Sub-buyer may as well have bought the Brooklyn Bridge. There is authority, however, protecting Sub-buyer if it can show that the sub-purchase is in the ordinary course of business. There are not many industries in which parties pay for goods before they receive them or before they receive a document of title covering them. In those cases where buyers prepay, they may be lending the seller money. They are certainly relying on the seller's trustworthiness. If the seller is not trustworthy or creditworthy, the buyers should take the loss, not the banks that have acted with commercial punctilio.

3. LETTERS OF CREDIT

Section 45. Letter of Credit Transactions

275. a. & b. Buyer has complied with the underlying contract. Note that §2-325(3) does not require a "confirmed" credit unless the contract speaks of a "confirmed" credit. Sellers want the credit confirmed so that they can present their documents at a bank local to them and so that they have a local bank on the hook. Sellers expect that banks local to them will advise the credit in order to provide the seller with verification of the credit. Issuers do not need to be told of this requirement. It is so common that everyone will assume that the foreign issuer will ask a bank in seller's market to advise. There is no assumption, however, that the credit will be confirmed. The seller has to ask for that.

Traditionally, banks did have signature books to verify signatures on letters they received through the mails. They also had telex codes, "keys" that identified the sender of a telex message. Now, most bank use SWIFT, which is a form of electronic data interchange (EDI), computerized transmission that permits banks to communicate over a dedicated communications network provided by a cooperative that the banks themselves own. SWIFT permits the banks to identify each other, to verify that messages are accurate and authentic, and to communicate quickly, all with a minimum of data.

276.   a. Dutch Bank is the issuer. *See* §5-103(1)(c).
            b. First Bank is the adviser. *See* §5-103(1)(e). An adviser will be a confirmer if it adds its confirmation to the advice. An advice could and sometimes does contain a recital to the effect that: "This is only an advice. The undersigned assumes no obligation under this advice beyond the authenticity of the information in this advice."
            c. Because it added its confirmation, First Bank is a confirming bank as well as an advising bank. Typically a confirmation will appear in the advice in language such as the following: "The undersigned hereby advises and confirms the credit of Dutch Bank and undertakes to honor your drafts accompanied by the designated documents if presented at our counters on or before the expiry date specified above."
            d. The buyer applied for the credit for its account and is sometimes referred to as the applicant, sometimes as the account party, and sometimes as the customer (of the issuing bank).

e.   Seller is the beneficiary of the credit.

f.   In a confirmed-credit transaction, almost always the beneficiary must submit his documents at the confirmer's place of business and must do so on or before the expiry.

g.   Typically, a commercial letter of credit such as this one will call for a draft, a negotiable bill of lading describing the goods, a commercial invoice, evidence of insurance (usually an insurance certificate), perhaps an inspection certificate, and, if necessary, official documents needed to bring the goods through customs.

277.   Credits should not contain this kind of language, which, unfortunately comes from real cases. Experienced letter-of-credit bankers will refuse to issue, advise, or confirm such a credit. The problem is that credits are supposed to be payable against the presentation by beneficiary of specified pieces of paper. Standby credits can serve the function the parties in this transaction want the standby to serve, but only if the credit calls for certification of default, not if it calls for payment on default. Bankers are not investigators. They will not know whether default has occurred and cannot determine whether to pay the beneficiary unless their task is confined to one of examining documents. They should not be required by the terms of the credit or by credit law to decide what documents are sufficient to show a default in the underlying transaction. Letters of credit, then, even standby letters of credit, should only call for documents and should not be payable against factual conditions. Some courts have wisely refused to apply letter-of-credit law to undertakings that the parties style as letters of credit but that call for factual determinations. Such undertakings are bonds, not letters of credit.

278.   When an issuer refuses to pay a beneficiary, the letter of credit is working. Letters of credit are not nullities when the issuer does not pay. Letters of credit are binary: pay or no pay. Thus the contract rule of construction does not suit letters of credit. A letter-of-credit issuer that refuses to pay against nonconforming documents has observed the credit's terms in a valid, commercial sense. It has protected its customer as it promised to do when it entered into the application agreement when the customer applied for the credit.

279.   It might make sense to construe a credit against the drafter, but not against the issuer. Why construe a vague credit drafted by the beneficiary against the issuer and thereby force the applicant to suffer a loss resulting from the beneficiary's vague language? Rules of contract law should supplement the law of letters of credit only if contract rules do not harm the unique features of the credit. The notion of substantial compliance, a common theme in contract law, does not mesh well in the document examination process, nor do rules on course of dealing or performance. Some courts have invoked these rules in the credit context, however, as the *Banco Espanol* court did.

280.   New York courts are common-law courts that can fashion the common law in a way that differs radically from that of the Code, that is similar to the Code, or that is identical to the Code. The New York nonconforming provision arguably is only a rule that says the New York courts are free to do as they please and are not bound by the Code when the credit incorpo-

rates the UCP. Thus, if the New York court wants to create a common-law warranty that will permit the issuer to recover payment from the beneficiary who presents fraudulent documents, nothing in the nonconforming amendment should stop them. That is not to say that the New York courts must adopt a warranty rule. The nonconforming amendment prevents that argument. It is only to say that the New York courts may adopt a warranty rule if it makes sense to them to do so.

281.   a. The invoice is not complying under Article 37(c) of UCP 500, which requires the description of the goods in the invoice to "correspond" to that of the credit. Most courts, commentators, and bankers read that article as requiring the invoice to contain an *in haec verba* repetition of the description in the credit.

b. Who knows? The benefit of the UCP is that it answers this kind of nitty gritty, often recurring, question.

c. A cautious seller will insist that his invoice procedures result in a word-for-word repetition in the invoice of the description in the credit.

Section 46. *Duties of the Credit Issuer*

282. The issuer that pays a stranger has not honored the credit and therefore should not be entitled to reimbursement, though some commentators disagree. Banks might include language in the reimbursement agreement requiring the applicant to pay even when the bank pays the wrong party. Courts would do well to hold such clauses unenforceable as unconscionable or as an attempt to contract away liability for lack of due care, *see* §4-103(a) [§4-103(1)], unless there are obvious risks that the applicant willingly undertakes.

283.   a. The issuer should not pay. Courts have construed §5-114(1) as requiring the issuer to pay the beneficiary only if his documents comply strictly with the terms of the credit. The bill of lading is noncomplying.

b. The air bill is nonconforming. This is from an actual case. The court held that it was not up to the bank to figure out whether shipment of the goods by air rather than by sea was detrimental to the goods.

c. In another case, the court held that it was not up to the bank to determine whether this defect was material and that the bank was justified in dishonoring the beneficiary's draft.

284.   a. It strikes most courts as unfair that an applicant, at a time when everyone knows that the documentary defect is inconsequential, should be able to avoid reimbursing the issuer. The reimbursement context and the reimbursement relationship are arguably different from the payment context and the issuer-beneficiary relationship, where the parties (the document examiners) do not know whether the defect matters and cannot take time to find out. Thus, even though §5-109(1) requires the issuer to observe banking usages when it examines documents, and even though general banking usage is that the bank should not pay over a defective bill of lading such as this one, most courts will not permit the applicant to avoid reimbursement. In all probability, the applicant is seeking to avoid reimbursement because the market has fallen and she no longer wants the goods. Market risks belong on commercial parties, not banks. The bank's error did not cause the market to fall. If the applicant is a dealer in documents (some kind of importer for an industry) and would be unable to dispose of the documents if they are defective in any way, perhaps the applicant should be able to avoid reimbursing the issuer.

    b.   If, on the other hand, the defect causes the applicant loss, as it does when the goods are destroyed on the dock while they are not covered by marine insurance, surely the applicant should be able to resist reimbursing the issuer.

285.   a.   The bank should not pay. If it does, it would not be justified in charging its customer's account. The courts generally have been quite strict in applying the expiry date of a letter of credit.

    b.   The expiry applies to the presentation of the documents. If the beneficiary gets the documents to the counters of the payor bank, in this case, the issuer, prior to the expiry, the beneficiary has satisfied the credit. It does not matter that the issuer does not pay or does not determine that the documents are conforming until after the credit expires.

    c.   There may have been a time when and courts where this kind of argument would work, but that time and those courts are long gone. As you may know, in every courtroom there is a boom; and when a bank lawyer makes this kind of argument, the judge lowers it. These facts are a classic candidate for estoppel. The bank delayed, and the beneficiary did nothing because of the delay. The beneficiary relied to its detriment. Under classic estoppel, the bank will not be heard to say that the certificate is unsigned. The courts have uniformly so held.

    d.   If there is no detrimental reliance, some courts will not estop the bank. Under Article 14(d) of the Uniform Customs and Practice for Documentary Credits (UCP 500) (1993), rules fashioned by the Banking Commission of the International Chamber of Commerce and incorporated by reference into most letter of credit forms, the bank must give notice of defects without delay, not more than seven days after it receives the documents. If it fails to give that notice or if it fails in the notice to specify all of the defects, the bank is precluded under Article 14(e) from saying that the documents are nonconforming. The rule of Article 14 applies without regard to reliance and detriment.

286.   a.   The issuer must pay. *See* §5-114(1) (first sentence).

    b.   No. If the bank is relying on the goods, perhaps it should require an independent inspector's certificate to the effect that the goods conform. Then the bank would have some protection. Otherwise it must pay against conforming documents, the nonconformity of the goods in the underlying transaction notwithstanding, as the section indicates. *Id.*

c. It is possible that the information the bank obtained clashes with the certificate sufficiently that the certificate is fraudulent. In that case, §5-114(2) permits the bank to dishonor. Note that the section also gives the bank the prerogative of honoring in these circumstances if it can do so in good faith. Article 5 does not require the bank to determine who is telling the truth: the person claiming defects or the independent inspector. Most letter of credit issuers, jealous of their reputation as issuers, will pay or will insist that their customer obtain an injunction stopping payment. *See* §5-114(2)(b). Courts have been properly concerned, however, that the fraud exception not swallow the general rule that banks must pay against facially conforming documents. The courts have, therefore, crafted serious limits on the fraud exception, as the following problems explain.

Section 47.   *The Exception for Fraud*

287. a. Yes. This is the type of case in which the courts are inclined to enter an injunction. Note the language of §5-114(1). Nonconformity of the goods or the documents to the underlying transaction will not justify a refusal to honor the beneficiary's draft. The kind of fraud in this problem is not just a case of nonconformity, of green diodes instead of red ones, or of 3/4-inch diodes instead of 3/8-inch diodes. The courts distinguish between breach of warranty cases and outright fraud: shipment of rubbish instead of bristles, just to pick an example out of the air. (The example comes from Sztejn v. J. Henry Schroder Banking Corp., 31 N.Y.S.2d 631 (Sup. Ct. 1941), which is the seminal case on the fraud exception.)

b. No, not unless the petitioner satisfies the equity prerequisites, most importantly by showing no adequate remedy at law and a probability of success on the merits.

288. This is a common scenario in Middle Eastern transactions. The Saudi buyer, the beneficiary of the Saudi bank's guaranty, understands the American law of letters of credit and the problem of the fraud exception. The buyer, therefore, has structured the transaction in a way that insulates the buyer from the risk of an injunction against payment. It is difficult under these facts for the U.S. bank to show that *its* beneficiary, the Saudi bank, has practiced fraud. The fraud, if there is any, is being practiced by the beneficiary of the foreign bank's guaranty. All is not lost, however. First, if the applicant, the U.S. seller, can show that the beneficiary of the credit and the guaranty beneficiary are in cahoots, there may be grounds for an injunction, assuming always that the equity prerequisites are satisfied. Even if the applicant cannot obtain an injunction, he can sue for fraud or its equivalent in Saudi Arabia. Bear in mind that he entered into the arrangement knowing that payment under the credit

could be effected by presentation of pieces of paper. Courts are generally unsympathetic to applicants that enter into agreements with foreign parties and then complain that they do not like to litigate in foreign courts. The Saudi Arabian system of law differs from the common law system, but it is a civilized system followed in many countries. Sellers in the United States that want petrodollars will have to adjust their prices or investigate the buyers' creditworthiness and commercial honor. If the sellers do not want to accept the risk of having to litigate in Saudi courts, they may have to satisfy themselves with the domestic market.

289. a. Most courts will not issue an injunction here. This dispute is really one in the underlying contract over the landlord's and the tenant's performance of the lease promises and covenants. The landlord has structured the transaction so that he will have the funds during the litigation of that underlying dispute, and most courts will not disturb this allocation of risks that the parties agreed on before the fact (ex ante). As long as the dispute is contractual and the beneficiary is acting under some color of right, most courts will not enter the injunction. There are other courts, however, that will issue it, to the detriment of the letter of credit and in conflict with the parties' ex ante allocation of risk.

  b. Same reasoning. The courts usually want to know whether the beneficiary is trying to take the applicant's money "without any shred of honest belief," as one commentator has put it, in its right to that money. These facts do not reflect that kind of egregiously fraudulent conduct.

290. a. If the large corporate beneficiary submits false documents, even if the corporation is practicing the most egregious fraud, the court should not enter the injunction unless the applicant can show that his remedy at law (a cause of action against the corporation for fraud) is not adequate. Normally, a cause of action for fraud against a solvent defendant is a sufficient remedy at law, and the court will put the applicant to his legal remedy and deny the injunction.

  b. Some courts appear to be moved by the applicant's charge that payment under the credit must be enjoined to avoid the applicant's bankruptcy. The notion that the embarrassment of the applicant should provide grounds for an injunction is a little bit silly, though at least one court has accepted it. Another court opined that the applicant should have been embarrassed to seek an injunction against payment.

  c. If the bank pays over facially nonconforming documents, it has breached its obligation to the customer-applicant under the application agreement; and the customer will have a cause of action against the bank to recover any damages that breach causes. Given that remedy at law against a solvent bank, the applicant has little cause to seek an injunction.

291. Lending bank is probably a holder in due course of the note, so that Applicant has no defense to Lending Bank's claim under the note, the fraud of the general partner being cut off by §3-305(b) [§3-305(2)]. Thus, Applicant has not demonstrated that it has a good chance of success on the merits. Applicant should lose on the merits, and to enter an injunction against payment would only make it necessary for Lending Bank to sue in order to recover. Injunctions should not be used to that wasteful end.

Section 48.   Transferring Interests in Letters of Credit

292.   a.   No. Second is entitled to enforce the credit under its terms. The credit does not call for payment to a holder in due course. Typically, a negotiation credit contains a negotiation clause: "We hereby engage with drawers, indorsers, and bona fide holders of drafts drawn under and in compliance with the terms of this credit that we will honor your draft if presented on or before the expiry." That language calls for payment to the holder of the beneficiary's draft.

b. & c.   If Second is a holder in due course, the injunction may not issue. *See* §5-114(2)(a). Normally, one would expect that Second would have the burden of showing that it is a holder in due course. *See* §3-308(b) [§3-307(3)]. Here, however, some authority holds that the petitioner seeking the injunction must allege facts showing that it is more likely than not that it will prevail on the merits. Because the petitioner will not prevail on the merits if Second is a holder in due course, those authorities put the burden on the applicant as petitioner to show that Second is not a holder in due course. One would guess that a petitioner that alleges that Second is not a holder in due course may have done enough, since no applicant will be in a position to disprove the holder in due course status of Second, which will be in possession of the facts on which that issue turns. Thus the burden of going forward with the evidence should perhaps fall to Second.

d.   If the credit is straight, Second's status as a holder in due course is irrelevant. If the petitioner can satisfy the prerequisites for an injunction, the court should not make the holder-in-due-course inquiry. The words "under the credit" in §5-114(2)(a) make this distinction. Those words mean that the negotiating bank must act "under the credit." A bank that negotiates the beneficiary's draft under a straight credit does not act under the credit because the straight credit does not run to "indorsers and bona fide holders."

e.   Most courts that have addressed the issue hold that once the issuer honors the time drafts and renders them acceptances, Article 3, not Article 5, governs. The cases arose under the old version of Article 3 and held further that under §3-305(2) the issuer must pay the holder in due course and, perhaps, must pay any holder. Presumably, the result will be the same under new Article 3. *See* §3-305(b). Certainly, the fraud defense to payment of the acceptances is cut off by the holder in due course rule.

293.   If the resulting company expects to draw on the letter of credit, it may want to have the credit amended so that its drafts and certificates, rather than those of the premerger subsidiary, will be acceptable under the credit. Corporate counsel and bankers claim that the hard-and-fast rule against transfer of the right to draw creates problems. The only case in point permitted the parent to draw.

294.   The courts have held almost uniformly that personal representatives — trustees, executors, and receivers — may draw under the credit. Some banks write into the application agreement a clause making it possible for the bank to honor the drafts of the beneficiary or its successors or personal representatives, including the trustee in bankruptcy.

295.   One case has permitted the FDIC to draw on a credit issued to a bank that later became insolvent. In the lower court, the judge ruled that when the FDIC acted as receiver, it could draw but that when, as receiver, it transferred the credit to the FDIC as insurer, the transfer was voluntary and not by operation of law and therefore forbidden by letter-of-credit law. On appeal, the court held that Congress' intent to facilitate the resolution of bank insolvencies by the federal agency overrides state letter-of-credit law and that the FDIC could draw whether it acted in its capacity as receiver or as insurer.

296.   a.   In either case, Exporter may want to assign the proceeds of the German credit to his bank. The credit is not transferable, but the proceeds of all credits may be assigned under a procedure that is the creation and perfection of a security interest. The Code treats the letter of credit as if it were an account but requires the lender to take possession of the credit as a method of perfecting the security interest. In practice, banks tend to use notification procedures to effect the assignment. A beneficiary must notify the paying bank of the assignment. The paying bank, the U.S. correspondent that confirmed the German bank's credit, will then pay the assignee rather than the beneficiary.

        b.   Exporter must draw the draft. The right to draw cannot be transferred unless the credit is transferable. This credit was not transferred; its proceeds were assigned. The original beneficiary is still Exporter, and Exporter must draw the draft.

Section 49.   Issuer Insolvency

297.   a.   The Supreme Court has held that despite confusing language in the Act, the beneficiary is not a depositor and not entitled to insurance under the deposit insurance scheme.

        b.   To the extent that the FDIC prefers the beneficiary out of the assets of the failed bank, the allocation would be in violation of the Act. To the extent that the FDIC provides its own funds to the liquidation or the sale of the failed bank, it may prefer one class of creditors over another.

c. No, not under the Code. *See* §5-117(1)(a). Whether this provision conflicts with the National Bank Act or the Federal Deposit Insurance Act has not been resolved by the courts, but there is ample non-Code authority and good reason to support the rule of the provision.

4. WIRE TRANSFERS

Section 50. Wire Transfers

298.   a. The San Francisco Fed charges the account of First Bank, which must maintain an account with the Fed.

b. If the receiving bank does not know that the name and the routing number do not refer to the same bank, it may credit the account according to the number. If it knows that the name and account differ, it cannot accept the order.

c. Acceptance occurs when the San Francisco Fed acts on the p/o, that is, when it sends the p/o to the Atlanta Fed. *See* UCC §4A-209(a).

d. Payment occurs when the Second Bank of Atlanta accepts it. It accepts the order in one of the ways specified in UCC §4A-209(b).

e. Under its contract with Insurance Co. or under wire transfer system rules a bank may have to accept, but the Code does not require it to accept. *See* UCC §4A-209, comment 5. Under Fedwire, the system used in the Problem, Second of Atlanta's account at the Atlanta Fed will be credited by the time Second receives the p/o. Under UCC §4A-209(b)(2), such an arrangement constitutes automatic acceptance of the p/o. *See* UCC §4A-209, comment 6.

299. It depends on the adoption by the bank of a security procedure. As §4A-202(b) suggests, no bank in its right mind will accept payment orders unless it has established such a procedure. If the bank does establish it and if it is commercially reasonable and the bank follows it in good faith, the employer will generally bear the loss. The customer can avoid the results of the general rule by proving that the unauthorized p/o was not the work of an employee entrusted with wire transfer duties or proves that the person responsible for the unauthorized p/o gained access to the system through the bank and not through the customer.

300. If the beneficiary's bank knows that the number and the name refer to different persons, it should not act on the order. The order cannot be accepted; it is an unacceptable payment order. If the beneficiary's bank pays the beneficiary, it will have to recover it from the beneficiary or bear the loss. *See* §4A-207(a) and comment 2 (third paragraph). If the bank does not know of the discrepancy, it will credit the account by number, or its computer technology will so credit it. That action by the beneficiary's

bank is proper. *See* §4A-207(b)(1). In that case, the originator, if the originator is a bank, will have to pay the beneficiary's bank. If the originator is not a bank, the originator's bank will bear the loss unless it can show that it has notified the originator in writing of the fact that the originator will bear the loss incurred by virtue of such a discrepancy. Comment 2 (third paragraph) discusses the scam cases. The originator can recover from the person whose account was credited unless that person gave value in good faith, as it did in the scam cases. *See* §4A-207(d) and comment three (second paragraph). The only other recourse for the originator that issued this discrepant order is against the fraudulent parties who have long since departed the scene.

301. a. Normally, yes, as long as beneficiary's bank receives the notice of cancellation in sufficient time to act on it before it executes the order in one of the ways specified in §4A-209(b). Note, however, that under §4A-209(b)(2) and Fedwire rules, Third will have accepted the p/o. *See id.* comment 6. Note further that the Code makes allowance for a different result if the beneficiary's bank consents. *See* §4A-211(b). It will consent if it can recover the funds from the beneficiary. It can recover funds from a bad-faith beneficiary if the funds are still in the beneficiary's account. *See* §4A-211, comment 4. Note also, that a receiving bank (not the beneficiary's bank) that has not executed the order by sending it on to the next bank must accept a cancellation. There is no reason it should not defer to the wishes of the sending bank, but the cancellation must arrive at the receiving bank in time for it to stop the order from its journey to the next bank.

b. No. Under §4A-211(b), the notice is late if the bank has accepted the order. Under §4A-209(b)(1), the bank that notifies the beneficiary has accepted the order.

302. Buyer's bank has acted erroneously. It may recover $1 million from the originator and must try to recover the balance from the beneficiary. *See* §4A-303(a).

303. No. *See* §4A-305. Bear in mind that Article 4A governs wholesale wire transfers. Consumers are seldom involved. The originator of a wire transfer that wants to play like a river boat gambler is going to take his losses. Users of the wire transfer systems will have to know that they should wire their funds early or arrange for their own verification procedures to see that the funds arrive on time. The rule may strike some as harsh, but it is a quite sound rule.

Table of Uniform Commercial Code Sections

References are to problem numbers unless indicated otherwise.

Table of Bankruptcy Code Sections

References are to problem numbers unless indicated otherwise.

Index

References are to problem numbers unless indicated otherwise.